| Oxford Shakespeare Topics

Shakespeare and Text

OXFORD SHAKESPEARE TOPICS
Published and forthcoming titles include:

Oxford Shakespeare Topics

GENERAL EDITORS: PETER HOLLAND AND STANLEY WELLS

Shakespeare and Text

JOHN JOWETT

OXFORD

UNIVERSITY PRESS

Great Clarendon Street, Oxford OX2 6DP

Oxford University Press is a department of the University of Oxford.
It furthers the University's objective of excellence in research, scholarship,
and education by publishing worldwide in

Oxford New York

Auckland Cape Town Dar es Salaam Hong Kong Karachi
Kuala Lumpur Madrid Melbourne Mexico City Nairobi
New Delhi Shanghai Taipei Toronto

With offices in

Argentina Austria Brazil Chile Czech Republic France Greece
Guatemala Hungary Italy Japan Poland Portugal Singapore
South Korea Switzerland Thailand Turkey Ukraine Vietnam

Oxford is a registered trade mark of Oxford University Press
in the UK and in certain other countries

Published in the United States
by Oxford University Press Inc., New York

© John Jowett 2007

British Library Cataloguing in Publication Data

Data available

Library of Congress Cataloging in Publication Data

Data available

Typeset by Laserwords Private Limited, Chennai, India
Printed in Great Britain
on acid-free paper by
Biddles Ltd., King's Lynn, Norfolk

ISBN 978–0–19–921707–6
ISBN 978–0–19–921706–9 (Pbk.)

10 9 8 7 6 5 4 3 2 1

Acknowledgements

This book has been encouraged from the beginning onwards above all by the series editors Peter Holland and Stanley Wells. Tom Perridge, Lizzie Robottom, and Fiona Smith at Oxford University Press, and the copy editor Hilary Walford, considerately and professionally helped it along its way. The library staff at the Shakespeare Institute Library continued to run a uniquely time-efficient research facility, and its library assistants were vitally helpful in checking references and the index. Sonia Massai and Lena Orlin kindly sent copies of their research work prior to publication. Will Sharpe gave valuable feedback such as can be expected only of a textual scholar. I am also grateful to Suzanne Gossett and Gordon McMullen for the ongoing dialogue about editing that surrounds our shared work on the Arden Early Modern Drama series. The British Academy generously funded travel to present work in progress at the Shakespeare World Congress, Brisbane, 2006. Chapter 5 of this book is based on my 'Editing Shakespeare's Plays in the Twentieth Century', in *Shakespeare Survey* 59 (2006). I am grateful to Sarah Stanton and Cambridge University Press for permission. Parts of Chapter 1 draw on my essay 'Varieties of Collaboration in Shakespeare's Problem and Late Plays', in Richard Dutton and Jean Howard (eds.), *A Companion to Shakespeare's Works*, vol. 4, *The Poems, Problem Comedies, Late Plays* (2003). My thanks for permission are here to Emma Bennett and Blackwell Publishing. My special personal gratitude goes to all colleagues, friends, and family who sustained me during the difficult period that followed the death of Davina Aldridge.

John Jowett
June 2007

Contents

List of Illustrations

As King Lear dies, he expresses anguished despair at the cruelty of his daughter Cordelia's death, and then, in his final words, imagines he sees breath in her lips:

> LEAR And my poor fool is hanged. No, no, no life?
>   Why should a dog, a horse, a rat have life,
>   And thou no breath at all? Thou'lt come no more.
>   Never, never, never, never, never.
>   [*To Kent*] Pray you, undo this button. Thank you, sir.
>   Do you see this? Look on her. Look, her lips.
>   Look there, look there.   *He dies*
> EDGAR He faints. (*To Lear*) My lord, my lord!
> KENT   (*to Lear*) Break, heart, I prithee break.

Such is the text as it appears in a modern edition. The 1623 Folio text on which it is based differs in spellings, punctuation, and presentation, and lacks the directional stage directions that the editors have supplied:

> *Lear.* And my poore Foole is hang'd: no, no, no life?
>   Why should a Dog, a Horse, a Rat haue life,
>   And thou no breath at all? Thou'lt come no more,
>   Neuer, neuer, neuer, neuer, neuer.
>   Pray you vndo this Button. Thanke you Sir,
>   Do you see this? Looke on her? Looke her lips,
>   Looke there, looke there.   *He dies.*
>   *Edg.* He faints, my Lord, my Lord.
>   *Kent.* Breake heart, I prythee breake.

In the pages that follow, we will consider amongst other things the book in which this passage appears, the form the play takes in that book, and the nature of the changes that editors make. But the Folio text is not one that readers would have found in any book issued in Shakespeare's lifetime. In the Quarto edition published in 1608 (and reprinted in 1619) the passage is significantly different:

> *Lear.* And my poore foole is hangd, no, no life, why should a dog, a horse, a rat of life and thou no breath at all, O thou wilt come no more, neuer, neuer, neuer, pray you vndo this button, thanke you sir, O, o, o, o. *Edgar.* He faints my Lord, my Lord.
> *Lear.* Breake hart, I prethe breake.

The passage is more crammed on the page—verse is set as prose, and Edgar's speech is not placed on a separate line. And, crucially, it is shorter. In this version Lear does not look on Cordelia's lips as he dies. There are other differences. The 1608 text (identified for brevity as Q1) refers to 'a rat of life'; the 1623 version (F) more plausibly has 'a rat haue life'. Only Q1 gives Lear the painful groans represented as text in 'O, o, o, o'. Lear's final speech in Q1 becomes Kent's line in F. Though Lear must die in the Q1 version too, he does so at a later point, and there is no stage direction to alert the reader to the moment.

These differences are both disconcerting and profound in their implications. There are almost certainly various different reasons why the texts are unlike. Q1, the text that appeared within two or three years of the play's first performance on stage, is incorrect both for setting 'of' instead of 'have' and in presenting verse as prose. But, according to current thinking, it is not a text to dismiss as simply inferior, but one to value as a distinct version in its own right. Looking at the two texts from this point of view, it can be said, then, that in Q1 Lear dies in the absolute knowledge that Cordelia is dead, whereas in F he dies in a state of enraptured delusion, thinking she does after all have breath, and so has no cause to say 'Break, heart, I prithee break'. This difference between the texts brings into focus at the moment of Lear's death some of the major issues that have sustained the action: Lear's mistaken apprehension at the beginning of the play about the 'breath' or words that issue from Cordelia's mouth, and the oscillations between hope and despair that have driven forward the play since Edgar declared that things could only improve ('The worst returns to laughter' (4.1.6)) and then, after meeting his blinded father, acknowledged 'O gods! Who is't can say "I am the worst"? | I am worse than e'er I was' (4.1.25–6).

Like any text, though more so than most, Q1 *King Lear* has its faults, but in the sustained and detailed differences between Q1 and F has been recognized a process of revision by Shakespeare. Life for the Shakespeare textualist would be easier but less interesting if Q1 and F were entirely accurate renditions of two authorial versions of the play, or if (as used to be assumed) they were both imperfect witnesses to a single lost original. The truth presumably lies somewhere in between. Exactly *where* in between is hard to pinpoint. But simple acceptance or simple rejection of a text will not suffice.

It is scarcely possible to negotiate such issues without making reference to the author, Shakespeare, as the most obvious criterion by which to judge whether two texts differ intentionally or as a result of error. This book belongs to a series based on the author's name, 'Oxford Shakespeare Topics'. Most titles in the series follow the formula 'Shakespeare and...', which puts Shakespeare in relation to something that affects his work and leaves its impression on his work. This formula partly applies to the present book. We might refer to 'Shakespeare and text' in the same way that we refer to 'Shakespeare and theatre'. 'Text' in this application can refer to the process by which Shakespeare wrote, the way the texts were brought into being first as manuscripts and then as printed books, and the study of those books as the textual objects that arose, indirectly, from his writing. The phrase clearly implies that we are viewing Shakespeare biographically as an author, separable from but largely responsible for the texts that bear his name.

Yet, in another way, the title of the present book, *Shakespeare and Text*, follows the series prescription in form but not in content. 'Text' is the mode in which Shakespeare's works exist. From this perspective, text is the very essence of Shakespeare. Locutions such as 'I often read Shakespeare' make the point. 'Shakespeare and text' might virtually mean 'Shakespeare as text'. 'Shakespeare as text' is potentially limitless. A Shakespeare text does not depend for its identity on the author's name appearing on the title page, for this would exclude some of the early and most authoritative printings. Nor does it depend on its appearance in Shakespeare's lifetime, for many of his now best-known plays remained unprinted until 1623, seven years after his death. 'Shakespeare as text' might reach out to refer to any and all Shakespeare works ever printed, copied, digitized, or remembered, from the early 1590s to today. Indeed, the term might be extended to adaptations, prompt books, film scripts, quotations, allusions, and to the words spoken in a performance.

It will be a premiss of this book that it does matter that a historical figure, William Shakespeare, creatively wrote the astonishing works associated with his name. But it matters too that Shakespeare wrote his plays in the first instance to be performed in the theatre. Though he might have anticipated that some of them would be published, there is little evidence that he was actively concerned with their appearance in print. During Shakespeare's lifetime there was no collected edition of his works. The plays that were printed all appeared in small, single-play volumes. They were issued typically two or more years after they had been written and performed, and the process leading from author's pen to printed book is highly variable. With the exception of a passage in *Sir Thomas More*, no manuscripts of Shakespeare's plays survive either from the theatre or in his hand. The earliest printed texts are, therefore, the only point of reference. They are both misrepresentations and the privileged and essential representations of the lost manuscripts on which they are based. They are secondary forms of publication that put the text into an entirely different form of circulation from the performance of plays on the stage, yet they are the very locus of the text as we first apprehend it. To understand Shakespeare as text, it is critical to keep hold of both halves of this critical paradox.

Work in the early twenty-first century epitomized in David Scott Kastan's title *Shakespeare and the Book* and Andrew Murphy's *Shakespeare in Print* has invaluably focused attention on Shakespeare in relation to the book industry in the early modern period and thereafter.[1] Such work is hugely informative on the history of Shakespeare as a cultural commodity, or at least the book-centred part of it. This area of study offers strong reminders that the materialization of texts in those specific physical objects known as books should not be ignored. The specific features of books need to be valued as more than noise that distorts the message emanating from that impossible ideal, the unsullied Shakespearian source. 'Bibliographical codes' inherent in print will, at times, demand close attention.[2] The charting of Shakespeare's emergence as a published author, the description of the printing and publishing industry that first gave us his works in the form in which they survive, and an account of the manufacturing process itself, are all key elements of the present volume.

Nevertheless, it would be partial in the extreme to assume all that mattered was the place of printed editions in the history of book culture. 'Text' is not 'the book'. The early editions of Shakespeare are not only textual objects and commodities in themselves, but also the surviving physical and textual evidence of something physically and textually different, the text as initially produced and, in the case of plays, as originally transmitted to theatre audiences on the stage. Theatre is a transitory phenomenon, and the manuscripts have proved short-lived. These circumstances present a challenge rather than an obstacle to intellectual enquiry. As long as we are interested in the literary and theatrical dynamic of Shakespeare's works, it will be both appropriate and important to consider the nature of Shakespeare as a writer, the stages by which his plays reached performance, and the essential differences between a performance culture and a culture of print.

The present study will present a textual world in which the categories by which we describe things are blurred, traditional interpretations are open to challenge, and the condition of text itself is unstable. To that extent it presents not so much a body of settled knowledge as an outline of ways of thinking about text. It will attempt to describe the complexion of textual issues rather than to offer solutions to them. Text is puzzling, Protean, and capable of shifting beyond reach at the very point where we try to grasp it. In that awareness lies the fascination of the subject.

1

Author and Collaborator

SHAKESPEARE IN PRINT

If today one speaks of a literary author, Shakespeare will seem to offer a good instance of such a figure, perhaps the pre-eminent one. The engraved portrait first published in the First Folio of 1623 has iconic status and is widely recognized. Shakespeare is taught in schools; he has been widely read. The term 'complete works' will be more readily associated with Shakespeare than any other writer. He is the prime example of the literary genius, and of the writer who combines literary longevity with worldwide recognition. The study of Shakespeare demands a historical adjustment to take into account four centuries of change, yet he is often thought to transcend the passage of time. He is deeply *established* in literary culture. At the same time, he retains a reputation for speaking to us, here and now, movingly, deeply, and sometimes challengingly about matters that concern us.

By 1623, Shakespeare had already acquired some of these attributes, or at least comparable ones. He had been published in an impressive Folio that brought together virtually all his dramatic works in one volume (see Chapter 4). He belonged to the past, albeit the past of living memory. Ben Jonson's commendatory poem in the Folio had presented him to readers as 'not of an age, but for all time'. He was already what we would now call 'literary', and was in the process of securing a place at the upper end of the literary marketplace.

In contrast, during his first few years as a dramatist Shakespeare's plays were unpublished. His first works to appear in print were non-dramatic: *Venus and Adonis* in 1593, followed by *The Rape of Lucrece* in

1594.[1] But he had made his mark as a writer of stage plays well before writing the narrative poems. It was probably some time after he arrived in London and began working as an actor that Shakespeare started to write. Sometimes he worked on plays in collaboration with other dramatists. Lacking the university education of the more prestigious dramatists of the day, such as John Lyly, Christopher Marlowe, and Robert Greene, he came to be criticized as a merely imitative writer. The attack came in the pamphlet *Greene's Groatsworth of Wit*, which Greene purportedly wrote on his deathbed in 1592. Greene in the pamphlet speaks of 'an upstart crow, beautified with our feathers, that with his "tiger's heart wrapped in a player's hide" supposes he is as well able to bombast out a blank verse as the best of you; and being an absolute *Johannes fac totum* [Jack of all trades], is in his own conceit the only Shake-scene in a country'.[2] The quoted line within this passage is a sharply satiric alteration of Shakespeare's 'O tiger's heart wrapped in a woman's hide', Richard Duke of York's denunciation of Queen Margaret in *Richard Duke of York* (*3 Henry VI*) 1.4.137.[3] The exact nature of Shakespeare's alleged trespass is unclear. But the underlying protest is against Shakespeare as a mere player who muscles into the craft of the playwright, arrogantly taking it upon himself to imitate or appropriate or pad out the plays of the established dramatists.

This is the first recorded reference to Shakespeare as a dramatist. It condemns him as a plagiarist and an intruder. Such an attack cannot help but act as a back-handed acknowledgement. Shakespeare is not named, but he is identified through the distortion of 'Shakespeare' to 'Shake-scene' and the similar distortion 'woman's hide' to 'player's hide'. The assumption is that one or both of these pointedly cryptic references will give away the identity of the person in question, even though the words are misquoted and the text of the play was not available in a printed edition. If the reader has not heard of Shakespeare, it seems to be implied that he or she ought to have done so, and should be capable of associating a memorable scene with its author's name.

Thus, before any of Shakespeare's plays were issued in print, he already had a reputation that could be exploited in print culture. The dramatist working for the commercial theatre in the early 1590s potentially had little or no status as an author. He (for women did not write for the professional theatre) would work for a fee, often in collaboration with other dramatists. Only a small proportion of plays appeared as printed books. The title pages of published plays almost always named the theatre company that had performed the play, and it was the theatre company that usually would have released the manuscript for publication. The dramatists' names were often not recorded in the printed texts of their plays, and there was no Copyright Act to recognize and protect their interests. Anonymity, collaboration, and the absence of authorial rights were the typical circumstances of dramatic writing.

If we consider this situation from the point of view of the 'university wits', young, sharp, intellectually aggressive men such as Christopher Marlowe, Robert Greene, and Thomas Nashe, coping with intellectual underemployment in London by turning to writing plays for the popular theatre, it is easy to see why they might have viewed their employers with resentment, and therefore have expressed a particular animosity to the player-turned-playwright. More to the point, the activity of professional theatre gave rise to opportunities in the field of book publication, by way of either the publication of a play or, as in the case of the *Groatsworth*, the publication of a pamphlet making journalistic capital out of the theatre. The *Groatsworth* suggests that the print medium had the potential to lift the dramatist out of anonymity; in other words, that the market conditions dictated by the theatre might be resisted by the common interests of dramatists and stationers.

The *Groatsworth* was edited and perhaps partly authored by Henry Chettle, who had served his apprenticeship as a stationer. Chettle himself later became a prolific dramatist working for the companies managed by Philip Henslowe, but in 1592 he was working in association with the part-printer of *Groatsworth*, John Danter. Danter was later to issue the first Shakespeare play in book form, *Titus Andronicus*, which appeared in 1594, perhaps not coincidentally the year Shakespeare became a member of the Lord Chamberlain's company.[4] Three years later he printed and published the first edition of *Romeo and Juliet*. There was scope, then, for Shakespeare to become an acknowledged writer of plays in the realm of print. By 1600 Shakespeare had become the most regularly published dramatist. We are used to thinking of him as a writer for the theatre; here, in contrast, we encounter him as an author many of whose works circulated in print during his lifetime.

In 1595 the anonymous play *Locrine* appeared in a quarto whose title page attributed the play to 'W.S.'. It may have been implied that Shakespeare was the author.[5] But it was another three years before Shakespeare's name began to appear in full for the first time on title pages. The first such editions were probably the reprints of *Richard II* and *Richard III* (see Appendix 2, which provides details of all early Shakespeare editions). The 1598 Quarto of *Love's Labour's Lost* and first editions of four plays issued in 1600 all named Shakespeare on the title page, as did most new editions published thereafter. It is hard to gauge how far these developments were driven by the print industry, the whole theatre company as the commercial organization that owned the manuscript, and Shakespeare as author. Lukas Erne has modified previous assumptions by arguing that Shakespeare wrote as a literary dramatist with an eye to publication in print as well as performance on stage.[6] This would certainly accord with the self-confident author of *Venus and Adonis* and *The Rape of Lucrece*, and the poet of the Sonnets with his insistence on the permanent worth of his work. If so, Shakespeare probably exerted some degree of control over his plays only after he had joined the newly formed Lord Chamberlain's Men in 1594. His interest was that of a 'sharer', the group of about ten leading actors who had financial ownership of the company. As both sharer and principal dramatist, he would have been in a position of unusual influence over decisions relating to publication.

Nevertheless, it cannot be claimed that Shakespeare's literary interests were paramount. Few if any of Shakespeare's plays were issued less than two years after the play in question had first been performed on the stage. The reason for this time lag has been disputed. By the older view, print would offer competition to the theatre, for publication would devalue the play as a text that otherwise could be experienced only in performance. Support has been found in Thomas Heywood's complaint that some of the actors 'think it against their peculiar profit to have them [plays] come in print'.[7] More recently, Erne has argued that, on the contrary, the theatre company were willing participants in the publication of plays.[8] These two explanations share in their view that the economic interest of the theatre, however that is identified, determined the timing of publication (except when it was unauthorized), and so prevented the plays of Shakespeare and other dramatists from being published until several years after they had finished writing them.

It may also have been the theatre company (which included Shakespeare) that decided to replace imperfect First Quarto editions of *Romeo and Juliet* and *Hamlet* with longer and more authorial second editions. It was the company rather than Shakespeare alone who in 1600 protected their interest in Shakespeare's *As You Like It*, *Henry V*, and *Much Ado about Nothing*, along with Jonson's *Every Man In his Humour*. They had these titles recorded in the regulatory Register of the Stationers' Company as 'staied' (i.e. 'stayed'; the exact meaning is disputed).[9]

After 1604 the players (as of 1603 called the King's Men) seem to have turned against publication. The reason has not been adequately explained. Only a further three Shakespeare plays appeared for the first time during the rest of his working life in the theatre. Of these plays, *Troilus and Cressida* was in the hands of the stationers as early as 1603, and *Pericles* was published probably without the company's authorization. The third play, *King Lear*, is therefore the only Shakespeare play likely to have been released by the King's Men and subsequently published in this period. In 1608, six months after the entry of *King Lear*, another play, *Antony and Cleopatra*, was entered in the Stationers' Register, but it remained unpublished until it appeared in the Folio of 1623. Only *Othello* (1622) appeared in the years between Shakespeare's death and the publication of the First Folio.

Shakespeare's status as a published author of plays from 1594 onwards can therefore be charted through the expansion and contraction of the number of works printed, and by the establishment of his name on the title pages. By 1623 twenty out of the thirty-six works included in the Folio had already been issued in smaller format. The availability of these plays over the preceding thirty years was far from uniform. It would depend on sales and on the decision to reprint, which would lie with the copy-holding stationer on the basis of his perception of demand. No edition of *2 Henry IV* and *Much Ado about Nothing* appeared between their first publication in 1600 and 1623. In contrast, *Richard III* had established itself as Shakespeare's most popular play with readers, having run to six editions. This in turn pales into insignificance alongside the non-dramatic *Venus and Adonis*, which had appeared in twelve editions by the same date.

The spectrum of titles available in the London bookshops at any one time, always a small fragment of the whole output of the book trade, varied considerably from year to year(see pp. 172–3). In 1600 the browser in the bookshops around St Paul's Churchyard would have found new editions of *Henry V*, *2 Henry IV*, *Much Ado about Nothing*, *A Midsummer Night's Dream*, and *The Merchant of Venice*. There were also new reprints of *First Part of the Contention* (*2 Henry VI*), *Richard Duke of York* (*3 Henry VI*), and *Titus Andronicus*. Stock may have remained from plays published over the previous two or three years: *Romeo and Juliet*, *1 Henry IV*, *Richard II*, *Richard III*, and *Love's Labour's Lost*. In contrast, in 1607 there were no new plays; stock may have remained of recently printed plays, namely one of the editions of *Hamlet* and the popular history plays *Richard III* and *1 Henry IV*. Surprisingly, the 1590s history plays *Richard II*, *Richard III*, and *1 Henry IV* made up the core of Shakespeare plays bought by Jacobean readers until 1623 and after. The records of court and provincial performance suggest that the King's Men offered a more up-to-date repertoire on stage.

The early history of publication tells us much about 'Shakespeare' as an institutionalized authorial figure in its earliest manifestations. Paradoxically, it leaves us at some remove from the act of writing that gave rise to these plays as textual entities in the first place. Little reference has been made so far to the manuscripts on which the printed texts were based. Apart from an adaptation of the *Henry IV* plays owned by the book-collector, antiquarian, and play-goer Sir Edward Dering, along with a few passages copied into commonplace books, the plays brought together in the First Folio no longer exist in manuscript form. One possible explanation is that the King's Men lost their stock of manuscripts in the fire that burnt down the Globe Theatre in 1613. But, to keep the matter in perspective, it should be remembered that Shakespeare is not unique. Of the hundreds or even thousands of plays written during the period, only a small handful survives in manuscript. We have no theatrical manuscripts of plays by Christopher Marlowe,

Thomas Kyd, George Chapman, Ben Jonson, John Webster, and other dramatists.

SIR THOMAS MORE

In Shakespeare's case there is, however, one fragment of dramatic writing of theatrical provenance that is probably in his hand. It is the 'Hand D' section of the manuscript play *Sir Thomas More*, which recent scholarship has shown with increasing clarity to be the hand of Shakespeare.[10] The passage was written as part of a complex set of revisions by four different dramatists to an 'Original Text' in the handwriting of Anthony Munday. We will return to this manuscript as a theatre document in Chapter 2, but discussion of its crucial evidence of Shakespeare as composer of dramatic dialogue belongs here. If the identification is right, this document restores the otherwise missing immediate access to Shakespeare's dramatic writing. The consistency of the evidence in admitting Shakespeare and excluding other dramatists is impressive, and a few details point firmly to Shakespeare and no other writer of the period, known or anonymous.

The overall appearance of the three leaves in Hand D is typical of a theatrical manuscript. The leaves have been lightly folded twice vertically, to create four vertical columns. The middle two are mostly taken up with verse dialogue. Prose extends into the fourth column. Each speech is separated by a rule extending from the left edge of the dialogue into the main block of dialogue. Speech prefixes are written in the column on the left, and some examples of slight and not-so-slight misalignment show that they were added after the dialogue had been written. The theatre annotator known simply as 'Hand C' has added some alterations and additions to speech prefixes.

Shakespeare's handwriting (if, as I will assume, it is his) can be described as an uneven version of the common script known as secretary hand. Many of the letter forms are unfamiliar. For example, the 'h' looks like a 'y' with an inverted descending loop, the 'c' looks more like a modern 'r', and the 'r' looks like a 'u' with a convex instead of concave curve at the bottom. The use of secretary hand was common in the period and would not in itself have presented any difficulty to the early modern reader. Hand D, however, was sometimes careless in his use of 'minims', the limbed vertical strokes that make up 'i', 'c', 'r', 'n', and 'm'. At l. 148 there is a word in which the combination of minims can be variously interpreted as 'momtanish' or 'moritanish'—neither of which gives very obvious or satisfactory sense—or 'mountanish', assuming that a minim is missing. There are other examples in Hand D of 'un' written as three rather than four minims in the words 'sounde', l. 125, and 'found', l. 155. This is a feature of Hand D's writing that might prove confusing to a copyist or a compositor, and so lead to errors in the resulting text.

The spellings are irregular, even by the standards of early modern English. 'Scilens', as a spelling of *silence*, is found in *Sir Thomas More* and recurrently in *2 Henry IV*, but in no known unShakespearian text of the period. Other spellings also shared between *Sir Thomas More* and Shakespeare plays as printed, but rarely if at all found elsewhere, include 'Iarman' for *German*, 'elamentes' for *elements*, 'a levenpence' for *elevenpence*, and 'deule' for *devil*.

The punctuation is very light, and at times irregular. At one point Shakespeare originally wrote:

> wash your foule mynds w^t teares and those same hand*e*s
> that yo^u lyke rebells lyft against the peace
> lift vp for peace, and your vnreuerent knees
> [that] make them your feet to kneele to be forgyven
> is safer warrs, then euer yo^u can make
> whose discipline is ryot; why euen yor [warrs] hurly
> cannot pr*o*ceed but by obedienc what rebell captaine
> as mutynes ar incident, by his name
> can still the rout who will obay [th] a traytor
> or howe can well that pr*o*clamation sounde
> when ther is no adicion but a rebell
> to quallyfy a rebell …

(Add. II, 231–42)[11]

The extent to which this rhetorically complex passage is misleadingly punctuated may be measured by comparing a modern-spelling version:

> Wash your foul minds with tears, and those same hands
> That you, like rebels, lift against the peace,
> Lift up for peace; and your unreverent knees,
> Make them your feet. To kneel to be forgiven

> Is safer wars than ever you can make
> Whose discipline is riot. Why, even your hurly
> Cannot proceed but by obedience. What rebel captain,
> As mutinies are incident, by his name
> Can still the rout? Who will obey a traitor?
> Or how can well that proclamation sound
> When there is no addition but 'a rebel'
> To qualify a rebel?

(6.121–34)

Four sentences in the modernized text close without any punctuation at all in Shakespeare's draft. The absence of such punctuation makes some of the pointing supplied in the manuscript confusing. An early modern reader would have been more accustomed than we are to features that we might now call irregularities. Lightish punctuation was common enough in play manuscripts of the period. But in this case the script's immediate early modern reader, Hand C, seems to have been confused. In the fourth line, the change of mind reflected in the deleted word 'that' combines with a particularly confusing lack of punctuation. Hand C responded by deleting two and a half lines from 'is safer' to 'obedienc'.

The passage also illustrates Shakespeare's own revisions of his script, both in the course of writing and afterwards. Comparable changes can be identified both within printings of individual texts, such as Q1 *Love's Labour's Lost* and Q2 *Romeo and Juliet*, and between the quarto and Folio texts of various plays, as will be seen later in this book. The first alteration in the passage quoted, the deletion of 'that' in l. 234, was made in the course of writing, and is known as a *currente calamo* correction. The layout of the manuscript makes it certain that the deleted word was immediately superseded. The status of a *currente calamo* correction within a sequence of writing and revision can be identified because it occurs immediately after the cancelled word has been written—whereas other local revisions could occur at various later stages. This second possibility is the case with the alteration of 'warrs' to 'hurly'. This is a literary improvement, replacing the more commonplace word with one that is far more unusual and that has more specific suggestions of civil commotion. Shakespeare also made a rather more substantial alteration by adding above this line the words 'in in to yor obedienc'. 'Obedience', specifically to royal authority, and the refusal of it, are major themes in the play as a whole, and Shakespeare can be seen adding further emphasis on it, repeating a word already supplied at l. 127 (in the Modern-Spelling version), just as he rhetorically repeated the word 'rebel' in the passage. The repeated words 'rebel' and 'obedience' (also 'obey' (l. 131)), and the key added words 'hurly' and 'obedience', are both sharply antithetical pairings.

One similar line involved alteration by both Shakespeare and Hand C. Shakespeare first made a running correction, crossing out the participle 'sayeng' and writing 'say' after it. He then added 'alas alas' as an interlineation, to give the extended line (in modernized form), 'To slip him like a hound. *Alas, alas!* Say now the King'. These two added words were deleted by Hand C. It seems that he was less tolerant of the metrical licence than was Shakespeare. But Shakespeare's tolerance is fully compatible with his writing elsewhere. The outcome of the interlineation has a close parallel for the metre in Shakespeare. Here, for instance, is *Measure for Measure*, 3.1.132–4:

> To what we fear of death.
> ISABELLA Alas, alas!
> CLAUDIO Sweet sister, let me live.

We cannot know whether Shakespeare again literally added Isabella's 'Alas, alas' at some point after writing 'To what we fear of death. Sweet sister let me live' as a single verse-line, but the words have the same effect of breaking up and adding to the regular pentameter as they do in *Sir Thomas More*. According to the chronological sequence of texts in the 1986 Oxford Shakespeare *Complete Works*, *Measure for Measure* was the next play Shakespeare wrote after revising *Sir Thomas More*.

If the manuscript had been used as printer's copy, the resulting book would have revealed various signs of an authorial draft, but would have concealed the fact that some key features were determined not by Shakespeare but by a theatre scribe. These include the deletion and the added bridging phrase discussed above. In making these changes to the dialogue the scribe altered the sense of what remained, for, whereas in Shakespeare's original a sentence ends at 'feet', Hand C's reading ends the sentence at 'forgyven'. He took care to avoid any discontinuity in the shortened text by introducing, before 'what rebell captaine', the bridge phrase 'tell me but this'. Again, it would be impossible to detect the non-authorial character of these changes if the play had appeared as a printed book.

It was Hand C who wrote the scene's opening stage direction on a previous leaf (see Chapter 2). The entire Hand D passage as Shakespeare left it contains only one entrance direction:

> Enter the L. maier Surrey
> Shrewsbury

This has posed considerable difficulties of interpretation, not least because there is no entrance anywhere in the scene for More himself. We are left wondering whether Shakespeare understood the staging that had been envisaged in the previous section, and indeed we might conjecture that he thought the episode he was writing began in the middle of a scene. Another possibility is that Shakespeare momentarily confused or conflated the Lord Mayor and his sheriff More, for this seems to be the most dramatically effective point for More to enter.

Such uncertainty in stage directions as to the presence of the major role in the entire play and the main speaker in the scene would be surprising in a play of continuous composition. Perhaps more routine, though striking to the modern eye, is Shakespeare's at times extreme casualness about the marking of speech prefixes. An unspecified 'other' (ll. 4 and 6) is quickly reduced to 'oth' (l. 10), and then to the most minimal identifier, the single letter 'o' (l. 16). It was left to Hand C to assign the lines to speakers. Shakespeare therefore left a draft that was in need of some adjustment and clarification for the stage. The dialogue was mostly fluent, but there are occasional errors that Shakespeare corrected, and he made a few minor improvements to his own script. This is very much the product of a working dramatist. The fragmentary nature of his task may have contributed to Shakespeare's lack of certainty over some details of staging. But Shakespeare was writing a draft in full knowledge that its functionality as a theatre script would be reviewed by someone else.[12] Not surprisingly, there are similar examples in printed texts, such as the uncertainties in identifying the Watchmen in Q1 *Much Ado about Nothing*, 3.3.

SHAKESPEARE AS CO-AUTHOR

It is common to think of Shakespeare as a writer who worked without the assistance of other dramatists. But, as the case of *Sir Thomas More* shows with uncompromising clarity, Shakespeare was also a collaborator. The way we think about the texts themselves can be reshaped by an awareness of the contribution of others.

Collaboration was so common in the period that Shakespeare, along with a few other dramatists such as Ben Jonson, was probably unusual in the extent to which he wrote as sole author. His position as a sharing actor with a stakehold in the theatre company probably placed him in an exceptionally strong position to control his own circumstances of work as a dramatist. But to this general and in itself remarkable habit of sole authorship there are significant exceptions. Plays in which Shakespeare wrote as collaborator probably include *1 Henry VI*,[13] *Titus Andronicus*,[14] *Edward III*,[15] and *Sir Thomas More*. Scholars are moving towards a consensus about the collaborative nature of *Pericles*, written with George Wilkins, and two plays written with John Fletcher, *All Is True* (the play identified in the Folio and most modern editions as *Henry VIII*) and *The Two Noble Kinsmen*. They draw attention to a lost play by Shakespeare and Fletcher called *Cardenio*. The problematic *Timon of Athens* is now explained as a collaboration with Thomas Middleton, a dramatist who had already established his skills in writing city comedy. Middleton's hand as an adapter has long been recognized in *Macbeth*, and the more recent case for Middleton treating *Measure for Measure* in a comparable way is slowly gaining acceptance.[16]

Simply listing the eleven plays that are not of Shakespeare's exclusive authorship immediately revises the picture that prevailed over much of the twentieth century of Shakespeare as a dramatist who avoided collaboration. That view is understandable. There is, after all, little specific documentation of Shakespeare as a collaborator—though it should not be forgotten that the very first known reference to him in *Greene's Groatsworth of Wit* seems to charge him with reworking the output of other dramatists. The 1623 Folio unhesitatingly presents him as a non-collaborating dramatist.

Title pages of other books can similarly offer unreliable or deficient information. As noted above, the earlier quarto editions of Shakespeare, and some later ones too, do not name him or any other dramatist. *Titus Andronicus*, first published as an anonymous play in 1594, later came to be associated exclusively with Shakespeare because it was included in the Folio, whereas *Edward III*, first published as an anonymous play in 1596, was excluded from the Folio and so came to be associated with Shakespeare only through the labours of later scholars of author attribution. Where information from Shakespeare's time is present, it can be misleading. Sometimes Shakespeare was credited on title pages with the authorship of plays he evidently did not write. Critics have occasionally and speculatively sought for evidence of his hand in *The London Prodigal* (1605) and *A Yorkshire Tragedy* (1608) on this basis, but it is highly unlikely that he made any significant contribution to them. In just one late case, *The Two Noble Kinsmen* (1634), he is named as co-author with John Fletcher. This late but credible identification of Shakespeare as a collaborator is the exception that proves the rule.

In principle, it is a sensible procedure to prefer documentary evidence such as title pages to 'internal' evidence based on language and stylistic preferences. It is not, however, strongly justified in circumstances where the documentary record is absent or unreliable. Title pages of plays from the early modern public theatres drastically under-represent collaboration. Yet scholars are well aware of the dangers of an impressionistic approach to 'internal' evidence. A number of studies appearing in the early twentieth century sought aggressively to take away from Shakespeare any writing that sounded to the investigator's ear like George Peele, or Robert Greene, or John Lyly, or Christopher Marlowe. In 1924 E. K. Chambers rightly castigated them.[17] Samuel Schoenbaum's later and detailed study of attribution techniques reinforced the scepticism that prevailed over much of the century.[18] Hence what Chambers had called the 'disintegration' of Shakespeare came to be seen as a disreputable activity. Since the 1970s scholars have struggled to find more reliable ways of analysing the texts themselves for evidence of collaboration. They have had some success, perhaps more than is generally realized, though they have not achieved final and definitive clarity.

One factor here is the uneven and sometimes anxious take-up of attribution studies. Objections will be found to even the most convincing study of authorship attribution by those who intuitively disagree with its findings. An edition of *Timon of Athens* briefly dismisses the strong case for collaboration without looking at the appropriate evidence.[19] In contrast, editors of three different *Complete Works* of Shakespeare appearing within a short span of time have accepted Shakespeare's authorship of 'A Funeral Elegy' on the basis of work whose findings have subsequently been decisively challenged and withdrawn by their instigator.[20] Gary Taylor's acceptance of an early manuscript attribution to Shakespeare of a minor poem beginning 'Shall I Die' proved to be a disproportionately controversial feature of the Oxford Shakespeare. Opposing statements can be found on the likelihood of Hand D in *Sir Thomas More* being Shakespeare's, some of them informed by close analysis of evidence, others not. Hand D sceptics rely on a recycled piece of information that is demonstrably incorrect—namely, that the distinctively Shakespearian spelling 'scilens' for *silence* is found in two non-Shakespeare plays; it is not. *Arden of Faversham* is rarely considered a Shakespearian play, yet it has recently been argued persuasively that Shakespeare probably did have a hand in it.[21] Outside observers could be forgiven for thinking that there is so much tortuous and impenetrable disagreement in this field that it should be left well alone.

Moreover, the highly technical studies falling under the heading of 'stylometry' have produced uneven results based on sometimes impenetrable statistical procedures. The humanities community is still struggling to understand how to identify a valid or invalid procedure and to negotiate an unexpected finding. Part of the difficulty lies in the interface between two different intellectual traditions and methodologies. But there are challenges for the investigator that go beyond cross-disciplinary communication. It is the nature of the text as a source of evidence that, though it is in some cases compliant, in other cases it may resist the expectation that, given the application of sufficient ingenuity, it will yield determinate statistics. One might suspect too that in some cases the investigator's expectation of certain results leads to an unconscious selection of data that seems to support those results and to a rejection as non-significant of comparable data that do not accord.

Nevertheless, there are grounds for optimism that computational analysis will make a convincing contribution to attribution study. The most widely applicable methods and the most coherent and persuasive results have come from investigations that depend on establishing a broad profile of different kinds of data, and results that conform in showing the same division of authorship, with each test having transparent evidence and procedures. Some of the techniques were established in the late 1950s in Cyrus Hoy's investigations of the 'Beaumont and Fletcher' plays, where the problem of distinguishing Francis Beaumont from John Fletcher was often compounded by the presence of other dramatists such as Philip Massinger and Thomas Middleton.[22] Hoy's concern was to avoid the impressionism of earlier studies that had relied on an unsophisticated and subjective use of verbal parallels between texts. He looked instead at grammatical and lexical choices that established an identifiable fingerprint for each writer. For example, a typical Fletcher characteristic is a high incidence of feminine endings to verse-lines, and, compared with other dramatists, he favours 'ye' over 'you'. Hoy was able to show that such features fluctuate in accord with each other; they indicate a sensible division of labour, and the identified Fletcher passages are reasonably in tune with most critics' sense of what sounds like Fletcherian writing.

The more recent studies of MacD. P. Jackson and Jonathan Hope have added sophistication to Hoy's approach.[23] Jackson establishes procedures for assessing statistical significance, extends the range of evidence, and applies it to plays in and around the Shakespeare canon. These might include grammatical preferences ('have' as against 'hath', for instance), habits of metre and rhyming (Middleton favoured rhyming couplets and was in the unShakespearian habit of mixing verse and prose in a single speech), preferred oaths and expletives, preferred contractions, and choice between doublets ('between' as against 'betwixt'). In recent work Jackson has defined a methodology for using the extensive database of the electronic resource *Literature Online* as a tool for extending and improving the accuracy of evidence previously identified by patient reading and counting. The same resource has enabled Jackson and others to refine the indentification of parallels of authorially distinctive words and phrases. It can be shown, for instance, that a word or phrase occurs only in a particular dramatist's work, and never elsewhere in the period as a whole. Hope, again focusing on Shakespeare, identifies linguistic variables characteristic of certain social populations, defined by age, status, or geographical region. Hence Shakespeare, as compared with Fletcher or Middleton, has identifiably old-fashioned and provincial preferences. Linguistic features of text no longer inhabit a vacuum, but are attached to the practices of a writer in a way that relates to his or her social background.

There remain limitations to this kind of testing. Some writers have more strongly individualized habits than others. Hoy himself recognized, for example, that Beaumont's hand is sometimes identified more on the basis of an absence of markers characteristic of Fletcher or another writer than on specific positive evidence for his own hand. Moreover, it is rare to find absolute consistency of usage. Even the ratio between one usage (such as 'ye') and its alternative ('you') can vary between different texts of the same authorship, sometimes for inexplicable reasons. Attribution studies aim nevertheless to find a goodness of fit between indicators that are reasonably stable within each author's habits, as well as significantly differentiated between authors.

Hoy's tests also assume, as do other forms of attribution study, that the writing of a play will break down into more-or-less self-contained sections, the typical unit being a scene. This premiss is reasonable in so far as shared playwrighting would usually begin with a division of labour so that each dramatist could write sections for which he held initial responsibility, and it often turns out to be valid in practice. But there was no fixed pattern for the sharing of work: a play might be divided by plot (as with Middleton and William Rowley's *The Changeling*), by act (as with *Pericles*), by character (as to some extent with the Steward in *Timon of Athens*), or by some combination of these. Moreover, individual scenes were sometimes split between more than one writer, and one writer might revise the work of another, or eventually copy out the entire play, superimposing his preferences over those of his colleague as he did so.

These considerations weaken the empirical value of attribution testing, because contrary evidence is not invalidating: indications of Hand A in a scene otherwise attributable to Hand B can readily be explained, and so they do not refute Hand B's authorship of the scene in the first instance. Such difficulties need careful and patient negotiation, and there is always a risk that the outcome will be to some extent influenced by the theoretical models of collaboration that the investigator deploys.

Other questions potentially complicate any simple division of a play between collaborators. Might the theory of 'accommodation' apply, whereby participants might congenially shift their usages towards each other, as Hope proposes for the disputed sections of *All Is True*? Might a scribe or compositor have complicated the picture by eliminating some part of the authorial fingerprint and imposing his own characteristics? These are real problems to which there are no standard answers. But they do not amount to a theoretical objection to the whole enterprise. If a situation arises where variation might reflect compositorial or scribal practices, such possibilities can be investigated. *Timon of Athens* is a good case in point. If, as has been suggested, a different compositor set one of the pages, his presence does not dispose of the evidence cited to support Middleton's hand. One editor attempted to explain the distinctive profile of contractions over part of the play in terms of an overlay introduced by the scribe Ralph Crane, but his findings have since then been decisively rejected.[24] Here, an anti-disintegrationist was keen to find an alternative to co-authorship, but the alternative can be ruled out.

One reason why an aura of conflict sometimes surrounds attribution studies is that the critical and ideological reasons for undertaking such investigations are themselves profoundly in dispute. For example, when Jeffrey Masten objects to the methods of the school of Hoy, his criticisms sound as though they address a failure to establish adequately grounded conclusions, but Masten's more fundamental concern lies elsewhere. He favours a principle of collaboration that erases authorial voice and describes the text in terms of socially constructed language that is not the special preserve of individual writers. His fundamental charge against attribution studies is that they act in accordance with the ideology of single authorship: they treat collaboration as abnormal, and cope with it by attempting to distribute the sections of a collaborative play into separate authorial canons.[25]

In other words, what presents itself as the dispassionate philological project of attribution study turns out, in this view, to support a conservatively romantic notion of the author that is inappropriate to early modern playwriting. Yet it is only through seeking to describe the artistic, cultural, and material aspects of authorship and collaboration with respect to particular texts that any notion of the author can be founded, whether romantic or post-dating Michel Foucault's metamorphosis of authorship from the act of writing to the construction of the authorial figure through acts of publication and reception.

Masten's provocative critique finds its anchorings in Gerald Eades Bentley's influential study of the profession of dramatist, which demonstrated the extent to which early modern dramatic authorship was shaped by the institutional circumstances of the theatre. Bentley considered that up to half the plays of the period probably involved the work of more than one dramatist, though this includes adaptations that were originally written by a single dramatist.[26] The figures are highly conjectural estimates, for a number of reasons. Most plays written in the period are now lost, and we know little or nothing about them. The plays that were preserved because they were published as printed books may be atypical of the drama as a whole, and, as we have seen, the preservation of a play does not ensure an accurate statement of its authorship on the title page. It is also by no means certain how typical are the practices uniquely recorded in the *Diary* of Philip Henslowe, whose records as financial manager of the Admiral's Men and other companies are crucial evidence. The magical watershed of 50 per cent, in any case, is not entirely the point. There was probably not a predominating and normative practice of collaborative authorship as described by Masten in the early years of the professional theatre. Rather, there seems to have been an acceptance and widespread practice of both single authorship and collaboration. Greene and Marlowe wrote both collaborations and plays of single authorship; the one collaborative play in Peele's hand is the otherwise Shakespearian *Titus Andronicus*; Kyd and Lyly are not know to have collaborated at all.

The authorship of a text is a matter of standard enquiry into one of the most fundamental matters we can expect to know of it, the central element in the question: how was this text produced? In cases such as *All Is True* and *Timon of Athens* the attempt to answer this question of who wrote what involves challenging the claim in the First Folio of 1623 that this play, along with the others, is, simply, 'Mr William Shakespeares'. In the Folio, silence on the whole subject of divided authorship enables an idealized image of Shakespeare to be kept apart from the contaminating and less prestigious activity of collaboration (see Chapter 4). No book has been more influential to English literature than this publication, and the assumptions underlying its production came to be absorbed into our way of thinking about Shakespeare, about authorship, and about literature itself. A succession of Shakespeare editions over nearly 400 years has perpetuated the image of Shakespeare as a genius who stands apart from his fellow dramatists, their feet clogged in the mud of contingency and early modernity that Shakespeare alone transcends.

A different picture emerged in the 1664 reissue of the Third Folio, which announced on an expanded title page that seven new plays were added to the established catalogue:

Mr WILLIAM SHAKESPEAR's Comedies, Histories, and Tragedies. Published according to the true Originall Copies. *The third Impression.* And unto this Impression is added seven Playes, never before Printed in Folio. viz, *Pericles Prince of Tyre. The London Prodigall.* The History of *Thomas* L^{d}. *Cromwell.* Sir *John Oldcastle* Lord *Cobham.* The *Puritan Widow.* A *York-shire* Tragedy. The Tragedy of *Locrine.*

All were seen as having some claim to be of Shakespeare's authorship, but in most cases the claim was weak. In this volume, and the later seventeenth- and eighteenth-century editions that followed it, *A Yorkshire Tragedy*, now attributed to Thomas Middleton, stands alongside the two plays now accepted as partly by Shakespeare, *Pericles* and *The Two Noble Kinsmen*. Recent attribution study offers the prospect of moving away from the 'Shakespeare apocrypha', a vaguely defined and slowly evolving grouping of plays 'assigned' to Shakespeare (typically by other, untrusted commentators), and towards a grouping of plays identified as collaborations and included within the canon of his works. But that process is incomplete, and a typical complete works of the twentieth century followed the First Folio precedent of ignoring or diminishing the issue of collaboration. Only the Oxford Shakespeare systematically re-evaluated the issue of collaboration.[27] In this edition, the title pages of plays thought to be collaborative clearly state that the play is by Shakespeare and whoever his partner(s) might have been. Here the reader will find that Shakespeare is presented as a working dramatist, and his shared labours are given recognition as such.

The study of attribution is an important prerequisite to the editing of Shakespeare's works as a whole and of some particular plays. It can affirm or interrogate the authorial context of a particular text, and affirm or interrogate the contents and complexion of an authorial canon. But its significance is not for editors alone. It can lead on to questions about the nature of authorship itself, especially in an environment where the modern concept of literary authorship had relatively little purchase and collaboration was common. It can address early figurations of collaborative authors and the relationship between them. It can develop towards analysis of a collaborative text as a harmonized or contestatory dialogue among different authorial voices within it. It can identify different contiguities between the text and the culture in which it participated. It can offer a means to explore the development through time of a text that presents itself in a simultaneous and linear fashion. It can restore a text to historical contexts through which it has passed between its original writing and its publication.

The internal dynamics of the collaborative play may be considered by again taking the example of *Timon of Athens*. Middleton, it is now believed, took responsibility for specific areas of the text: the banquet scene (1.2), the creditor scenes and the banishment of Alcibiades (all of Act 3 except the middle part of the mock-banquet scene 3.7), and most of the lines dealing with Timon's Steward (Flavius) in Act 4. He may also have contributed oddments such as the closing ten lines of 1.1 and parts of 2.2. Shakespeare's Timon, both in Athens and in the woods, defies all customary behaviour; it is Middleton who most crucially articulates these opposite, social forms of expression. Where Shakespeare's language is metaphoric and hyperexpressive, Middleton's is satiric and reductive; most of his speakers fend off sincere self-expression rather than articulate their feelings. This is not to say that Shakespeare contributed no irony or satire to *Timon of Athens*, or that Middleton contributed no emotional sincerity. Rather, Middleton gave the play a distinctive quality that is not Shakespearian, creating a dialogue or tension between different styles and areas of represented experience. Different parts of the play contrast in authorial ideolect. They are also differently rooted in early modern society and culture. Shakespeare wrote about gold; Middleton wrote about debt.[28] To understand the play, it is helpful to understand it as a collaboration, whilst viewing collaboration itself as a valid and *different* mode of play production.

Theatre

THEATRICAL MANUSCRIPTS

Early modern playwrights were working in a commercial situation that accorded no intellectual prestige and no proprietary rights over the texts they delivered to the company. To judge by the records kept by Philip Henslowe, the financial manager of the Admiral's Men, the turnover of plays was astonishingly high. As Tiffany Stern relates:

In January 1596, the same [Admiral's] Company played on every day except Sunday and presented fourteen different plays. Of these, six were only ever given one performance. The next month their new play, Chapman's *The Blind Beggar of Alexandria*, first performed on 12 February, was followed by a play they had not performed for 140 days, Marlowe's *Dr Faustus*. During the 140 days that intervened between one *Faustus* and the next, the Admiral's Company had played 107 performances of twenty-one other works.[1]

The demand for new plays evidently eased after 1612, by which time the companies had established a body of old plays suitable for revival, but by this time Shakespeare was about to retire as a playwright.

The writing was often on a topic proposed by the company, and the dramatist or dramatists often drew up an initial 'plot' for approval by the company. Once drafted, the play would be subject to one or more read-throughs by the dramatist or the company, and further alterations at the request of the company might follow. In constructing the play the dramatist had to make best use of the available actors. Plays were written with an inbuilt awareness of the size of the company, and parts were scripted so that more than one could be played by a single actor. The sharers in the company—typically about ten of them—took most of the parts; minor and non-speaking roles were distributed between hired men. There was a certain amount of typecasting. For most of Shakespeare's writing career the leading male roles were taken by Richard Burbage. Shakespeare's scripting of clowns' roles changed to reflect the abilities of the actor. William Kemp left the company in late 1599, evidently to be succeeded by the more melancholic and wistful Robert Armin. Kemp probably played Bottom and Falstaff. Feste and the Fool in *King Lear* are in Armin's vein.

The dramatist sometimes delivered a manuscript that was fit for use in the theatre; in other cases it needed copying out by a scribe. In either case, it was then usually marked up in the theatre to become the company 'book' or 'prompt book'. The theatrical manuscript is a site for textual alteration. Both the author-centred text and the theatre-centred text that emerges from it might coexist in the self-same document. Where text is replaced, it is usually nevertheless still present on the page and visible to the reader. Authorial stage directions and speech prefixes may sometimes stay unaltered, even where they are inconsistent. The theatre-centred text would by no means be fully consistent and regularized. It could remain in use for many years, accumulating new annotations for each revival.

The surviving theatre playbooks, about twenty in number, are far from homogeneous. They vary in three important respects: whether they were written out by a dramatist or a scribe, whether (and to what extent) they have been annotated by subsequent hands, and whether at the end of the manuscript there is a note from the office of the Master of the Revels showing that the manuscript was submitted for licensing for the stage. Henry Glapthorne's *The Lady Mother* (1635) has a licence but no annotation. A number of manuscripts, such as *Edmund Ironside* and *The Two Noble Ladies*, have annotation but no sign of the hand of the Master of the Revels. Arthur Brown, editor of Heywood's *The Captives* (1634) for Malone Society Reprints, describes that manuscript as probably 'a manuscript handed in by the author and annotated by the book-keeper for the guidance of the scribe for whom the official "book" was to be prepared'.[2] Yet the manuscript's annotation may, after all, have been made with respect to the text as it was laid out in the manuscript, rather than in anticipation of a transcript.[3] If this is so, the term 'theatrical manuscript' would seem appropriate irrespective of whether a transcription was made. Such a text blurs the distinction between authorial papers and theatrical manuscript.

In the normal course of things, the theatrical manuscript would be submitted to the office of the Master of the Revels, a court official appointed by the Lord Chamberlain whose duties included regulation of plays performed in the public theatres. He would write into the manuscript an unconditional licence to perform. Or he would license the play subject to certain changes: 'This second Maiden's Tragedy—for it hath no name inscribed—may with the reformations be acted publicly, 31 October 1611. By me, G. Buc.' Or the company might have to demonstrate that the required changes had been made, as is the case in the following licence, which begins as a conditional permission but after a change of mind ends as a requirement to resubmit: 'This play, called *The Seaman's Honest Wife*, all the oaths left out in the action as they are crossed out in the book, and all other reformations strictly observed, may be acted, not otherwise. This 27 June 1633. Henry Herbert. I command your book-keeper to present me with a fair copy hereafter, and to leave out all oaths, profaneness, and public ribaldry, as he will answer at his peril. Herbert.'

The absence of a licence from a number of these plays does not mean that licensing was optional or occasional. All plays required licensing. As evidently with Massinger's *The Parliament of Love* (1624), the licence may sometimes have been lost or removed at a later date. But we must countenance the other possibility, that some of the surviving theatrical manuscripts were not the official 'book' and that a second theatre manuscript must therefore have been prepared. This may have depended on theatre personnel or company practice; the surviving manuscripts of plays prepared for the Chamberlain's/King's Men were mostly submitted for licence.

Janet Clare has presented a picture of censorship that suggests individually minded dramatists struggling against an oppressive state system.[4] Indeed, the fortunes of dramatists and theatre companies could be marred when they came into conflict with the authorities. Ben Jonson, George Chapman, and John Marston all suffered imprisonment for satirising the Scots in *Eastward Ho!* The early Jacobean boys' company the Children of the Revels was driven out of existence after a series of scandals in which it infringed the prohibition against satirizing royalty and leading courtiers. However, the overriding interest of the Master of the Revels was to keep the theatre functioning and well governed. He was responsible not only for censorship but also for the provision of entertainment at court. Plays from the public theatre were performed at court during periods of festivity such as New Year. Consequently the court had a particular interest in protecting the theatres from the hostility of the anti-theatrical lobby, which was influential with the City of London authorities. There were concerns about law and order as well as questions of morality and religion. The court's regulation of the theatre, though sometimes detrimental to particular plays, had an overall objective in ensuring that a well-governed theatre industry survived.[5] Dramatists were occasionally imprisoned; though they might be threatened with further physical punishment, there is no known case where this actually happened.

With this proviso we may consider one of the most notorious instances of the censorship of plays in the period, an instance that came to involve Shakespeare himself. When the theatre company sought a licence to perform *Sir Thomas More*, they did not get it. Players were prohibited from showing sedition on stage, and the Master of the Revels, Edmund Tilney, saw the play's depiction of riots against European immigrants resident in London as an offence, presumably seeing potential for the play to provoke violence of a similar kind. The licence he issued was highly conditional, demanding such drastic alterations that he probably stopped the projected staging in its tracks. He wrote in the margin opposite the play's opening lines:

Leave out the insurrection wholly, and the cause thereof, and begin with Sir Thomas More at the Mayor's sessions, with a report afterwards of his good service done being Sheriff of London upon a mutiny against the Lombards—only by a short report, and not otherwise. At your own perils. E. Tilney.

Tilney also introduced a number of marginal notes, alterations, crossings-out (sometimes very heavy cross-hatching), and marks for omission (typically a line drawn vertically down the left-hand edge of the dialogue). His attention was not confined to the insurrection scenes. The dramatists had handled their depiction of More's downfall with such circumspection that Henry VIII never appears on stage and is never given his personal name, and the contents of the 'articles' More refuses to sign are carefully left unspecified. Tilney nevertheless marked a number of passages in this part of the play for omission or revision, including the passage showing More's arrest in the Council, and his later criticism of

> the prince, in all his sweet-gorged maw,
> And his rank flesh that sinfully renews
> The noon's excess in the night's dangerous surfeits

(A5.23)

Tilney's injunction and omission marks, though they fell short of banning the play outright, probably led the company at first to abandon it as impaired beyond all possibility of performance. The insurrection they were instructed to omit makes up the main plot in the first half of the play. But later, when a second attempt was made to complete the play and bring it to the stage, Shakespeare was commissioned to replace one of the insurrection scenes, perhaps because he was recognized as having a special ability to depict a popular riot in such a way as to fall short of giving further offence to Tilney. The result was the episode already encountered in Chapter 1.

Sir Thomas More is an extreme case. But Tilney may have initiated a severe example of censorship of another Shakespeare play. It is *Richard II*, where the 'deposition scene' was not printed in the First Quarto of 1597. Like *Sir Thomas More*, the play dealt with moments in English history of extraordinary political sensitivity to Queen Elizabeth, the one dealing obliquely with Henry VIII's break with the Catholic Church, the other showing directly the dethroning of a legitimate anointed monarch. Like the arrest of More, the episode in question is the fulcrum of the play's political narrative, representing the moment where the leading character definitively loses his power and begins his journey to death at the monarch's hand. The exact explanation as to how *Richard II* came to be deprived of its key scene must remain a matter of speculation (and we cannot entirely exclude the possibility that the 1597 text was later augmented rather than itself being subject to cutting), but it is most plausible that theatre censorship lies behind Q1's omission.

Other Shakespeare plays may have been dealt with similarly. If, as has been suspected, some lines were cut from Folio *King Lear* for reasons of censorship, the Master of the Revels is likely to have been responsible. The passage most strongly to be suspected as censored in the Folio is the Fool's satire on monopolies in the Quarto text (*History of King Lear*, 4.135–50). Elsewhere, the effects of censorship are not confined to cuts. In *1 Henry IV* the character more familiar as Sir John Falstaff was originally called Sir John Oldcastle. The change to the now familiar name evidently came in response to protests from Lord Brooke of the Cobham family, as Shakespeare's play scurrilously caricatured Oldcastle, an earlier bearer of the title Lord Cobham.

The evidence marked in a manuscript of the control exercised by the Master of the Revels establishes that the manuscript was intended to act as the company's official document of the play. If the play is fully licensed, we can infer that it actually served in this capacity. But the feature that most obviously identifies some of the manuscripts as designed for practical use in the theatre is the presence of annotations by theatre personnel. Annotations might add stage directions such as missing entrances and exits, calls for music (commonly 'flourish'; more specifically 'The lute strikes, and then the song' in Massinger's *Believe As You List*, ll. 2003–4), for other sounds ('Thunder') or for properties (examples in *Believe As You List* include 'with three papers', 'with poinard and halter', 'with bread and water').[6] They sometimes anticipated action in advance ('Fellows ready', 'Bar ready' in *The Captives*, l. 1464, l. 2834; 'Table ready and six chairs', 'Mr Hobs called up', 'Gascoigne and Hubert below, ready to open the trapdoor for Mr Taylor', 'Harry Wilson and boy ready for the song at the arras' in *Believe As You List*, ll. 654–6, ll. 661–2, ll. 1825–31, ll. 1968–71). They might alter existing stage directions, whether by supplementing them or copying them from the right margin to the left. They sometimes supply actors' names ('Messenger: T. Goodal' in *Sir Thomas More*, 9.0.1). The evidential value of actors' names is in itself dubious, in that the author himself may have occasionally written them. In quartos closely based on an authorial script such as Q2 *Romeo and Juliet* the appearance of an actor's name does not in itself constitute evidence for annotation by the theatre employee whose function Henry Herbert described as the book-keeper—though that possibility certainly exists. The Clown called Peter is given the entry 'Enter Will Kemp' at 4.4.127.2. The following dialogue runs:

> PETER Musicians, O, musicians! 'Heart's ease, 'Heart's ease';
>   O, an you will have me live, play 'Heart's ease'.
> [FIRST] MUSICIAN Why 'Heart's ease'?
> PETER O, musicians, because my heart itself plays 'My heart
>   is full of woe'.

Kemp, the company's famous clown, may be named specifically at this point because he was himself associated with singing the popular song called 'Heart's ease'. For *his* heart to be full of woe is particularly exceptional. Peter's call for the familiar and sanguine 'Heart's ease' suggests a pointed contrast between the song's possibly direct association with the actor Kemp and the character Peter's need to be cured of woe. In this case there is no obvious dissociation from Shakespeare. But in a text such as Folio *3 Henry VI* the names 'Gabriel' (1.2.47.1 and 49) and 'Sinklo' and 'Humphrey' (both 3.1.0.1) can be identified and associated with players active several years after the original composition. In such a case it is clearer that their presence has theatrical provenance.[7]

A theatre book-keeper's annotations, as they can be seen in surviving manuscripts, might occasionally clarify or alter speech prefixes. So in Shakespeare's contribution to *Sir Thomas More* Hand C distributed the speeches Shakespeare had casually assigned to 'other' between George Betts, his brother the Clown Betts, and Williamson. He also clarified that an undifferentiated 'bettes' was George Betts by adding 'Ge' for George; he cogently sorted out two speeches that Shakespeare impossibly gave to a figure he identified as 'Sher' by reassigning them to the Mayor and Williamson, and transferred a speech from 'all' the citizens to the citizens' leader Lincoln.

Hand C was also involved with the stage directions, and here his interventions were less successful. The scene begins with an entrance direction written or copied out by Hand C at the bottom of the leaf before Shakespeare's contribution:

> *Enter Lincoln. Doll. Clown. George betts williamson others*
> *And A sergaunt at armes*

Hand C had transcribed the previous episode, and finished the job with this entry anticipating the Shakespeare passage. But his inclusion of the Sergeant at Arms contradicts a change he made in the Shakespearian portion of the manuscript, where Hand C added 'Enter' above the first speech prefix for the Sergeant at Arms. If the combined opening entry and annotation provide the Sergeant with two entries, Hand C, like Shakespeare, evidently did not realize that Sir Thomas More had no entry at all. It is possible that he annotated the passage before he copied the previous episode and wrote in the opening entry direction for Shakespeare's scene, in which case these deficiencies would not have been apparent to him. Hand C's failure to resolve the staging of the episode is at all events probably connected to a circumstantial detail of the make-up and sequence of preparation of the revisions. The exact situation is not typical of theatrical manuscripts generally, but is nevertheless analogous to other unpredictable and equally circumstantial details that might be found in other manuscripts.

As seen in Chapter 1, Hand C deleted lines, probably because the under-punctuation confused him, and he deleted two words, probably because he judged them to be unmetrical. Elsewhere, theatre annotators might mark larger passages of dialogue for omission. But the manuscript might also gain new material. In some cases the dramatist might be brought back to add in revisions, as happened in the play known variously as *The Second Maiden's Tragedy* or *The Lady's Tragedy*, where Thomas Middleton wrote out new passages on slips of paper that were then pasted into the manuscript.

Almost all the surviving manuscripts that have been described as prompt books contain at least some theatrical annotation. Given the variety of feature and the thinness of external documentation, it is hard to piece together a picture of how these manuscripts were used, but, in addition to serving as the immediate source for the actors' parts and as the official document of the play, they seem to have assumed an active role in the preparation and perhaps the regulation of performance, as is suggested by the examples of annotation cited above. The manuscript of the anonymous play *Woodstock* demonstrates the stability and continuity of staging practice over a series of revivals.[8] The same manuscript was used from one production to the next. For each revival minor alterations were made by way of annotation. The dialogue was affected by deletion marks but was generally kept intact.

Stage directions as originally supplied were kept in place when new stage directions were added.

Though the term 'prompt book' was used for most of the twentieth century to describe such manuscripts, it has been criticized as a misleading and anachronistic word. The suggestion is that there was no prompter as we now understand it. In support of describing theatre manuscripts as 'prompt books' it may be recalled that theatre manuscripts sometimes record the need for particular properties several lines before they are actually required, suggesting that some of them at least were used in connection with the time-bound flow of rehearsal or performance. The term 'prompt book' remains in place in Stern's discussions on rehearsal. She has adduced evidence for the function of prompter in the early modern theatre. This figure, perhaps the same person as the book-keeper, played a major role, and not only in prompting actors; he 'managed the entrances and exits, arranged the basic blocking on the stage, and saw to it that the timing was right *during performance*, rather like a modern musical conductor'.[9] The emphasis on 'during performance' is a reminder that there was little rehearsal as we know it. Whereas we now understand a theatrical performance to emerge from a long period of preparation, the conditions of performance in early modern England allowed very little time for such activity. There is correspondingly all the more reason why it would be important for someone to regulate the actual passage of performance.

If we think of a 'book-keeper' who annotates a 'playbook', we will develop an image of that document as having a documentary, even archival function. If, instead, we refer to a 'prompter' who maintains a 'prompt book', the implication is that the text in the manuscript has a more immediate connection with the play as spoken and performed on the stage. But is it really possible that the plays in the Shakespeare Folio thought to have been based on theatre manuscripts represent a text that could have been played on stage? The potential objection is they are simply too long.

We do not know with any certainty how long the performance of an Elizabethan or Jacobean play would take. But many critics have found it difficult to reconcile the length of a Shakespeare play—not least, emphatically long plays such as *Richard III* and *Hamlet*—with

Shakespeare's own reference to 'two-hours' traffic of our stage' (*Romeo and Juliet*, Prologue, 12). We need not take the 'two hours' any more at face value than when the opening Chorus to *Henry V* describes the theatre as a 'cock-pit' (*Henry V*, Prologue, 9 and 11). The Chorus to *Henry V* also implies a time length for performance—the events span 'many years' but they will be represented within the time measured by 'an hourglass' (ll. 30–1). The implication is less precise than in *Romeo and Juliet* (does it refer to all the events or only some of them?), and indeed no one would set forward this passage to argue that the performance time might have been a single hour. Although the Chorus in *Romeo and Juliet* seems more prescriptive as to what is contained in the time limit, for he summarizes the entire plot, we should likewise take into account his rhetorical strategies. Like the Chorus in *Henry V*, he disarmingly belittles the theatrical event in order to contrast it with the import of the play's subject matter. In contrast, he also uses a trope of analogy that explains the specific number two: 'Two households' have become 'the two-hours' traffic'. The speech has the artifice of a sonnet; it is not a document of performance practice.

But there are several other references in the period to plays taking two hours on stage. In the most detailed treatment of the topic Andrew Gurr argues that the 'maximal' texts preserved in the plays as most reliably printed are significantly longer than the plays as performed. He concludes that it is possible that some of the texts castigated as 'bad' quartos, significantly shorter than their 'good' counterparts, may well preserve the length and structural features of a play as performed, even though they have been textually deformed.[10] Gurr suggests that, as Q1 *Henry V* lacks the speeches of the Chorus, these were probably not performed in Shakespeare's theatre.

Gurr admits that actual performance time might have run up to three hours. Lines would probably have been delivered somewhat faster than in modern theatre practice, and in the public theatre there were no act intervals. Allowing for these factors, up to 3,000 lines could be performed in three hours.[11] Nevertheless, the longer plays of Shakespeare present a problem. The survival of Shakespeare texts of varying length might be related to this problem. *Hamlet* provides the best insight, both because in its full form it is a very long play, and because it survives in three versions of different length. Q2 (1604–5) is agreed to be the most immediately author-based text; it is 3,668 lines long.[12] The text in F has been revised and is closer to theatre practice; it is about 160 lines shorter. Q1 (1603) has been regarded by most recent scholars as a memorially corrupted text based on a staged version of the play; it runs to approximately 2,200 lines, between half and two-thirds of Q2. If F is based directly or indirectly on a theatrical manuscript, the text in that manuscript is still so long that one might question whether it could have been staged in full. But the persistent lack of correspondence between lines in Q1 and anything in Q2 or F makes it impossible to identify Q1 as an accurate reflection of the play as staged. Passages in Q2/F are persistently reduced by short and inexact paraphrase, rather than, or as well as, by determinate cuts of the kind witnessed in play manuscripts. It would be incautious if not absurd to suppose that all the shortening of this and other 'bad' quartos arises from deliberate cutting for the stage. Q1 and Folio *Hamlet* may well offer false alternatives in determining the form of the play as performed.

Shakespeare's plays, along with Jonson's, Webster's, and some of Fletcher's, tend to be longer than is typical of plays of the period. It is significant that, of the four statements in published editions that are usually cited to substantiate the claim that printed plays are longer than plays on the stage, three are from editions of plays by these dramatists. The 1600 Quarto of Jonson's *Every Man Out of his Humour* claims to contain 'more than hath been publicly spoken or acted'. Webster's *Duchess of Malfi* is said to include 'more than was presented upon the stage, and left out of presentation for superfluous length (as some of the players pretended)'. And the publisher Humphrey Moseley explained in his preface to the Beaumont and Fletcher Folio of 1647 that, 'When these comedies or tragedies were presented on the stage, the actors omitted some scenes and passages, with the author's consent, as occasion led them...But now you have both all that was acted, and all that was not.'[13] Shakespeare may be a similar case. The claim in the Folio preliminaries that the plays in that volume are 'absolute in their numbers', though susceptible to other interpretations, may indicate as much. But some of the quoted pronouncements affirm that the long text is the 'maximal' basis from which performance was derived, and so the status of, for instance, Folio *Hamlet* as a theatre-oriented text based on a 'playbook' or 'prompt book' is not challenged by this evidence. If the actors omitted 'some scenes and passages' that are printed in the Shakespeare Folio, and if (as one would only expect) those omitted passages are also omitted in the shorter and textually altered quartos, it does not follow by any means that texts such as Q1 *Henry V* and Q1 *Hamlet* accurately reflect the plays as staged by the Lord Chamberlain's Men.

PLOTS AND PARTS

The theatre of Shakespeare's time generated a number of documents other than full manuscripts in the process of bringing the play to the stage. There would be an initial plot, sometimes usefully distinguished as the 'author-plot', which was used as the basis on which the company and dramatist agreed the plan for the play before it was written.[14] This is probably distinct from the document, also called a plot and usefully distinguished as the 'theatre-plot', which was used in some way to prepare for or to regulate performance.[15] A small number of these survive.[16] They consist of a single leaf, mounted on card, with a rectangular hole above the centre. The play is divided into scenes, with a series of stage directions naming both the roles and the actors, who were to play them. For instance, the anonymous play *1 Tamar Cham* (1592) survives only in the form of a plot preserved in the Shakespeare editor George Steevens's print facsimile published in 1803; the first scene reads as follows:

Sound	Enter Mango Cham, 3 noblemen: Mr.
Sennet.	Denygten 1 w. Cart. 2 & Tho. Marbeck
	& W. Parr. attendants: Parsons & George:
	To them Otanes: Tamar: & Colmogra:
	H. Jeffs: Mr. Allen & Mr. Burne. exit
Sound	Mango & nobles: manet the rest Exit Tamor
flourish.	& Otanes manet Colmogra Exit.

At first sight the information presented here looks confused, but this is only on account of the inefficiency, by modern standards, of the punctuation and layout in discriminating between the different items and kinds of information. Once these initial difficulties are addressed, the plot for this scene emerges as presenting an exceptionally well-ordered account of the action. The scene is constructed around the following entrances and exits:

1. Sound sennet. Enter Mango Cham and three noblemen.
2. Enter to them Otanes, Tamar, and Colmogra.
3. Sound flourish. Exeunt Mango and nobles; the rest remain.
4. Exeunt Tamor and Otanes; Colmogra remains.
5. Exit Colmogra.

These are normalized versions of the stage directions as they might have appeared in a theatrical manuscript, or as they would appear in a modern edition based on such a manuscript or an edition printed from it. The directions for sennet and flourish, marked in a separate box, establish Mango Cham as the authority figure who enters and exits to fanfares of trumpets. Colmogra speaks a soliloquy at the end, presumably commenting on what has happened during the scene or projecting what will happen subsequently.

The plot adds in the names of the actors after each entry, enabling us to establish the following casting:

'Mango Cham': played by 'Mr. Denygten' (Thomas Downton)
'3 noblemen': played by 'w. Cart.', 'Tho. Marbeck', 'W. Parr' (William Cartwright, Thomas Marbeck, and William Parr)
'attendants': played by 'Parsons' and 'George' (Thomas Parsons and George Somerset)
'Otanes': played by 'H. Jeffs' (Humphrey Jeffes)
'Tamar': played by 'Mr. Allen' (Edward Alleyn)
'Colmogra': played by 'Mr. Burne' (understood to be Steevens's error for 'Bird', i.e. William Bird).

Where the plot designates an actor as 'Mr.' it is naming one of the principal actors and sharers of the company, the Lord Admiral's Men. The remaining actors include minor or journeymen adult actors (Cartwright, Marbeck, Parr, Jeffes) and boy actors (Parsons and perhaps Somerset).

This and other plots are crucial documents in the development of a play towards staged performance. Probably because papers from the company were better preserved than those of other troupes, most of the surviving examples relate to plays performed by the Lord Admiral's Men at dates ranging between the early-to-mid-1590s and 1602.[17]

Greg understood these mounted documents to have been designed with a rectangular hole cut in order for them to be hung on pegs in the theatre. The prompter would have taken the plot for the play in question and used it to regulate performance. David Bradley has concluded differently: their purpose was 'not, as Greg supposed, to direct performances, but to count the actors, to construct a framework for the correct making-out of their acting scrolls, to create a mutual accommodation between the cast and the text, and to direct rehearsals in the absence of the Book'.[18] If Bradley is right, the plot was prepared after the playbook, but before the parts or scrolls from which the actors learnt their lines. The plot would establish which actors needed which scrolls, and the playbook itself would be the source for the words that were written into the scrolls. But Stern reverts to a variant on Greg's position, suggesting that the plots were used by 'call-boys', assistants to the prompter who ensured that actors were ready to enter at the required times.[19]

The best-known actor's part to survive from the period is Edward Alleyn's for Orlando in Robert Greene's *Orlando Furioso*. The part—or the surviving sections of it—consists of strips of paper pasted together to make a long roll.[20] We can compare Alleyn's lines as written in it with the text as printed in John Danter's 1594 edition of the play; unfortunately Danter issued a shortened and evidently much altered text that relates problematically to the manuscript of the actor's part (and happens to demonstrate a marked lack of correspondence between a 'short' or 'bad' quarto and a standard performance text). How close the part is to the theatrical manuscript from which it was copied is impossible to judge. But the key characteristic is that the part is confined to the actor's lines, along with stage directions such as 'here he harkens' and 'he walketh up and down',[21] and merely the shortest of cues, sometimes no more than one or two words.

The actors' parts were the crucial intermediary document, the last written script before the lines were committed to memory and later performed. Consideration of the actor's part returns us to the relation between the playbook and the performed text. Such questions continue to vex and intrigue textual and theatre historians, and the surviving part of Orlando offers no clear answers to them.

REVISION AND ADAPTATION

To this point, our discussion has taken us away from the dramatist to investigate the treatment of the text by the theatre company. As we have seen, the distinction cannot be upheld rigorously, for the theatre company was involved in the original instigation of the work, and the dramatist, or dramatists, could remain involved after completing a draft by way of copying and revision as the rough draft evolved towards the licensed playbook. But dramatists might be required once more at a later stage. If the play was revived, it might be injected with new appeal, or, to quote the phrase in use in the period, with 'new additions'.

In the case of *King Lear* we witness in the variants between the First Quarto and Folio what is now widely regarded as a revision for the theatre in which Shakespeare himself played the decisive role. In 1978 Michael Warren influentially asserted that 'what we as scholars, editors, interpreters, and servants of the theatrical craft have to accept and learn to live by is the knowledge that we have two plays of *King Lear* sufficiently different to require that all further work on the play be based on either Q1 or F, but not the conflation of both'.[22]

Like other revised plays, *King Lear* was probably altered some years after its original performances in order to give it renewed appeal in the theatre. In contrast with the First Quarto, the Folio is supplied with act divisions. Act breaks reflect the act breaks that were needed in the indoor Blackfriars theatre but not the outdoor Globe. Illumination was by the artificial light of candles. These candles needed to be 'trimmed' or replaced several times during the performance. For this reason, the classical device of act divisions, to all practical purposes ignored in the amphitheatres, became necessary to the practicalities of staging. The performance was halted, and musicians played while the candles were trimmed. The King's Men began to play at the Blackfriars in about 1608. Any earlier Globe play that was revived for that theatre would need marking with act intervals. If the revisions of *King Lear* were made for a Blackfriars performance, they followed several years after the play's original composition in 1605–6. Vocabulary links with Shakespeare's other plays place the revision later still, in about 1610.[23] If these inferences are right, the distance in time and the changes in the physical setting for performance affirm the distinct identities of the two versions.

King Lear evidently conforms to the process of revision whereby the original dramatist was brought in to make the changes. A few scenes acquire a distinctly different shape, usually through cutting lines from the earlier text or adding new passages. The most striking and substantial omission in the Folio is of the 'mock trial' of Goneril and Regan during the storm when Lear is at the height of his madness. Like Ludwig van Beethoven's *Grosse Fuge* originally written as the last movement of his Opus 130 String Quartet in B Flat but then removed, the scene's absence from the final text does not argue against its greatness as writing, even if its removal was sanctioned by the author. The revisionist critics, noting the experimental dramaturgy of this episode and its lack of contribution to the plot, urged that the cut might have been made in response to the actors' experience of the play on stage. This point has been contested with reference to modern stagings in which directors have seen the scene as integral to the play's dramatic impact,[24] but it is hard to separate out such justifications from the predisposition of the reader towards the more familiar text. Despite changes such as these, the alterations manifested in Folio *King Lear* were not primarily structural, and go beyond the theatrical need to adjust the text for a revival in a different theatre. They typically introduced much more detailed cuts, small additions, and local rephrasings. Critics have located the effect of the changes not so much in the theatrical structure as in the treatment of specific roles (Lear, the Fool, Albany, and Edgar).[25] In these respects the revision has an authorial rather than theatrical complexion.

But the original dramatist was not always available; he might have moved on from the company or died. What happened when Shakespeare was not on hand to revise his own plays can be studied in *Macbeth* and *Measure for Measure*. Of the two plays, *Macbeth* is the better known and longer established example. The curious thing about *Macbeth* for a student of Shakespeare's text is that, as first printed in the 1623 First Folio, it includes cues for songs found also in a tragicomedy by Middleton called *The Witch*.[26] This play was evidently written in about 1616, by which time Shakespeare was no longer active as a writer. Closer examination of the songs in the two plays shows that they seem to have originated in *The Witch* and to have been subsequently transferred to *Macbeth*. It seems, then, that these songs were imported into *Macbeth* as part of a revival performed probably after Shakespeare's death. Other Middleton characteristics have been identified in the Hecate scenes (3.5; 4.1.39–60 and 141–8) in which the songs are performed and, locally, elsewhere in the play.

The theory that in 1621 Middleton adapted *Measure for Measure* in a similar manner is newer and less familiar, but the evidence in its favour is if anything stronger. Of initial interest are two strong indications that the Folio was printed, indirectly, from a manuscript that had been in use in the theatre several years after Shakespeare originally wrote the play. The absence of offensive oaths and references to God is striking, especially given the play's inclusion of scurrilous low-life characters and its concern with religious matters. This otherwise puzzling purity of diction points to a revival after 1606, when a new instrument of censorship, the Act to Restrain Abuses of Players, made it necessary to avoid performing profanity on stage. After 1606, profanity had to be removed from plays written under the earlier dispensation when they were revived. Likewise, the presence of act breaks probably reflects staging at the Blackfriars theatre after 1608. As we have seen was probably the case with *King Lear*, *Measure for Measure* would have been written for the Globe theatre, but would have needed act intervals for a revival at the Blackfriars.

The dating can be pushed markedly later by the appearance of the one conspicuously solitary song in *Measure for Measure*, 'Take Oh take those lips away', because the same song also occurs, with a second stanza, in *Rollo, Duke of Normandy* (alternatively known as *The Bloody Brother*). The situation is conspicuously similar to that with *Macbeth*. Every indication is that the song originated in the non-Shakespeare play, which was written in 1617–20, and that the first stanza was borrowed for *Measure for Measure*. Act intervals had been introduced, and the song provided an effective beginning to the new Act 4. A brief passage of dialogue after the song must have been added to lock it into the dramatic action. This part of the adaptation evidently also entailed transposition of the Duke's soliloquies 'O place and greatness' and 'He who the sword of heaven will bear', so as to produce a stronger close to the new Act 3.

By comparison, a passage at the beginning of 1.2 is a more straight-forward and sustained piece of dramatic composition, but it too can be seen to date from after Shakespeare's death. Most of the play's editors have accepted that there is a duplication in the second scene, and it now seems that Middleton wrote the first eighty-two lines. It is Middleton who favours the linguistic forms that mark this passage out from the rest of the play and from Shakespeare's usage more generally. Moreover, an array of individual words, distinctive phrases, and idiosyncratic turns of thought can be paralleled in Middleton but not Shakespeare. There are also striking Middleton parallels for the passage's staging, structure, and dramatic function, all contributing to a strongly Shakespeare-negative, Middleton-positive profile.

Middleton evidently added a few other lines and short passages, and in the adaptation the location was probably changed from a city in Italy (perhaps Ferrara) to Vienna.[27] Italian names such as Isabella, Angelo, and Lucio are the most immediate evidence of the former location. But the expansion of 1.2 and restructuring of 4.1 were his main contributions. With the opening of 1.2 Middleton updated the play by inserting a passage that was intensely topical to the early 1620s. It both added to and thematized the play's participation in public debate, at a time when King James was attempting to stifle it, and when Parliament was insisting on its rights to debate foreign policy. Lucio's conversation with his companions supplies a sensationalizing but localizing environment variously for the Duke's supposed urgent affairs out of Vienna, for Claudio's sexual misdemeanour as a topic for rumour-mongering, and for Lucio's role as news-bringer to Isabella in the convent, not to mention the rumours he later promotes about the Duke's sexual conduct. The allusions to the Thirty Years War are especially significant. Middleton seizes on the significance of the new location Vienna to the moment of the revival. By 1621 it was the seat of the Catholic Emperor Ferdinand II, and a city at war. It is in this context that the audience would have understood the opening exchange:

> LUCIO If the Duke with the other dukes come not to compo-
> sition with the King of Hungary, why then, all the dukes
> fall upon the King.
> FIRST GENTLEMAN Heaven grant us its peace, but not the
> King of Hungary's!
>
> (1.2.1–5)

The Hungarian prince Bethlen Gàbor had joined the Protestant alliance; as a gesture of defiance towards the Emperor's title of King of Hungary, he was elected king in 1620, so making a 'King of Hungary' an enemy of Vienna. His troops made incursions against Austrian strongholds in Bohemia, and into Austria itself; by mid-September 1621 they were within sight of the walls of Vienna. The passage is not only topical to 1621; its matter is more in line with Middleton's interest in the religious politics of continental Europe.

The revision was concerned not only to make the play topical, but also to make the play's structure, style, and fascinations match the dramaturgy of an indoor hall theatre in the early 1620s. The introduction of a song takes advantage of the beginning of the new fourth act to impose a new two-part structure in which the song is a formal marker of a turning point, opening on a realm of experience remote from Vienna's rigorous nexus between sexual crime and punishment.

Revision and adaptation return the play to dramatists. But they are engaged in particular kinds of alteration that, in the first instance at least, reflect the needs of the theatre company rather than the aspirations of the reviser. In their revisions of *Sir Thomas More* Hand C and Heywood created a new role in the insurrection scenes, that of the clown Betts. The new comic matter is an end in itself, but it might also be designed to ward off the Master of the Revels, by defusing the political urgency of the insurrection and making its supporters look more foolish. In *Measure for Measure* the roles of Lucio and Pompey seem to have been similarly expanded to augment the play's comic appeal. Songs, too, were staple fare of adapted texts. The title page of the 1617 edition of Thomas Middleton and William Rowley's *A Fair Quarrel* advertised that the play as printed included 'new Additions of M^r. *Chaughs* and *Tristrams* Roaring, and the Bauds Song', thus demonstrating the appeal of both kinds of addition.[28] Adaptation, therefore, compresses the space between the interests of dramatist and theatre. But, as we have seen, those interests were always closely interconnected.

The Material Book

ASPECT OF AN EARLY MODERN BOOK: Q1 *TROILUS AND CRESSIDA*

Investigations of how Shakespeare's plays were written and prepared for the theatre deal with lost manuscripts and proceed largely
by inference. In considering Shakespeare's plays in print, one can
access the immediate objects in question, and situate them within
perhaps the best-documented industrial practice in early modern
England. The printed editions of plays that appeared in London
bookshops during and shortly after his life are primary evidence for
the study of Shakespeare, and the basis for the editions in regular use
today. The present chapter will focus on a single play, *Troilus and
Cressida*. It will reconstruct the preparation and printing of the 1609
Quarto. But the value of *Troilus and Cressida* as the chosen example
is that bibliographical features of both the Quarto and Folio texts
provide intriguing evidence as to the publishers' larger strategies in
issuing these books. This chapter will therefore encompass both the
manufacture of physical objects and the position of those objects in
the marketplace of print.

An opening of two pages in any early modern book will display a
number of features unfamiliar to the modern reader. Examples could
be drawn from anywhere, but the following discussion is based on
a single opening of two pages in the 1609 Quarto of *Troilus and
Cressida*, the pages identified—as will be explained below—as B1^v–2
(see Fig. 1). The spellings are to a modern eye irregular: 'ſmyling' for
smiling, 'Dooes' for *Does*, 'heare' for *hair*, 'Queene' for *Queen*, and so
on. 'Heare', in the line 'And ſhee takes vpon her to ſpie a white heare on

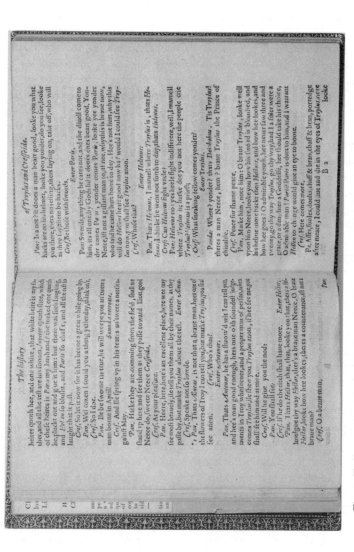

Fig. 1. *Troilus and Cressida*, Q1 (1609), British Library Halliwell-Phillipps copy, C.34.k.61, sig. B1ʳ–2.

his chinne' is potentially an ambiguous form, as it could alternatively stand for the verb *hear* and, taken in isolation, would more obviously do so. Only the context can show that the less obvious modernization is required. These various examples of *spelling* can be distinguished from the details of *typography*. Particularly confusing to the modern eye are the types 'ſ', which is the long form of 's' but resembles 'f' without a forward crossbar, and the unexpected distribution of 'u' and 'v', as in 'loue' and 'vpon'. Both are also features of early modern handwriting.

The bottom line of type does not usually contain any part of the main run of text. In the bottom right-hand corner is placed the *catchword*, in our case '*Pan:*' and 'looke'. This anticipates the first word printed on the following page. It may look at first sight as though it is designed to help the reader join up the end of one page with the beginning of the next, but its main use was as an aid to the compositor who set the type. As we will see, the arrangement of pages to make up one side of a printed sheet is not straightforward, and, as there are no page numbers in most books of the period including Q1 *Troilus and Cressida*, some guidance as to continuity was helpful.

Even more important information about the structure and continuity of the book is to be found in a second element on the bottom line of type. This is the *signature*. It consists of a letter (or, in long books, letters), usually followed by a number, and is a system identifying the book's physical make-up. The entirely typical sequence of page signatures in this part of *Troilus and Cressida* is as follows:

B, [blank], B2, [blank], B3, [blank], [blank], [blank], C.

The signature appears on the first three right-hand pages, or rectos. The left-hand pages, or versos, are blank, as is the final recto of the 'B' sequence. The page that in this example from *Troilus and Cressida* is signed 'B3' is also blank in some quarto editions.

The signature 'B' identifies a sequence of four leaves. We can infer that 'B' is B1. The last leaf is unsigned, and the signature must be inferred. Thus the leaves are B1, B2, B3, and inferred B4. A similar pattern is seen throughout the book. In the alphabetical sequence, each letter refers to four leaves, or eight pages. This sequence in *Troilus and Cressida* runs up to M, this final section having one leaf signed 'M' and a blank leaf following.

This system of identifying leaves by letter and number is the only alternative offered to page numbers. Signatures originated in the early days of printing; page numbers gradually came in later. The only pre-1623 edition of Shakespeare to have page numbers is the 1622 Quarto of *Othello*. Though the 1623 Folio has page numbering, the volume is split into sections devoted to Comedies, Histories, and Tragedies, and a separate sequence of pagination is devoted to each section.

A superscript 'v' is conventionally used to identify verso pages.[1] The pages designated B in Q1 *Troilus and Cressida* can be identified bibliographically as follows:

B1, B1^v, B2, B2^v, B3, B3^v, B4, B4^v.

Scholars working with early modern books, or photographic reproductions of them, use this system of signatures when making references to a book. This still holds true when the book has page numbers, as with the 1623 Folio, because mistakes in the page numbering were relatively common. A page in the Folio is usually cited by its signature, not its section title and page number. The abbreviation 'sig.' is used as a prefix instead of 'p.'. So one would say, for example, that the Folio text of *Hamlet* begins on sig. Nn4^v (the verso of the fourth leaf of quire Nn). In the Folio and other large books, the letters of the alphabet run out, and have to return doubled, trebled, or sometimes even quadrupled.

The second reason why signatures are important is that they relate to the physical construction of the book, which needs to be considered in more detail. In *Troilus and Cressida* the four leaves under consideration make up a single quire, or gathering. As with quartos generally, the four leaves of a quire are all part of a single sheet. The four pages that make up one side of the sheet were printed together. And here we need to introduce another technical term from printing. One side of a sheet is known as a forme. The forme that contains the first page of the quire is referred to as the outer forme. The other is, correspondingly, the inner forme. From the printer's point of view, the forme is the fundamental unit of text, being the unit that will go under the press at one time when the sheet is printed. Each sheet will therefore need running through the press a second time to be completed or, to use the technical term, perfected.

The arrangement of pages on a quarto sheet can be simply demonstrated by folding a sheet of paper into a four-leaf booklet, and then marking the pages with page numbers and signatures. When the sheet is unfolded the position of pages on the sheet is immediately evident. It will be noticed that the pages of the inner formes are not adjacent to each other on the unfolded sheet, but lie head-to-head. The outer forme is made up of the outer pages (the first and eighth, B1 and B4^v) and the two pages facing each other in the middle of the forme (the fourth and fifth, B2^v and B3). The inner forme consists of the two pairs of facing pages making up the gaps (the second and third, B1^v and B2, and the sixth and seventh, B3^v and B4).

Q1 *TROILUS AND CRESSIDA*: THE PUBLISHER'S ARRANGEMENTS

Troilus and Cressida survives in two editions that are significantly different: the Quarto edition of 1609 and the version printed in the collected Folio of Shakespeare's plays of 1623. They are both 'substantive' editions. This means that they have independent sources, being based on two different manuscripts. Both the Quarto and Folio can be taken as representatives of their formats. They both also have individual features. These two printings between them contribute to an intriguing early textual history for this play. There are implications for its performance history, its generic identity, and its placement as a cultural product in the world of books and readers.

The play was written in about 1602. On 7 February the following year (unusually soon after composition) the play was entered in the Stationers' Register as follows:

M^r. Robertes. Entred for his copie in full Court
holden this day. to print when
he hath gotten sufficient aucthority
for yt. The booke of
Troilus and Cresseda as
yt is acted by my lo: Chamb[er]lens
Men

We see here the standard process by which a prospective publisher would register his (very rarely 'her') right to publish a title. All publishers, printers, and booksellers needed to belong to the Stationers' Company in order to conduct their trade, and without the Company's allowance to print and publish a book the stationer would fall foul of the Company's powerful Court, which could exact fines and punish members for irregular or illegal practices.[2] As author's copyright did not exist in the period, the publisher would normally have exclusive rights of ownership over the manuscript and the book printed from it. Each title needed the licence of the Company, in the form of authorization to print written into the manuscript itself. The Company's wardens, or, as in this case, its full Court, would check that the title had not been previously granted to another stationer. If a play was published without entry in the Stationers' Register, it was not necessarily a surreptitious publication. A book apparently could be and occasionally was issued with a licence on the manuscript itself without entry in the Register, which would save the stationer from paying the separate fee that was required for entry.[3] Nevertheless, the Register provided a central record of entitlement, and it was usually in the issuing stationer's interest to pay that fee.

The Company wardens would also review the content to check that it contained nothing offensive from the point of view of censorship. If the text fell under suspicion in this respect, it was referred to ecclesiastical authorities, usually the office of the Bishop of London in Southwark. The operation of this process of ecclesiastical allowance was uneven, varying on individual perceptions and the political climate of the moment. Within a matter of weeks, *Richard III* was licensed without allowance, but *Richard II* was referred to William Barlow of the Bishop's office for his allowance, which was duly given. Both plays deal with the deposition or overthrow of an anointed monarch, a matter of extreme sensitivity to the politics of their day. For reasons we can only surmise, one was sent to the Church authorities whereas the other was treated by the Stationers' Company as being without offence.

Troilus and Cressida was not referred for allowance. But the Stationers' Court was concerned about the validity of the stationer's entitlement, which was an issue of trade regulation rather than control of the book's content. The provisional wording 'to print when he hath gotten sufficient aucthority for yt' demanded further evidence on the question.

The stationer in question was James Roberts, who was to enter his title to *Hamlet* a few months later on 26 July. He went on to print but not publish the Second Quarto of *Hamlet*, and he was neither to publish nor to print *Troilus and Cressida*. After a lapse of some six years during which no edition appeared, on 28 January 1609 the play was entered in the Register once again:

Ri. Bonion	Entred for their Copy vnder thandes of M[r]
Henry Walleys	Segar deputy to S[r] George Bucke &
	m[r] war[d]. Lownes a booke called, The
	history of Troylus & Cressida

Perhaps Roberts had failed to secure the required 'aucthority' to publish and his claim lapsed. Richard Bonian and Henry Walley were duly the publishers of the edition that appeared in 1609.

Whereas the conditional licence of 1603 had been issued without referral for allowance, the unqualified licence of 1609 was endorsed by Sir George Buc, acting on behalf of the Bishop of London's office. Buc's original interest in the regulation of plays was as Master of the Revels. Our present brief encounter with regulation of the book trade may be compared with the account of regulation of the theatre by the Master of the Revels in Chapter 2. The two systems were separate, with the theatre falling under the ultimate jurisdiction of the royal court and the book under the Church authorities. But for some years beginning in 1606 the Master of the Revels acted as a specialist censor on behalf of the Bishop's office. *Troilus and Cressida* was the first but not the only example of a Shakespeare play to come to Buc's attention before publication in print. Buc also issued allowance for *King Lear*, *Pericles*, and *Othello*, and his successor as Master of the Revels, Henry Herbert, did likewise for *The Two Noble Kinsmen*.

Having bought the manuscript and secured his entitlement to print from it, the publisher would have to make decisions about the format and size of the book. These would depend on the length of the text, but also on decisions such as type size, spacing, and the use of ornaments. What influenced these decisions would be the publisher's sense of readership. To what kinds of reader would the book appeal? How many copies could the publisher expect to sell? Apart from the securing of copy, the main costs would relate to the purchase of paper and the printing; unlike the costs relating to securing copy, these outlays would vary according to the design of the book and the print run.

These calculations were delicate and critical. It was a rule of the Stationers' Company that a print run should not exceed 1,500 copies. But editions would not necessarily extend to the maximum. A publisher would risk making an unrecoupable expenditure if the print run significantly overran sales. In his influential study of the economics of printing and publishing plays, Peter W. M. Blayney suggests that there was little money to be made out of a first edition, and that the publisher would depend on a reprint for making a significant gain. In the light of Blayney's work, it is impossible now to argue that publishers eagerly seized on plays because they offered the prospect of quick profit.[4] His calculations are, however, vulnerable for the extent to which they rely on suppositions and approximations. Only about 48 per cent of plays were reprinted. It is scarcely credible that publishers would repeatedly have invested in plays if they stood a chance of less than 50 per cent of making an acceptable profit. Moreover, plays were not intrinsically more expensive to produce than other works of a similar length, and publishers were prepared to invest in works that stood even less chance of reprinting.[5] These considerations suggest that the potential for profit for a play or an early modern quarto of equivalent length might have been higher than Blayney indicates—though still no doubt fairly modest.

Blayney suggests that the printer chosen by the publisher would provide an estimate of the number of sheets required for the book, based on his sense of appropriate format and design unless the publisher instructed otherwise.[6] The number of sheets would provide an indication of the cost of typesetting, which would be the same irrespective of the number of copies printed. By multiplying the number of sheets in the book by the print run, the printer and publisher would be able to estimate the labour costs of presswork and the outlay on paper.

It was in order to produce these crucial figures that the printer would cast off the copy. This involved working through the manuscript keeping in mind the determined information about format, type size, length of the measure (that is, the width of the type on the page as determined by the width set on the compositor's stick), extent of ornamentation, layout of headings (and, with plays, layout of stage directions), and so on, in order to calculate where the page breaks would fall in the printed book. This was a skilled job, and plays presented special challenges. They usually alternated between passages of verse, where one manuscript line would equate with one type line, and prose, where the casting-off would be based on a ratio between manuscript lines and the typically shorter lines of print. Casting-off would be inaccurate if it either counted manuscript lines or applied a fixed arithmetical conversion. Plays also included stage directions, some of which might be situated in the margins of the manuscript but normally needed setting on separate type-lines in the printed book. A compositor would have various expedients for correcting mistakes in casting off, and it is common to find inconsistent spacing round stage directions, stretching or squeezing of text to waste or save a type-line, or pages with one more or less line of type than was regular. But the casting-off was usually performed to a good standard of accuracy.

For *Troilus and Cressida* it was determined that twelve quarto sheets would be needed, though the final sheet would need to accommodate only the last two pages. A final leaf was allowed to protect the unbound copies. The book's construction can be expressed as a collation formula thus: '4°: A–L^4 M$^{2\prime}$'. This means that the format is quarto, and a regular sequence of sheets folded into four leaves with signatures from A to L is followed by half-sheet M. The publisher and printer determined that the title would be printed on A1, which would be followed by a blank verso page. The play itself would begin on A2, and continue to M1^v, leaving the final leaf M2 blank. At this stage the printer could finally begin work on setting the play.

COMPOSITION AND PRESS CORRECTION

It is beyond the scope of this book to examine the mechanics of composition and printing in any detail. The printer's sequence of work would depend on the number of compositors available to him, the number of presses in his shop, and the volume of other work in which he was currently engaged. He would need to decide between one of two commonly used procedures for setting type. Pages could be composed either seriatim, that is, in the order of the text, or by forme, which entails setting the pages of one of the formes before its opposite (or 'forme-mate') on the same sheet.[7] Setting by forme would make use of casting-off marks in the manuscript indicating where the page breaks would fall. This would have the possible advantage that the forme output from the compositor(s) would be regular, occurring after the fourth and eighth pages of a quarto, rather than after the seventh and eighth pages as with seriatim setting.

Composition—that is, the setting of type to make up rows and eventually whole pages and formes ready for printing—is a complex process in its own right. The type would first be placed in the compositor's 'stick', a shallow tray whose width could be adjusted to the determined measure of print on the page. The stick was held in the hand with the bottom edge horizontal and with the flat back-plate at a steep angle. The first line of type lay on a 'setting rule' placed on the bottom edge. Types were set upside down with their faces outward. The inversion of the type face as a reverse image of the printed letter was counteracted by the inversion caused by setting type upside down, so the compositor could proceed from left to right in the normal sequence of reading. The vertical turn-about enabled the second line of type to rest on top of the first, and so on. About four lines of type could be composed and stacked up in the compositor's stick before they were carefully transferred to a flat tray. By repeating this process, the compositor gradually built up a page of type.

When the pages making up a forme had been set, including the running titles (that is, the book titles or section titles as printed at the top of the page), catchwords, signatures, and any ornaments or rules that might be required, the pages were placed within a wooden frame and surrounded by pieces of wood known as 'furniture'. The type was then locked into a solid block by hammering wooden wedges or 'quoins' between the furniture and the outer frame. This process of laying out and consolidating the forme is known as 'imposition'.

Once the forme was tight and the surface level, it could be transferred to the press stone of the hand-press for printing. The parts of the hand-press are shown in Fig. 2. The sheet of paper that was to be printed was held in a two-part wooden framework known as the tympan and frisket. This was hinged onto the end of the coffin, the shallow horizontal box that held the press stone. To initiate the printing of the sheet, the coffin was pulled clear of the press mechanism, the tympan was opened on its hinge, as in Fig.2 and the sheet of paper was placed on a parchment covering the frame of the tympan. The sheet

Fig. 2. A modern replica of a hand-press.

was held in position by two adjustable pins, or points. The frisket was a second frame, hinged onto the end of the tympan. It too was covered with parchment (or paper), but, unlike the tympan parchment, this was cut with rectangular holes corresponding to the pages of type. These holes allowed the type to come into contact with the paper. Once the paper was pinned onto the tympan, the frisket was lowered onto the tympan and paper to secure the paper round the edge. Then the whole unit was folded over the forme of type assembled on the press stone, with the windowed parchment of the frisket lying between the type and the paper. The pressman slid the coffin, press stone, tympan, and frisket as a unit on rails (known as 'ribs') under the press mechanism. He then pulled a bar, which lowered the platen, a flat, horizontal piece of wood. This pressed the paper evenly onto the raised inked surface of the type.

The printing of the First Quarto of *Troilus and Cressida* has been studied in some detail.[8] As is stated on the title page, the printer was George Eld, who also happens to have printed Shakespeare's *Sonnets* in the same year (1609). Three compositors have been identified; as we do not know their actual names, we refer to them as Eld A, Eld B, and Eld C. There is an example of a change of compositors within Sheet B, at the beginning of sig. B3, where the compositor identified as Eld B took over from Eld A. One slight difference between the compositors' stints as seen in Sheet B is that the measure, or width of the full type-line, is a bit shorter in sig. B3 and thereafter. This reflects Eld B setting the measure on his stick a shade narrower than did Eld A.

Compositors, and their role in the process of manufacture, can be investigated by means of detailed attention to mechanical features such as the measure, the recurrence of headlines, the recirculation of type, and variables of text-setting such as punctuation, spelling, and spacing. It was part of the compositor's job to normalize spelling and punctuation, but, given the extreme variability of forms current in the period, there was scope for compositors to impose standards that were as much personal as common to the printing house. It is demonstrable that different compositors, in the 1623 Folio, for instance, used punctuation marks in different proportions and preferred different spellings. In general, however, bibliographers have come to rely more on the 'mechanical' forms of evidence such as spacing before or after punctuation, or habits of indentation.[9] The success of bibliographers in identifying compositors varies considerably from text to text, and depends on variables such as the length of the text, the format (a folio page holds more text and therefore supplies more potential evidence than a quarto page), and the distinctiveness or otherwise of the different compositors' work.

Some parts of the printing process affect the text as we read it. There are specific if minor textual variants between different copies of Q1 *Troilus and Cressida*. Here are some of them:

Line	*Before correction*	*After correction*
2.3.224	Yon [turned letter]	You
3.2.84	thene/then [duplication across line-break]	then
3.2.92	to to faire [another duplication]	to faire
5.2.155	*Ariathna's* [misreading or misprint]	*Ariachna's*

These pairs of readings are known as press variants. They arise through the second of two routine kinds of correction. The first, a term familiar today, is proof correction, where a sample copy of the forme is printed before the main print run so that it can be checked for imperfection and error. A few proof sheets of the period survive, including examples from the Shakespeare First Folio.[10] But the rejected reading in the proof sheet will not normally appear in any copy of the finished book, as the proof sheet, marked up by hand with instructions for correction, is not fit to be used for any other purpose. In contrast, press correction during the print run results in variants in completed copies of the book of the kind represented in our four examples. Though a standard practice, it was not routine.

The changes introduced in press correction might be 'mechanical'—in which case they correct imperfections of printing resulting from loose or uneven type and the like—or 'textual'—in which case they alter actual or perceived errors of spelling, punctuation, or wording. Textual corrections are themselves of two different kinds. The forme may be checked against the manuscript, or alternatively corrections may be made purely on the initiative of the corrector. In the present cases, the error is self-evident, and there is no need to assume that the manuscript was consulted. A complex set of press corrections in Q1 *King Lear* often seem to be based on the corrector's guesswork,

as can be seen when the corrector makes mistakes. At 7.121 'ausrent'
is corrected to 'miscreant'; F reads 'ansient', which is evidently the
required reading. Likewise, at 7.127 'Stobing' is altered to 'Stopping';
here F much more plausibly reads 'Stoking'. In contrast, a corrected
forme in Q1 *2 Henry IV* contains readings that are clearly authoritative.
They include:

Line	Before correction	After correction
3.2.206	Clemham	Clements inne
3.2.227	my dames sake	my old dames sake
3.2.309	gemies	genius
4.1.12	could	would
4.1.30	Vnto your grace	Then my L.	Vnto your Grace

Which state is corrected can usually be inferred from the nature of the
changes. In the readings listed, 'Clemham' and 'gemies' are manifestly
wrong. It is inconceivable that a compositor should deliberately alter
'Clements inne' and 'genius' to establish these readings. On the basis of
an accumulation of such evidence, sometimes augmented by the correction of flaws in the alignment of type of a more mechanical nature,
the direction of the correction is more often than not unambiguous
for each forme.

In the case of the forme in *2 Henry IV* we can make a further
inference about the source of the corrected reading. In the cited
readings either there is no self-evident error, or the nature of the
required correction is not apparent from the uncorrected reading.
The corrector must, then, have found the readings in the manuscript.
Having established this, an editor can then adopt the corrected
state of the forme as the preferred base text where there are less
clearly differentiated readings.[11] He or she will need to keep in mind,
however, that it does not *necessarily* follow that all corrections in
the forme are authoritative, and that there is scope for the corrector
misunderstanding the manuscript, or the compositor misinterpreting
the corrector's marks.

Press corrections in Q1 *King Lear* contribute to two notorious
cruces. At 11.99 'come on bee true' is press-corrected to 'come on'. The
First Folio, which is set with reference to an independent manuscript,
reads 'Come, vnbutton heere'. The Folio's 'heere' can be regarded
as an exclusive reading, but it is possible that 'on bee true' in the

original setting of Q1 reflects a misreading of 'vnbuttone'. If the press corrections were authoritative, this is unlikely, for the correction would confirm the validity of the words 'come on'. But the unreliability of press corrections elsewhere in this text leaves it open for the editor to consider whether a text based on Q1 should be emended to 'come, unbutton'. Later in Q1 *King Lear*, at 16.28, the original text 'My foote vsurps my body' is corrected to 'A foole vsurps my bed'. Q2, here based on the uncorrected text of Q1, alters instead to 'My foote vsurps my head'. F's version is 'My Foole vsurps my body'. Any understanding of these perplexing alternatives will need to take into account the degree of authority that can be attributed to the Q1 correction, as well as the complexities of transmission from Q1 and/or Q2 to F.

Of the four examples of press correction in *Troilus and Cressida* listed above, the first three are self-evident: they need involve no consultation of the copy manuscript. The fifth represents another puzzling crux. The corrected reading, which is found similarly in F, is usually explained as a conflation of 'Ariadne's' and 'Arachne's'. So 'Ariachne's broken woof' alludes both to the thread left by Ariadne to enable Theseus to find his way through the Cretan labyrinth and to the work of Arachne, who was punished by being turned into a spider for her presumption in weaving cloth as well as Pallas. A corrector with a basic schooling in the classics might realize that '*Ariathna's*' was a misprint for either '*Ariadna's*' or '*Arachna's*', but is unlikely to have intuited that it is a misleading form of a portmanteau combining the two.

Press correction has interesting implications beyond the establishment of the text. The four examples of press correction from *Troilus and Cressida* listed above appear on three different formes. The uncorrected sheets were not discarded, but came to be sewn into normal copies of the book. The three uncorrected formes were not necessarily present in the same copies, so there are not three but eight different states of individual copies that arise even from this very limited variation (the permutations are: aaa, aab, aba, abb, baa, bab, bba, bbb). When press correction is used more extensively, it can happen that every single surviving copy of a text will be unique in its combination of readings. It is also possible that, whenever a new copy from an edition is inspected, it may turn out to have readings that occur in no other surviving copy. Textual scholars spend many hours happily or unhappily collating copies of the edition, reading each copy letter by letter, usually against a photocopy of one copy that is used as a control text, on the lookout for unrecorded press variants. Just occasionally, this painstaking practical work reveals something of vital interest about the text, or provides important clues as to the printing process. The consequent theoretical point challenges our notion, more pertinently belonging to a later stage in the technology of printing, that an edition consists of identical copies. In the conditions of early modern book production, any copy of an edition might be unique.

THE PARATEXTS OF Q1 *TROILUS AND CRESSIDA*

Much more immediately important to the study specifically of *Troilus and Cressida* are the major changes introduced in printing the preliminaries in Q1. These affect the introductory matter at the beginning of the book that falls under the heading of the term 'paratext'—the marginal and introductory material that surrounds the text itself and gives contextual guidance as to its interest and how it should be read.[12] Here we recover a sense of the Quarto not just as a material object (or, rather, a set of nearly but not fully identical material objects), but as a cultural object that exists in relation to posited readers and that includes a specific and unusual text.

The title page exists in two completely different settings. Eld had originally printed the title as 'The Historie of Troylus and Cresseida. *As it was acted by the Kings Maiesties* seruants at the Globe'. This echoes the information in the Stationers' Register that the play was acted by the Lord Chamberlain's Men, but updates the name of the company, which had changed to the King's Men in 1603. Eld now defined the play as 'The Famous Historie of Troylus and Cresseid'. Information about performance by the King's Men at the Globe was removed. In its place the reader finds details praising the literary excellence of the play: '*Excellently expressing the beginning* of their loues, with the conceited wooing of *Pandarus* Prince of Licia'. The second setting of the title is followed on a new second leaf by an unsigned epistle, headed '*A neuer writer, to an euer Reader. Newes*'.

From an examination of the physical make-up of the book the sequence of events can be established. We can tell that the 'Globe' title was set first because it belongs to the regular sheet A; the verso is blank, as is commonly the case with title pages. The title is without a signature, as again is more usually than not the case with title pages, but the next leaf, on which the play begins, is signed 'A2'. Careful inspection of an actual copy of Q1 shows that the title page belongs to a regular quarto sheet. In contrast, the altered title page and the epistle make up an irregular half-sheet that has the anomalous signature '¶'. As the new title page is unsigned, this symbol appears uniquely on the first page of the epistle, which bears the signature '¶2'. The original title page has been cut off from sheet A and replaced with a new half-sheet. The collation formula expressing the resulting second issue is: $4°$: $A^4(-A1+¶^2) B-L^4 M^2$.

Contrary to appearances, the new half-sheet was not printed alone. Philip Williams's study of the typographical evidence shows that the new title page and epistle were printed on the same sheet as the two-leaf part-sheet M that appears at the end of the book, where M1 contains text on both sides and M2 is blank. It follows that the cancel was made when the end of the book was being printed. The decision was taken to include the epistle before the main run of printing was complete. This meant that the paper available from the part-sheet M at the end of the book could therefore be utilized for part-sheet ¶ at the beginning. Along with the final pages, the reset title page and epistle were the last parts of the book to be set in type. When the sheet had been run through the press, it was cut in half, and the two halves placed in the required positions.

Eld was presumably instructed to make the change by the publishers Bonian and Walley. It is a remarkable intervention. The deletion of the playing company's name is all the more noteworthy because in the usual course of things the playing company was almost always identified. The second impression was presumably made to bring the information it contains, with its advertisement value, into line with the new material that was included at the same time, the text of the epistle to the reader. This epistle declares: 'Eternal reader, you have here a new play, never staled with the stage, never clapper-clawed with the palms of the vulgar', and later describes the play as 'not being sullied with the smoky breath of the multitude'. The contradiction between original title page and new epistle could not stand. Moreover, the epistle too makes much of the play's literary qualities, in particular its 'wit'. This much-repeated term implies both humour and intellectual polish. It correlates closely with the reset title page's word 'conceited', which has very similar connotations. The original title page advertised a routine play from the popular theatre. The new one put the play alongside the comedies of the ancient Roman dramatists Terence and Plautus, and affirmed its classicizing, scholarly bent by leaving the reader with a Latin 'Vale' (meaning 'farewell'). And this all correlates with the information on the reset title page that Pandarus was Prince of Licia: information found nowhere in the play, and so from an independent and learned source. In short, the reset and expanded preliminaries target the play towards an educated elite reader. Some critics have suggested that the publisher or epistle-writer is specifically addressing the smart intellectual students of the Inns of Court, London's law schools.[13]

The evidence of the preliminaries can therefore be interpreted in terms of the historical sociology of publishing. How does a publisher negotiate the interface between a play by a popular dramatist and a putative elite readership? Q1 *Troilus and Cressida* is unique, in that it is the only Shakespeare play issued during his lifetime with an epistle to the reader. But Ben Jonson had over the previous few years been supplying similar epistles before his own plays. Eld had published Jonson's *Sejanus* in 1605. In this epistle Jonson justifies his use of marginal notes alongside the text providing references to his source material. He also deals with the relationship between the text as a derivative from a stage play and this apparatus of scholarly learning. So he informs the reader that 'this book in all numbers is not the same with that which was acted on the public stage, wherein a second pen had good share; in place of which I have rather chosen to put weaker, and no doubt less pleasing, of mine own'. The promotion of this play's classicism and refutation of the text as a stage play strongly anticipate the changes made in the second issue of Q1 *Troilus and Cressida*.

How far do we read such paratextual statements as the truth, and how far do we see them as gestures of cultural positioning in which the truth is not entirely to the point? Perhaps there was indeed a second hand in the stage version of *Sejanus*. But the assertion that it has been removed is very much part and parcel with the Jonsonian project of claiming a new and more elevated cultural space for stage plays. In *Troilus and Cressida* we are again faced with a play on a classical subject that is poised somewhere between tragedy and satire, and that, like *Sejanus*, has been regarded as 'difficult' in its literary style. We are faced with evidence—but *cancelled* evidence—that the play was performed by Shakespeare's company, the King's Men. If this statement is true, the statement in the epistle that the play was 'never staled with the stage' would seem to be untrue. Gary Taylor generously speculates that 'the publishers came to believe that the play had never been performed'.[14] This may be so, especially if, as Taylor argues, the epistle had been written several years earlier for the edition anticipated in the 1603 Stationers' Register entry. But we cannot ignore the possibility that Bonian and Walley, perhaps in consort with Eld, perhaps influenced by the example of *Sejanus*, made the change with regard to the potential buyers. If so, they decided that a change of presentational strategy would help to sell a play that by no reckoning could be expected to appeal in the manner of a *Richard III* or a *Hamlet*. But the change was not systematic. The original title page was left in place in a minority of copies, perhaps in order to sell the book to the regular purchaser of plays from the Globe as well as the coterie readership that the reset preliminaries seem to court.

TROILUS AND CRESSIDA IN THE FIRST FOLIO

The First Folio of 1623, more fully the subject of Chapter 4, is a monumental collection. *Troilus and Cressida* appeared there in a new text, based on Q1 but introducing numerous verbal variants through reference to an independent manuscript. By a strange coincidence, the play, having undergone a cancel that added new preliminaries in Q1, underwent a similar cancel when it was reissued in the Folio. As a result, the anomalous signature '¶', again signalling the presence of material that does not fall within the regular sequence of signatures, occurs in this text too. Stranger still, the textual alteration also involves a repositioning of the play in terms of its affinities with other drama.

Quite literally, Folio *Troilus and Cressida* was physically repositioned within the volume. It should have been placed in the middle of the Tragedies section, but ended up in a ghetto between the Histories and Tragedies. A bibliographically aware reader of the Folio might wonder whether some subtle point was being made about the play's ambiguous genre. After all, the Quarto had proclaimed the play as a 'History' in both versions of the title page, and the epistle's praise of the play's 'savoured salt of wit' scarcely suggests a tragedy. As it transpires, the play's journey into exile has nothing to do with literary perceptions of its genre, and depends instead on a matter pertaining to the book trade, that of copyright.

Before examining this issue in any detail we need some basic information about the format of the Shakespeare Folio. There, *Troilus and Cressida* begins on two unsigned leaves, identified by convention as χ1 and χ2, followed by two regular quires, signed '¶' and '¶¶', followed by a single leaf, signed '¶¶¶', the verso of which is blank. The irregular leaves at the beginning and end relate to the relocation of the play, as will become apparent. The full quires follow the standard format of the volume. Each consists of twelve pages, or six leaves. Three separate sheets were folded together to make a booklet of one quire. This format, called 'folio in sixes', was common in the printing of such books. A quire such as this is a very large unit of text equivalent to between a third and a half of an entire Shakespeare play, or about five quarto sheets. With its large, double-column pages, a quire in the Folio holds about 1560 type-lines. As a consequence, the outer forme of the outer sheet contains two pages of widely separated text; there are about 1,300 lines between the end of the first page of the sheet and the beginning of the last.

With the Shakespeare Folio, we know that detailed casting off and planning went well ahead of the printing. We also know that the usual pattern of composition took advantage of the casting-off marks. Following a pattern of work that was common in folio typesetting, the compositors began with the inner pages of the inner sheet and worked outwards. Usually two compositors worked on a quire, one setting the first half in reverse page order, the other setting the second half in normal page order.

Charlton Hinman's studies based on evidence such as the recirculation of distinctive types from one page to another have built up a detailed and comprehensive picture of the sequence of printing of the Folio.[15] It is to Hinman that we owe most of our knowledge of the printing of *Troilus and Cressida* itself. Hinman noted, for example, that in one surviving copy of the Folio the first page of the *Troilus* section was filled not with the Prologue to *Troilus and Cressida* but with the last page of *Romeo and Juliet*, deleted by the simple if crude expedient of crossing it out by hand. This is a key piece of evidence, which, put together with the outcome of Hinman's other investigations, leads to the following conclusions. *Troilus and Cressida* was originally planned to follow immediately after *Romeo and Juliet*. Work actually began on printing it in this position in the Folio Tragedies section, but after several pages had been set the compositors abandoned the printing. The play was subsequently replaced by the play that actually follows *Romeo and Juliet*, which is *Timon of Athens*. When work was resumed on *Troilus and Cressida* the space originally allocated to it was unavailable. Indeed the entire Folio volume was so near completion that in the table of contents, which falls in the very last section to be printed apart from *Troilus and Cressida* itself, the play is not named. This explains the play's anomalous position in the volume.

Why was work on *Troilus and Cressida* suspended in the first place? It is generally agreed that the Folio editors must have run into a problem with copyright. The entitlement to the play remained with the surviving member of the partners who had published the play in 1609, Henry Walley. The conjecture is that Walley initially refused to come to an arrangement with the syndicate of stationers who financed the publication of the Folio. Presumably they managed to persuade him to change his mind at the very last minute. The editors' persistence in attempting to secure an agreement and succeeding even when the volume was virtually ready for publication without *Troilus and Cressida* says much about their desire to make sure that the play did not escape inclusion. How did they manage to succeed? At some point in between the setting of the first pages for inclusion after *Romeo and Juliet* and the final setting of *Troilus and Cressida*, something happened that may have had a bearing on the outcome. The Folio editors acquired an independent manuscript on which to base their text. They were no longer manifestly dependent on simply reprinting Bonian and Walley's Quarto.

We know this because one page of the play exists in two states. When it was finally decided to print the play between the Histories and Tragedies, the staff in the printing shop had to deal with the three Folio pages that had already been printed from the Q1. Initially, these were recycled to become part of the new full text, along with the crossed-out page on which *Romeo and Juliet* ended, inseparable from the first page of *Troilus and Cressida* as it occupied the other side of the same leaf. After these four pages, the printing of the rest of the play resumed. The reuse of pages originally printed for the setting of *Troilus and Cressida* in the Tragedies section saved time, and it avoided wasting the costs of labour and paper that had already been invested.

But the gains were halved when it was decided to replace the intrusive and obviously redundant final page of *Romeo and Juliet*. The leaf containing this page on the recto and the opening page of *Troilus and Cressida* on the verso could not have been utilized if the Prologue had been included. The Prologue is not in Q1, and therefore was not in the initial Folio printing directly from Q1. The Prologue itself, consisting of a heading and thirty-one lines of verse, was set in a single column of large type to fill the page. As its initial exclusion is explained by the reuse of existing printed sheets, there is no need to suppose that it was missing from the manuscript from which the compositors set the main part of *Troilus and Cressida*; it was probably part and parcel of the manuscript. The exercise of removing the end of *Romeo and Juliet* and printing the Prologue meant reprinting the first page of the play itself, as this page appeared on the verso of the same leaf. The opportunity was taken to introduce into this page the variant readings from the play manuscript, and so bring it into line with the rest of the play. So the final text of Folio *Troilus and Cressida* begins with:

- the Prologue, replacing the last page of *Romeo and Juliet*;
- the first page, now reprinted on the verso of the Prologue with reference to the manuscript;
- two subsequent pages, still printed directly from Q1 and retrieved from the original printing that had been abandoned.

Thereafter the play is printed with reference to the manuscript—which means in practice that the compositors set from what must often have been difficult copy, an exemplar of the quarto into which readings from the manuscript had been written by way of interlineations, deletions, and hundreds of verbal corrections.

We can, then, examine the opening passages of the play in three states: the Quarto, the cancelled Folio text, and the final Folio text. The specific details of the printing of the first Quarto and the Folio are bibliographical puzzles that relate to more than the manufacture of the books. They take us back to the Shakespeare text, and to questions relating to performance and to genre.[16] The Quarto offers explicit but contradictory information about performance. No matter how we interpret the underlying facts relating to stage history, our attention is also drawn to the intents of the publisher in offering the play in book form, a process that has been described as 'a recentring of the play around a particular publishing speciality, a particular niche in the marketplace of print'.[17] Here questions of intended readership and marketing publicity come to the fore. This historical and bibliographical knowledge is an important precondition for our understanding of the play, its origins, and its early reception both on the stage and in print. It is clear from the example of *Troilus and Cressida* that the book trade plays an active role in the making not only of the book but also of the text, and that publishers could take active steps to determine the manner in which it would circulate amongst readers.

The First Folio

A SUBSTANTIAL BOOK

The First Folio, published seven years after Shakespeare's death in 1623, is one of the most famous and most studied books in the world. The first collected edition of Shakespeare's plays, it claims to offer a defining, complete, and authentic text. As its common appellation suggests, the book was printed in a folio format, meaning that it consists of paper sheets folded just once, to give a substantial book. The page was large enough to allow two columns and so about 130 lines of text on a single page. The folio format was more usually regarded as suitable for law books, bibles, and works of learning. The only precedent for stage plays to be issued in folio format was the Folio of Ben Jonson's works published under his personal supervision in 1616. Even that daring and eccentric volume was not devoted entirely to plays from the public stage, as it included the text of masques and non-dramatic poetry and prose. Seven years after its publication, its even more provocative Shakespearian successor therefore became the first collection in folio format that was devoted entirely to plays from the public theatre. Both volumes challenged the usual assumptions that stage plays were of low cultural status. These folios of dramatic works monumentalized their respective authors.

THE PAVIER QUARTOS

The 1623 Folio stands in marked contrast with an earlier attempt to publish Shakespeare's dramatic works, or at least some of them. Three years after the Jonson Folio, in 1619, an irregular collection of ten plays attributed to Shakespeare was published in quarto by Thomas Pavier. Though his name appears nowhere, the plays were all printed by William Jaggard, who just a couple of years later was engaged as printer of the First Folio. The 1619 collection's make-up is curious. All ten quartos are reprints. The group includes five plays that would prove to be substantially variant on, and inferior to, the texts later published in F. They are *The Whole Contention* (the plays identified in F as the second and third parts of *Henry VI*),[1] *Henry V*, *The Merry Wives of Windsor*, and *King Lear*. Just two plays appear in texts similar to those in F, *A Midsummer Night's Dream*, which in F was actually set from the 1619 edition, and *The Merchant of Venice*. The other three plays were to be excluded from F entirely: *Pericles*, *A Yorkshire Tragedy*, and *Sir John Oldcastle*.

These are in various ways irregular editions, notable not only for the dubious choice of plays and the questionable quality of the texts. Pavier's publishing strategy is also unusual, if not bizarre. There are existing copies of the ten plays bound as a single volume, but plays were also issued individually and in smaller groupings. Bibliographical study reveals an initial plan to issue a collection of plays in a single volume that evolved into more diversified forms of publication. Imprints of the six last plays to be printed are notable for false dates or incorrect information as to the stationers.

First to be printed were *The First Part of the Contention* and *Richard Duke of York*, which shared an undated title page naming the pair as *The Whole Contention*. They had continuous signatures, though *Richard Duke of York* begins on a new gathering. The next play, *Pericles*, was dated 1619; it continued the signatures from *The Whole Contention*, but abandoned the page numbering entirely. The title page was printed on a separate leaf, which was not used when the play was sewn together with *The Whole Contention*. Middleton's *A Yorkshire Tragedy* was printed at the same time as *Pericles* and was also dated 1619. Its ascription to Shakespeare repeated the details found on the title page of Pavier's previous edition of 1608. Along with the remainder of the plays printed after it, it was bibliographically independent in that it had an independent set of signatures.

The remaining plays were published with at least one element of false information in each imprint. *The Merchant of Venice* was issued as 'Printed by I. Roberts, 1600', which falsely repeats the originally correct information given in the imprint of the first edition, 'Printed by *I. R....*1600'. Pavier's edition of *The Merry Wives of Windsor* reprints the 1602 'bad' Quarto; though the date is correctly given as 1619, the imprint repeats and expands on the 1602 edition in naming Arthur Johnson as publisher. *King Lear* reiterates both the date and the publisher of the 1608 Quarto, 'Printed for *Nathaniel Butter.* 1608'. Pavier's *Henry V* recognizes 'T.P.' as publisher, but echoes the date 1608 used for *King Lear*, even though Pavier himself held the title to *Henry V* from his edition of 1602 (Q2). This play was followed by another Pavier had published previously, the unShakespearian *Sir John Oldcastle*; the 1619 edition, like that of *Henry V*, was attributed to 'T.P.', and again was given a false date, 1600, the date of Pavier's earlier issue. Finally, *A Midsummer Night's Dream* follows the example of *The Merry Wives of Windsor* in that the information as to both publisher and date repeats that of the first edition: 'Printed by James Roberts, 1600', though the entitlement lay with Thomas Fisher.

Significantly, the King's Men took a measure to prevent unauthorized publication of their plays that coincides with Pavier's project. On 13 May 1619 the Court of the Stationers' Company considered a letter from the Lord Chamberlain, perhaps presented by John Heminge, the leading actor and co-writer of preliminary epistles in the Folio. In response the Court declared: 'It is thought fit and so ordered that no plays that his Majesty's players do play shall be printed without consent of some of them.' Probably there is some kind of connection with the Pavier project, as no other Shakespeare play had appeared in print since the 1615 reissue of *Richard II*.

From a standard publishing point of view, Pavier did not need to conceal his responsibility for issuing many of these plays, as either he held the entitlement or (for *Pericles*) the ownership had probably expired. Johnson, Roberts, and Thomas Heyes, the probable title-holder of *The Merchant of Venice*, would not themselves have been taken in by Pavier's misrepresentations. Pavier's project was initially reputable in that he held rights to the first plays to be printed and they were issued without any falsification beyond the missing date of *The Whole Contention*. One explanation of the project's development is that the Lord Chamberlain's intervention pushed the project underground, making Pavier resort to false imprints designed to avoid the appearance of an ongoing venture. If the title pages were taken at face value, Pavier appeared to comply with the order.

It is possible, however, that the theatre company, like the stationers, was able to recognize the ruse. If so, they might have asked the Lord Chamberlain to act on their behalf because they wished to stop imitators of Pavier issuing other plays that would more damagingly pre-empt the Folio.[2] Pavier's collection, binding together new editions with books apparently taken from old stock and separately published in 1600 or 1608, would have offered far more competition to the Folio if it had declared itself to be issued uniformly in 1619. In the form it took the Pavier collection may even have been useful as a preparation of the market for the Folio. It revived the visibility of Shakespeare in the print medium at a time when it had faded away, while at the same time creating the very conditions in which the 1623 collection could claim to offer a superior and more authoritative text than those that had come before.

Were vague plans for the Folio already in place before 1619? It is at least possible. In his will Shakespeare left the leading actors Heminge, Burbage, and Condell '26*s* 8*d* apiece to buy them rings'. Perhaps this commemorative gift was connected with a wish that his works also should be remembered, in Heminge and Condell's words in their epistle '*To the great Variety of Readers*', 'to keep the memory of so worthy a friend and fellow as was our Shakespeare'. Perhaps Shakespeare, as he looked on death, was aware that Jonson's works would soon appear in impressive Folio format. If so, one can understand the delay: actors were not in the business of playing the role of editor or surrogate author, the project would be hugely time-consuming, and publishers may have been wisely reluctant to risk the capital investment. If plans had stalled for any of these reasons or others, it is easy to see how the Pavier collection might have jolted the actors into action.

THE FOLIO AS PUBLISHING VENTURE

John Heminge and Henry Condell were old and long-standing members of the King's Men. They supplied the volume with two epistles, the first dedicating the volume to the Herbert brothers William Earl of

Pembroke and Philip Earl of Montgomery, and the second addressing '*the great Variety of Readers*'. Heminge and Condell must have made available the King's Men's stock of manuscripts, though, as we shall see, these documents by and large seem not to have been used directly in the printing house.

The actors worked in association with a syndicate of publishers, identified in the colophon (the details of publication printed at the end of the volume), below the end of the final play *Cymbeline*: '*Printed at the Charges of W. Jaggard, Ed. Blount, I. Smithweeke, and W. Aspley, 1623.*' This supplements and clarifies the information in the title page that the book was 'Printed by Isaac Iaggard, and Ed. Blount'. Blount was not involved in the printing. Work had begun in the printing house of William Jaggard in 1621, which was taken over by his son Isaac as William grew blind. Hence in the catalogue of the Frankfurt book fair of 1622 there is notice of 'Playes, written by M. William Shakespeare, all in one volume, printed by Isaak Iaggard, in fol.'. But, like Blount, Isaac had an interest also as publisher, as the colophon testifies. The title-page imprint can be understood to mean 'Printed by Isaac Jaggard for Isaac Jaggard and Edward Blount'. It was Jaggard and Blount who on 8 November 1623 entered the titles of sixteen previously unpublished plays in the Stationers' Register. Evidently they had a larger interest in the project than John Smethwick and William Aspley, who were evidently brought on board because they held the copyright to some of the plays that had previously appeared in print. Jaggard and Blount are likely to have been the main organizers of the project. Though Heminge and Condell probably determined the content of the volume and perhaps helped to decide on its organization, Jaggard's and/or Blount's involvement may have run to include some of the other activities described later in this chapter that in today's terminology would be called editing.

Peter W. M. Blayney describes Jaggard and Blount as 'an ill-assorted pair who had never collaborated before and never would again'.[3] Jaggard had newly succeeded to his father's business, which had held a monopoly on the printing of playbills, but was inexperienced as a publisher. In contrast, Blount was an important publisher of literary texts, including the first English editions of Montaigne's *Essays*, translated by John Florio (1603), and Miguel de Cervantes's *Don Quixote* (Part 1 in 1612, Part 2 in 1620). He had previously published the first collection of plays written in English, William Alexander's *Monarchic Tragedies*, which appeared as a two-volume set in 1604 and as an expanded four-volume set in 1607. His contributions to collected editions of drama continued in 1632 with Lyly's *Six Court Comedies*.[4]

The Folio project might be seen as a triumphal aggrandisement of the leading theatre company's leading player—in other words, as a piece of publicity on the part of the King's Men. The volume was planned as a marketing venture with meticulous care, yet it is difficult to see it entirely as a shrewd business venture motivated by expectation of profit. Recent studies suggest that it was not only an expensive project but also risky. The careful marketing of the volume through its preliminaries was probably designed to avoid loss rather than to ensure fast profit. The fact that it was nine years before there was a second edition (1632) tells us that the team of publishers must have regained their investment only slowly. This may have been expected. Speedy reprint, though possible with a successful quarto, was not at best to be looked for in a book that required so much preparation, and a folio collection of stage plays was far from an established formula for success. So there may be no contradiction between interpreting the Folio as a gesture of homage, as a promotion of the King's Men as the theatre company of the highest cultural prestige, and as a financial venture.

It would be hard to overstate the importance of this book to the establishment of the Shakespeare canon: what is included, how it is sequenced, how it is presented. There are no non-dramatic poems. The plays are divided into three sections, identified in the page of contents or 'Catalogue', each section having its own sequence of page numbering. The contents, as identified in the Catalogue, are as follows:[5]

Comedies: *The Tempest*; *The Two Gentlemen of Verona*; *The Merry Wives of Windsor*; *Measure for Measure*; *The Comedy of Errors*; *Much Ado About Nothing*; *Love's Labour's Lost*; *Midsummer Night's Dream*; *The Merchant of Venice*; *As You Like It*; *The Taming of the Shrew*; *All Is Well That Ends Well*; *Twelfth Night, Or, What You Will*; *The Winter's Tale*.

Histories: *The Life and Death of King John*; *The Life and Death of Richard the Second*; *The First Part of King Henry the Fourth*; *The Second Part of King Henry the Fourth*; *The Life of King Henry the Fifth*; *The First Part of King Henry the*

Sixth; *The Second Part of King Henry the Sixth*; *The Third Part of King Henry the Sixth*; *The Life and Death of Richard the Third*; *The Life of King Henry the Eighth*.

Tragedies: *The Tragedy of Coriolanus*; *Titus Andronicus*; *Romeo and Juliet*; *Timon of Athens*; *The Life and Death of Julius Caesar*; *The Tragedy of Macbeth*; *The Tragedy of Hamlet*; *King Lear*; *Othello, the Moor of Venice*; *Antony and Cleopatra*; *Cymbeline, King of Britain*.

For reasons already explained (see Chapter 3), the Catalogue omits *Troilus and Cressida*, which was added at the last minute and placed between the Histories and Tragedies.

Sixteen of the plays listed had not appeared in print before. For these plays, the Folio is our only authoritative text. Without it, we would not know them. Because most of the Shakespeare quartos had first appeared by 1605, there is a preponderance of mature and late plays among those printed for the first time in the Folio; they include *The Tempest, The Winter's Tale, All Is True, Coriolanus, Macbeth, Antony and Cleopatra*, and *Cymbeline*. If it were not for the Folio, the only play to survive that was written after *King Lear* would be *Pericles*, which, paradoxically, is one of only two extant plays substantially by Shakespeare that are not included in the Folio. There would be no *Julius Caesar*. We would also miss the experimental plays *Measure for Measure, All's Well That Ends Well*, and *Timon of Athens*. The histories would retain their core but would lack *King John* and *1 Henry VI* as well as *All Is True*. Of the comedies, *The Two Gentlemen of Verona, The Comedy of Errors, As You Like It*, and *Twelfth Night* would all be missing. So would *The Taming of the Shrew*, for the short play issued in 1594 as *The Taming of A Shrew* is so linguistically and structurally different from the Folio that it is generally considered a separate and unShakespearian play.

Some other plays had already been issued in a radically different form. Of these, *The Merry Wives of Windsor, 2 Henry VI, 3 Henry VI*, and *Henry V* are printed in the Folio in significantly more reliable texts. There are also a number of plays that were previously printed in a relatively good text that are now offered in an alternative version. The most significant cases are *2 Henry IV, Richard III, Troilus and Cressida, Hamlet, King Lear*, and *Othello*. Over the past few decades, many variants that were previously understood to be the result of corruption have been reassessed, to be interpreted as an effect of

Shakespeare's revising hand in these plays. And this can also apply, if to a lesser extent, to the plays where the earlier quarto text is clearly less authorial. There are far-reaching implications as regards our conception of Shakespeare as a creative writer, his relationship with the theatre, and the nature of the editorial enterprise itself. These matters are considered in the section below headed 'The Folio as Representation and Misrepresentation'. More immediately, we consider the procedures the editors and printers went through in order to establish new and different texts.

THE COPY FOR THE FOLIO

As Charlton Hinman demonstrated in unprecedented detail, the process of work on the Folio was complex, involving delays, and switches from one part of the volume to another. There were spells of time when the Folio was left unattended while Jaggard's compositors and pressmen worked towards completion of two books that would be published by Jaggard and therefore took priority and on other books. According to Hinman, the printing of the Folio took from February–March 1622 to November 1623.[6] The compositors usually set by formes, as was necessary in view of the large volume of type committed to each page and the number of pages (twelve) in a single gathering. They usually began with the middle of each gathering—that is to say, the sixth and seventh of the twelve pages—and worked outwards—backwards and forwards—from there towards the first and last pages of the gathering.

Most of the book was set by the compositors identified as A, B, and C, with more occasional contributions from D and others, some of them less securely identified. Sometimes two compositors worked from different cases of type in setting the two pages of a forme; at other times a single compositor set both pages. During the setting of the Tragedies, an apprentice compositor, E, having demonstrated his ineptitude in following manuscript copy, was assigned to setting from printed copy only. Unfortunately, work was at this stage proceeding on plays for which no printed copy was available, so Compositor E was assigned to work on a later section of the Tragedies. The formes that he set are described as intercalary, meaning that they intermittently interrupt the main run of work. So, for instance, during a break in Compositor B and C's setting of quire kk, which is part of *Julius Caesar* and follows manuscript copy, Compositor E set pages of *Titus Andronicus*, following a very lightly annotated copy of Q3 (1611).

A play such as *Titus Andronicus* was reprinted from an earlier quarto with limited reference to a manuscript. Absolutely unannotated quarto copy is rarely encountered. Most Folio texts based on earlier quarto texts involve a more complicated cross-fertilization between those editions and manuscripts. Typically, readings would be copied from the manuscript to a quarto. The editorial process sometimes, as with *Richard III*, must have involved very heavy copying, to the extent that the annotated print must have been difficult for a compositor to follow. In the case of *Richard III*, more than one quarto edition was used for this purpose. The task was further complicated by the need to include longer passages, which must have been written out separately from the manuscript to supplement the annotated quartos.

The manuscript in question must have been a document accessible to Heminge and Condell. It does not follow automatically that such a manuscript would be a playbook, but in practice it seems most often to have been so. There are one or two exceptions, including *Richard III*. But there was an obstacle to using a playbook directly. A manuscript could not be committed to the printers without the certainty of marking-up and the risk of heavy damage, perhaps even loss. For the actors, a playbook would represent their authoritative statement of the text, their essential guide to cuts and staging, and the repository of the licence that allowed them to perform the play.[7] It would be of little surprise if the company insisted on retaining it in their possession.

In its direct or (more often) indirect recourse to theatrical manuscripts, the Folio contrasts with the various quartos that seem to have been printed from manuscripts released earlier by Shakespeare or the theatre company, where theatre influence is not apparent, and the text has a less mediated, more authorial, complexion. The contrast may be less absolute than has been claimed, for certain theatrical features such as act divisions belong to the period of theatre history after most of the substantive quartos had been printed, and so could not be expected to appear in them under any circumstances. But the differences remain. There are corresponding differences between the situation of the printer of a substantive quarto and that of the Folio printers. The latter's supplementary use of the quartos themselves was, of course, an expedient that was unavailable to the printers of those original editions. And the Folio publishers may have been prepared to commission new transcripts for use in the printing house — something more likely to occur in circumstances where the actors had a close interest in a major, prestigious, and orchestrated publishing venture than in the more haphazard event of a quarto publication.

What is the evidence for playbook influence on a Folio text? Two key elements have already been identified in *Measure for Measure*: the presence of act division in a play written for performance before Shakespeare's company began to perform with act breaks in about 1608, and the signs that profanity has been removed from plays written for performance before the 1606 Act to Restrain Abuses of Players (see Chapter 2). They both relate to revivals after 1606. As already noted, most of the quarto texts with which we are able to compare the Folio were printed before 1606. Consequently, in these cases there is a good chance that the playbook will show significant changes from the quarto version, provided that the play was sufficiently in demand for it to have been revived. This proves to be true, and with particular clarity as regards act division. Of the quartos, only the late *Othello* (1622) has act divisions. In contrast, they are a common (though not universal) feature of Folio texts, whether printed directly from manuscript or from annotated quarto copy.

A Midsummer Night's Dream is a valuable case in point of theatrical act divisions being added in the Folio. Though the Folio is essentially a reprint of Pavier's 1619 Quarto, the copy received light annotation, and the appearance of act divisions offers the clearest indication that the source lies in a playbook. The act division beginning Act 4 strikingly reveals its theatrical origin. Immediately above '*Actus Quartus*' is the stage direction '*They sleepe all the Act*'. '*They*' refers to the four young lovers who, we are told, '*all start vp*' from sleep some lines later when they are awakened by Theseus' horns and the shouts of hunting. The first of these directions tells us that these figures remain sleeping on stage during the act break ('act' was an accepted theatrical term for an act break). The playbook annotator, unable to locate a convenient scene break to adopt as the act interval, split a long and continuous scene in two. The unusual expedient of leaving actors on stage during the break palpably belongs to theatre practice, and so testifies to the origin of the act breaks that were transferred from the playbook to the Q2 copy.

Folio *A Midsummer Night's Dream* benefited from various alterations to stage directions apart from the one discussed already. The first exit to be marked in either text is in the middle of the first scene at 1.1.127. Where Q1 read simply '*Exeunt*', F expanded the direction by adding '*Manet Lysander and Hermia*', calling for these figures to remain on stage as the action requires. At 2.2.30 F provides a new direction for Titania: '*Shee sleepes*'. Stage directions were particularly susceptible to alteration throughout F, and, with certain exceptions, the changes are often more specific as to the staging requirements.

Some similar attention was paid to speech prefixes. For instance, in *A Midsummer Night's Dream* 5.1, where in Q1 Theseus reads the descriptions of the plays on offer for performance at the wedding feast, in F these lines, four speeches in all, are assigned to Lysander. In the same scene, the lines Q1 gives to Philostrate are reattributed to Egeus, a deliberate theatrical change that affects a stage direction as well as speech prefixes, and is even picked up in the dialogue at 5.1.38, where F alters Q's 'Call *Philostrate*' to 'Call *Egeus*'. This is one of the very few readings in the dialogue in F that can be attributed to the manuscript.

The changes introduced in *A Midsummer Night's Dream* are therefore predominantly related to the theatre. But some are of another complexion. Perhaps not coincidentally, one non-theatrical variant reading occurs later in the same scene as the changes in theatrical roles. It presents a difficult crux because few editors have had confidence in either the Quarto or Folio reading. In Q1 and Q2, when Wall makes his exit in the Pyramus and Thisbe play, Theseus comments: 'Now is the Moon vsed between the two neighbors.' F alters this to: 'Now is the morall downe between the two Neighbours' (5.1.205–6). Q is virtually nonsense (Starveling as Moonshine is not on stage at this point), and it is difficult to explain as an error. As for F, Pope emended 'morall' to 'Mural', meaning 'wall'; others have suggested 'mure all', or just 'mure', or, indeed, 'wall'. Here F has been recognized as providing independent witness, and its new reading 'downe' as a replacement for 'vsed' has been accepted. It looks as though F may not simply make a bad job of restoring the reading that is misprinted in Q, but make a bad job of transmitting a different reading.

Elsewhere in *A Midsummer Night's Dream*, the annotator's neglect of variants that one would expect to have been available in the manuscript can be seen from the survival of errors in F that are inherited from Q1 or Q2. Where Q2 introduces an error, F typically agrees with Q2 against Q1, or exacerbates the error. Q1's errors must be inferred, but F seems often to follow them. In a passage of rhyming verse, the quartos and F agree in printing the following sequence of line-endings: 'sweld', 'meete', 'eyes', 'strange companions' (1.1.216–19). Editors since Lewis Theobald (1733) have accepted that 'meet' should rhyme with 'sweet' rather than 'sweld' in the previous line, and that 'eyes' should rhyme with 'stranger companies' rather than 'strange companions'. At 2.1.101 Titania complains that 'The humane mortals want their winter heere' in F as in the quartos; editors again accept Theobald's suggestion that 'heere' is an error for 'cheere'. F's failure to correct these and other errors demonstrates the superficiality of the annotation against the manuscript.

A more persistent level of annotation is found in *Richard II*. The Folio was printed from a copy of Q3 (1598) that had been annotated against a late playbook. F again introduces act divisions, and, as in many Folio plays, scene divisions. It provides a new set of stage directions that amplify the directions in Q1. The episode showing the deposition of Richard in 4.1 is absent in Q1 and Q3; though it had appeared in Q4 (1608), it is now printed in a fuller and evidently more accurate text, presumably copied from the playbook when the annotations were taken from it. F considerably reduces the quantity of profanity, and restores many of the errors introduced in Q2 and Q3 to the original Q1 reading; it also corrects what are manifestly or probably errors in Q1. A number of cuts in F are likely to be of theatrical origin. It also introduces variants on Q1 where both readings make good sense and an error of transmission would not be expected; these are probably Shakespeare's second thoughts (see Chapter 6, where an example is discussed). The Folio therefore again brings us close to performance, specifically to performances after 1608. It reverses what is evidently the censorship of the deposition episode in Q1, while introducing a new form of censorship, the removal of profanity that would have been allowed in the earlier performances. But, although F takes us towards a late-performance text, it does not deliver it to us; it can be seen from the correction of Q2 and Q3 error that the annotation is only about 50 per cent efficient. F therefore gives us a substantial but still *partial* view of a *multilayered* text that has been through a variety of changes.

Plays such as *King Lear, Hamlet, Richard III, Troilus and Cressida,* and *Richard II* were printed in F through a complex and dense inter-mixing of quarto copy and readings or annotations from manuscript; the exact way in which the two (or more) documents were used as copy has been much debated. There was a clear purpose to present a distinctively different version of these and other plays, even when an earlier quarto text had been printed from a manuscript close to Shakespeare's papers, as evidently with most of the plays listed above. But even when the textual differences between quarto and Folio were slight, as with *A Midsummer Night's Dream,* alterations such as the addition of act divisions and introduction of reworded stage directions were conspicuous. Throughout F, act divisions were as a matter of course printed in large italic type with extra spacing and ink-lines above and below, and stage directions were printed in italic, centred on the page, and usually with blank space above, and sometimes blank space below. These are areas of text that draw the reader's attention. Alteration of them drew attention to the Folio's provision of different (and, by implication, better) texts, even when there was in reality little other change.

The plays printed wholly or mainly from a previously printed text contrast with those where the copy was a manuscript. The procedure of setting directly from manuscript was inevitable where plays had not been previously printed. In addition, the editors rejected the earlier printings in favour of an independent manuscript for *2* and *3 Henry VI, The Merry Wives of Windsor, 2 Henry IV, Henry V,* and *Othello.*[8] To these texts we may add the unShakespearian *Taming of A Shrew* and the two-part *The Troublesome Reign of King John* (1591). The rejected editions vary from the short and textually deformed *Merry Wives* to the highly authorial *2 Henry IV.* Taking into account both the Folio alternative texts based directly on manuscript and the plays that had never previously been printed, twenty-three Folio texts were set from manuscript copy. The remaining thirteen were set from a copy of an earlier edition, usually to a greater or lesser extent annotated.

Where 'literary' transcripts were utilized, were they prepared, in the first instance, to supply printers with copy? Instead, they could, potentially at least, have been written out earlier for the benefit of private patrons. This appears to have been a relatively common practice at least by the time the publisher Humphrey Moseley remembered, in his prefatory letter in the 1647 Beaumont and Fletcher Folio: 'when private friends desired a copy, they then, and justly too, transcribed what they acted'. Ralph Crane, the scribe responsible for the copy for several Folio texts, prepared other transcripts in both literary and theatrical contexts. Surviving manuscripts in his hand include the presentation copy of Middleton's *The Witch* (transcribed 1624-5) and the theatre playbook of Fletcher and Massinger's *Sir John van Olden Barnavelt* (1619).

If anything, however, Crane's involvement points to the preparation of copy immediately for the Folio. The 1623 Quarto of Webster's *The Duchess of Malfi* was evidently set from a Crane transcript, and was printed by a different publisher (John Waterson). It seems more likely that Crane was supplying copies of King's Men plays to publishers than that different publishers were able to retrieve various Crane manuscripts from private patrons. Moreover, the Crane transcripts do not appear at random. Crane was evidently responsible for supplying copy for *The Tempest, The Two Gentlemen of Verona, The Merry Wives of Windsor, Measure for Measure, The Comedy of Errors, The Winter's Tale, 2 Henry IV*, and *Othello*. These are the first five and the last plays in the Comedies section, along with the only two plays that had previously been issued in full and relatively reliable quartos that were replaced with texts based directly on manuscripts. The distribution of Crane texts suggests more than an element of editorial planning. It is possible that an initial intention to use Crane transcripts extensively might have been abandoned because it committed the scrivener to too much work. We can only guess how far Crane was involved in the Folio project beyond the mere copying of plays. Trevor Howard-Hill goes as far as to identify Crane as the Folio's editor.[9] As already suggested, Isaac Jaggard and Edward Blount are other likely candidates, and one cannot rule out some kind of editorial participation by Jonson. But, as Howard-Hill points out, it is Crane who in his work elsewhere demonstrates some of the attributes of a textual editor.

The texts thought to have been set from Crane transcripts bear close comparison with surviving manuscripts in Crane's hand, and with other printed texts such as *The Duchess of Malfi*. Webster's play also belonged to the King's Men. Crane's habits of spelling, hyphenation, and use of apostrophes were idiosyncratic, and, precisely because they were distinctive, they survived the normalizing habits of the Folio compositors. His peculiar hyphenation can be seen both in his transcripts—'hangs ore-me', 'barkes-out' (*Demetrius and Enanthe*, 2909 and 2934), and the Folio texts set from his hand—'wide-chopt-rascall', 'dark-backward' (*The Tempest*, TLN 66, 140).[10] His eccentric apostrophes are also found in both. Crane makes widespread use of parentheses:

> But remember
> (For that's my businesse to you) that you three
> From *Millaine* did supplant good *Prospero*,
> Expos'd vnto the Sea (which hath requit it)
> Him, and his innocent childe: for which foule deed,
> The Powres, delaying (not forgetting) haue
> Incens'd the Seas, and Shores; yea, all the Creatures
> Against your peace: Thee of thy Sonne, *Alonso*
> They haue bereft; and doe pronounce by me
> Lingring perdition (worse then any death
> Can be at once) shall step, by step attend
> You, and your wayes …

> (*The Tempest*, TLN 1601–12)

In this passage the parentheses are effective in delineating the complex syntax of Shakespeare's late style.

This styling attracts descriptions such as 'mannered', 'Jonsonian', 'affected', or 'courtly'. It is designed to set the text forth as a literary artefact, and so to draw it away from the environment of theatre. Perhaps it is not surprising, then, that Crane paid special attention to restyling stage directions. In texts such as *The Two Gentlemen of Verona* and *The Merry Wives of Windsor*, he reformulated the entrances as 'massed' staged directions. This means that a single direction at the beginning of a scene names all the characters to appear in that scene, not just those who enter at the beginning. The resulting texts stand somewhere between the usual system as it functioned in the theatre and the classical system adopted by Jonson when he prepared his plays for print. In Jonson's plays a new scene typically begins whenever a new character enters, with no requirement for a cleared stage; the term 'Enter' is dropped, and the initial list of names is all that is required and supplied. Crane keeps the term 'Enter', and keeps the more extended and fluid scene unit of stage practice, but misleadingly includes the characters who actually enter during it under the 'Enter' at the beginning of the scene.

Crane's texts are as a result sparse in their provision of stage directions, and the impression of paucity extends to texts such as *The Winter's Tale*, where there is no massing. But he appears to have afforded different treatment to *The Tempest*. It is likely that Crane supplied rich if rather nebulously descriptive detail such as 'with a quaint device' and 'several strange shapes'. Here he adopts the complimentary language of the stage directions in court masques, and so is once again expressing the influence of Jonson.

Despite the opportunity for post-theatrical restyling afforded by transcripts, their use was in the first instance probably prompted by the same consideration that led to the annotation of quarto copy. Both measures ensured that the actors' playbooks remained under the control of the company. A few Folio plays may have been set from transcripts in other hands (*King John, Othello, Coriolanus*). Others may have been set from authorial papers (*Henry V, All's Well That Ends Well, Timon of Athens*). The Folio text of a few plays shows signs of use in the theatre and no signs of post-theatrical transcription (*Julius Caesar, As You Like It*), though such transcription cannot be ruled out, and may have been considered necessary. We can say that the King's Men must have minimized the extent to which their manuscripts were exposed to the risk of loss and damage. But the exact character of many of the lost manuscripts used as Folio copy remains elusive, hence it cannot be asserted with confidence that a playbook was never sent to the Jaggards' shop.

THE FOLIO AS REPRESENTATION
AND MISREPRESENTATION

The Folio gives us more Shakespeare, much more, and it gives us different Shakespeare, allowing us often to compare one form of a play with another. In its own time, it also enabled readers for the first time to think about 'Shakespeare' as a totality, as an author of a canon of works. This book gave formal definition to 'Shakespeare' as author. Quite specifically, it established an organic linkage between the author's body and his works as represented in the Folio itself. Jonson's short poem 'To the Reader' placed on the page facing the title page with Martin Droeshout's engraving is vital here. Referring to the engraved image of Shakespeare, Jonson wrote:

> This figure that thou here seest put
> It was for gentle Shakespeare cut,
> Wherein the graver had a strife
> With Nature to out-do the life.
> O, could he but have drawn his wit
> As well in brass as he hath hit
> His face! The print would then surpass
> All that was ever writ in brass.
> But, since he cannot, reader, look
> Not on his picture, but his Book.

Jonson makes full use of his awareness of the relationship between the visual image and the textual word, something that goes back to his writing of masques for the court of King James. He contrasts the qualities of mind epitomized in the word 'wit', meaning 'intellectual capacity and dexterity', with Shakespeare's body, as reflected in the 'picture'. The word 'print' acts as a crucial hinge between pictorial engraving of the person and the poet's words as set in type.

In his longer poem, the first of the commendatory verses printed after Heminge and Condell's epistle to the readers, Jonson presents another image of the canon, now seen as a body of writing that takes its place alongside other, established canonical writers. Jonson places Shakespeare alongside the English non-dramatic poets Chaucer and Spenser, as well as other contemporary dramatists such as Beaumont, Kyd, and Marlowe, and classical dramatists such as Aeschylus, Euripides, and Sophocles. He gives us the famous phrase 'Sweet swan of Avon', making strong claims for Shakespeare both as a writer of nature and as a conscious artist who produced 'well-turnèd and true-filèd lines'. This is the real beginning of Shakespeare as literary figure—notions of his belonging to literary tradition, of his pre-eminence, and of his distinctive quality are all here.

It might be supposed that the Folio, in its fullness and greatness, gives an accurate account of the canon it brings into being, that there is a goodness of fit between the book and the canon. But Margreta de Grazia's influential account of this volume's strong orientation to the market reminds us that the publishers set out a body of works that was defined to promote the idea of exclusivity, edited with a view to establishing textual differentiation from the quartos that came before it, and organized to present a specific image of Shakespeare that might owe as much to the market or to ideological forces as to any objective truth about the author.[11] De Grazia's question about how we read the preliminaries can be taken onwards to address the text itself. What, specifically, are its limitations?

The first deficiency, as compared with any modern edition of Shakespeare's complete works, is that it does not include the non-dramatic poems. This is one of the major differences between the Shakespeare and Jonson Folios. The Shakespeare Folio, of course, steers clear of the ridicule to which Jonson was exposed when he called his volume *Works*, though Heminge and Condell's epistle to the reader does claim that they 'have collected and published' Shakespeare's 'writings', and that they 'gather his works'. One possible reason why the volume does not include the poems is that there might have been insuperable difficulties in securing entitlement to print the poems. Whether as a result of such a necessity or by initial design, this Shakespeare is exclusively a writer of plays, and his poems are not only left out of the book but rendered invisible. The image stuck: it was not until Malone's edition of 1790 that the poems were included in Shakespeare editions, notwithstanding the Jonsonian title of *Works* adopted by Nicholas Rowe and other early eighteenth-century editors.

A second limitation is that the Folio organized the range of Shakespeare's plays in an arbitrary way that remains familiar today and yet creates difficulties in seeing some of the plays for what they are. Within the three headings of Comedies, Histories, and Tragedies, the plays are presented in an order that bears little or no relation to the chronological sequence of composition or first performance. The Histories were presented in the order of the events shown in the play, which bears an uneven relation to the order of writing. The sequence within the Comedies and Tragedies seems to have been aimed at placing previously unpublished plays written late in Shakespeare's career at the beginning and end of each section. Availability of copy may also have played its part in the ordering. From the reader's point of view, there is little discernible logic to the progression from one play to the next.

As for the categories themselves, the editors recognized the classical genres of drama going back to ancient Greece, comedy and tragedy. But there had never before been a substantial collection of plays called 'histories'. A glance at the catalogue shows that not all the history plays were put in this section: *Macbeth*, *Julius Caesar*, and *Troilus and Cressida* are examples of plays based on historical events that in the Folio appear in the tragedies section. What the term means in effect is 'English histories'. A grand narrative transcending the individual play is implied by the organization of the plays in the order of the events they portray, and in the standardization of titles to display the individual plays and 'parts' of sequences as centred on the figure of the king. This is in marked contrast with the seemingly random order of the other two sections.

The 'Histories' category recognizes a distinctly Shakespearian species of play, at the risk of presenting Shakespeare as an old-fashioned dramatist—though there may have been capital in that too: nostalgia has its commercial value, and some of the history plays had proved of durable interest to Jacobean readers of Shakespeare. There is something generative and positive in the Folio's shaping of our image of Shakespeare by focusing on the English histories as a mighty sequence. We can see too the beginnings of the myth of the national poet, or one aspect of it: Shakespeare is the poet of English nationhood. The Folio elevates Shakespeare by aggrandising this aspect of his writing. The histories are all named after English kings. To achieve this uniformity, previous unconformable titles such as *The Contention between the Houses of York and Lancaster* and *The True Tragedy of Richard Duke of York* were dropped in favour of *The Second Part of King Henry the Sixth* and *The Third Part of King Henry the Sixth*. The previously unpublished play that had been performed under the title *All Is True* was similarly restyled *Henry VIII*. The Folio catalogue of Histories leaves little evident space for the local, the demotic, the anti-heroic, the comic, the conscience-stricken, all aspects of the history plays as we encounter them individually, and some of them reflected in a quarto title such as 'The history of Henrie the Fovrth; with the battell at Shrewsburie, betweene the King and Lord Henry Percy, surnamed Henrie Hotspur of the North. With the humorous conceits of Sir Iohn Falstalffe'.

The overall picture of Shakespeare as a writer of three kinds of play and three only is a serious distortion. Modern criticism slowly found alternative labels: romantic comedy, Roman plays, problem plays, late plays. It has been repeatedly stressed that Shakespeare is a writer whose works constantly overflow the narrow bounds of genre. Shakespeare's plays are hard to categorize because they often experiment with or deconstruct the genres on which they are based. We have encountered a particularly acute example of the generic instability in *Troilus and Cressida* (see Chapter 3). One might wonder why the Folio editors rejected the option of presenting a fourth section called 'Tragicomedies'. This would have been appropriate to the plays that criticism has labelled by the modern terms 'problem plays' (based on a nineteenth-century Ibsenite view of drama) and 'late plays' (based on a post-Romantic notion of the great artist's biographical development). 'Tragicomedy' intrinsically suggests instability of genre, and was a term in use and indeed fashionable in the Jacobean period. Perhaps it was considered something different from Shakespeare's dramatic art; perhaps the actors remembered that it had come into prominence in the theatres of the boy companies that were the rivals to the King's Men.

Thirdly, perhaps as a sales pitch, the Folio gave an over-pessimistic picture of the editions that came before it. Heminge and Condell said in their epistle that 'before you were abused with diverse stolen and surreptitious copies, maimed and deformed by the frauds and stealths of injurious imposters'. It took centuries before scholars were able to rehabilitate most of the quarto editions that seemed to have been written off as frauds in this statement. The actors' scathing remark may have been directed against the Pavier Quartos,[12] yet it is of a piece with much else in the preliminaries that is designed to emphasize what is claimed to be the unprecedented and unique access that this book offers to the mind of the author.

And here we encounter the fourth limitation, which is that the Folio misrepresents Shakespeare as a dramatist by isolating him from the theatre. Heminge and Condell stress the immediacy of the texts in their book to what is called, conspicuously, on the title page the

'True Originall Copies'. It is as though nothing stood in between Shakespeare's pen and the text. The phrase 'True Originall Copies' is damagingly misleading. W. W. Greg, who placed as much credence in the words of Heminge and Condell as he could muster, understood the phrase to mean that the Folio plays 'had either been printed from or verified by comparison with playhouse manuscripts'. He commented: 'Thus interpreted it is probably substantially true, though it will not bear pressing in every case.'[13] Greg used a footnote to deal with this important issue, and the varieties of hedging with which he surrounds his endorsement of the Folio editors' claim further suggest an attempt to brush the dust under the carpet. Greg evidently takes 'original copies' to mean 'first transcripts'—in other words, it points to the 'fair copies' of the author's 'foul papers' from which the prompt book would emerge after annotation and licensing. The view has more recently been accepted in modified form by De Grazia and Julie Stone Peters.[14] But it is probably wrong. Peters suggests that such phrases consolidated around the authorial manuscript only at a later date. Hence, in Moseley's claim in the 1647 Beaumont and Fletcher Folio that it is 'published by the Authours Originall Copies', the manuscripts are finally said to be original in the sense that they originate directly from the author (being copies in the sense that they provided the compositors with their copy-text). But this is surely how any reader in 1623 would have interpreted the phrase 'True Originall Copies'. These words appear immediately above the engraved image of Shakespeare the author, and so stand in complex emblematic relation to that image as a 'copy', or, in Jonson's term, 'figure', of the man himself.[15] Moseley's word 'Authours' merely sets in type what is already conspicuously manifested in the presentation of the 1623 Shakespeare Folio.

Further reading of the preliminaries would reinforce the impression that the texts are immediately authorial. If, as we have seen, previous editions are corrupt because injurious imposters have maimed them, in contrast, Heminge and Condell have taken the 'care and pain to have collected and published them' (thus writing as editors, not as members of the theatre company); they continue: 'His mind and hand went together. And what he thought, he uttered with that easiness that we have scarce received from him a blot in his papers'; hence the plays 'are now offered to your view cured and perfect of their limbs'. The project here is to construct the impression that the book gives immediate access to the authorial manuscript, which itself gives immediate access to the authorial mind: 'his mind and hand went together'. This fantasy of transparent access to the mind reinforces the equivalence between the two aspects of the authorial *corpus*: the physical body of the person and the collection of works. To paraphrase Jonson's poem 'To the Reader', unlike Shakespeare's 'figure', his 'wit' cannot be engraved in brass, but it can be represented in lead type. This poem stands directly facing not only the engraving, but also the claim 'Published according to the True Originall Copies'. Taking all into account, the implication as regards the nature of those copies could scarcely be clearer, and the implication is false. Plays were not for the most part published from manuscripts where printed texts were available. Even where manuscript readings are copied into the quarto copy, the primary copy is the print, not the manuscript. That print is not even the most reliable edition, for, in line with usual early modern printing practice, the most recent edition was regarded as the most satisfactory (and usually would be the most readily available). Moreover, when a quarto was printed from a reliable authorial manuscript, the Folio editors' reference to an alternative manuscript takes us further away from anything resembling the 'True Originall Copies'. Folio texts are very often distinctive because they have been through the theatre; they include adjustments for the stage, introduction of act intervals for performance in the private Blackfriars theatre, music cues, alterations for revival, censorship changes, and so on. In the case of *2 Henry IV* the highly authorial Quarto is replaced with a text that has been copied and verbally softened by a scribe. On both counts there is a mismatch between the advertised access to Shakespeare's mind and the actual editorial practice, and it could scarcely be more stark.

Fifth, and just as important, the impression we get of Shakespeare as a dramatist from the Folio is of a writer isolated from other writers. This is not true, and again it has taken centuries of scholarship to correct this impression. The Folio established a definitive canon of what was and was not 'Shakespeare'. The plays are said to be 'absolute in their numbers, as he conceived them', and so to represent a complete picture of Shakespeare's dramatic achievement. But the Folio actually included two plays that are thought to have been adapted after Shakespeare's death by Thomas Middleton, *Macbeth* and *Measure*

for Measure (see Chapter 2). It also included some collaborations—
1 Henry VI, possibly *3 Henry VI*, *Titus Andronicus*, *Timon of Athens*, and
All Is True. But it left out a number of other collaborative plays: *Edward
III*, *Sir Thomas More*, *Pericles*, *The Two Noble Kinsmen*, and possibly
Arden of Faversham. Though a play was more likely to be included if
it was predominantly by Shakespeare, there was no consistent policy:
it is likely that only about one-third of the included play *1 Henry
VI* was written by Shakespeare, whereas the excluded *Pericles* seems
to be about three-fifths in his hand. One play, *Timon of Athens*, was
probably included only to fill a gap in the Folio that was left when the
editors faced difficulties in securing copyright for another play, *Troilus
and Cressida*. If it had not been for these very particular circumstances,
Timon of Athens would probably be a lost play of which there would
be no record.

In addition to the plays already mentioned, we do have references
to two plays that are indeed lost, a sequel to *Love's Labour's Lost*
called *Love's Labour's Won* and a collaboration with Fletcher called
Cardenio. *Pericles*, which was issued in several quarto editions during
Shakespeare's lifetime, was accepted into the Shakespeare canon in
the eighteenth century, to be followed much later by *The Two Noble
Kinsmen* and then *Edward III* in the late twentieth century. Before
the twenty-first century, *Sir Thomas More* only once appeared in full
in a Shakespeare edition.[16] The 2004 Oxford *Timon of Athens* was
the first separate edition to present this play as a collaboration,[17]
and a comparable separate edition of *Titus Andronicus* has yet to
appear.

There is, therefore, an important aspect of Shakespeare that the
Folio fails to acknowledge, presumably because the cultural status of
Shakespeare would seem more impressive without it. This assumption—that a Shakespeare who mixed with other writers might be
judged inferior—applied in 1623, when it took a deliberate effort to
accord Shakespeare high cultural status. It applied in the nineteenth
century, when in an almost blasphemous sentence of bardolatry the
editor Charles Knight wrote of Shakespeare in relationship to his
early competitors that 'he lived amongst them, but we may readily
believe that he was not of them'.[18] Shakespeare-as-Jesus, dwelling
among but not of humanity, is unlikely to join with lesser mortals to
write a collaborative play. And these nineteenth-century attitudes still

echo residually, belatedly, every time, for instance, we call Shakespeare the Bard.

The status of the First Folio as one of the most important books ever printed remains unchallenged, and is indeed reflected in current market prices. At a sale at Sotheby's in 2006, a copy changed hands at £2,808,000. This is the book that gave us Shakespeare (or most of Shakespeare). Nothing detracts from that remarkable fact. But the way it presented Shakespeare was very carefully calculated to make a collection of theatre works look plausible as what we would now call works of literature. The book not only gives us the texts; it gives us Shakespeare as a cultural icon. Ultimately, it succeeded: not in immediate acclaim and fast sales, but by establishing Shakespeare's presence at the upper end of the print market. This position was entrenched by the reprints of 1632 (F2), 1663–4 (F3), and 1685 (F4). Shakespeare's eighteenth-century editors continued to work (usually indirectly) from the Folio text, and even today many editions of his works might be described as elaborations on the Folio. If one finds Shakespeare's late play *The Tempest* at the beginning of the volume, as in the 1951 edition by Peter Alexander, that apparently random way of organizing the book goes back to the Folio. We might usefully be aware, then, that this cultural icon is not in all respects accurate, or truthful, or objective in its presentation of Shakespeare. This is a book edited with a strong sense of purpose. Shakespeare was more of a collaborator, more a man of the theatre, than the Folio allowed. His plays were constantly undermining rather than conforming to the narrow confines of genre. In this respect Shakespeare was a more experimental dramatist than the Folio recognizes; perhaps we might say a writer more attuned to modern sensibilities.

Mapping the Text

LOCATING BADNESS

When an editor describes the manufacture, make-up, and mode of circulation of the printed book that presents the play, he or she is writing as a bibliographer, and is likely to attend to the bibliographical codes operating in the typography and layout:[1] matters that have been touched on in the earlier discussions in this book of Quarto and Folio *Troilus and Cressida* and the Folio as a whole. This focus is essential for understanding the book as a physical object and its relation to the world in which it was made, sold, and read. In contrast, for the purposes of establishing the text the editor will focus on the content of the book, its words, and their meaning. The book is now the repository for a text, a vehicle within a semiotic process of complex origin and multiple outcomes.[2] Inked letters are now regarded as the constituents of words as signifiers. The code is linguistic. The material artefact of the book is now examined not as an object in its own right, but as a conveyor of meaning. The editor's activity is textual criticism.

Under the Shakespeare-centred school of textual and bibliographical study that dominated most of the twentieth century known as the New Bibliography, it became important to analyse the individual text not in isolation but in relation to a general description of the genesis and evolution of the Shakespeare text. The contours of the twentieth century's editorial work on Shakespeare were set in place in Alfred W. Pollard's work on the classification of texts.[3] Previous textual critics had developed some sense that the quartos varied in character, and indeed the suggestion that the First Quartos of *Hamlet* and *Romeo and Juliet* might derive from memorial reconstruction by actors goes back to Tycho Mommsen in 1857. But Pollard transformed the field of study by generating an overall hypothesis as to textual origins.

His most crucial intervention came in the chapter in his *Shakespeare Folios and Quartos* headed 'The Good and Bad Quartos'.[4] Investigating the regulation of entitlement to publication as evidenced in the Stationers' Register, he noted a high level of correspondence between textual 'goodness' and regular, authorized publication. One criterion of textual virtue was the implied verdict of the Folio editors in accepting printed copy; Pollard also took into account the quality of the text on its own terms. The criterion for authorized publication was regular entry in the Stationers' Register. As W. W. Greg later summarized:

> The novel feature in Pollard's argument was the demonstration that the issue of each of these five 'bad' quartos was in some way peculiar: *Romeo and Juliet* and *Henry V* were not entered in the Stationers' Register at all; *Hamlet* and *Pericles* were published by stationers other than those who had made the entrance; *The Merry Wives of Windsor* was entered by one stationer and transferred to another the same day.[5]

Pollard interpreted certain entries in the Stationers' Register of 1598 and 1600 as successful attempts by the Lord Chamberlain's Men to block unauthorized publication of their plays. They indicated, therefore, that Shakespeare and his company were doing battle with 'pirates' who sought to steal their plays and publish them surreptitiously. Where previous critics had often been suspicious of the quartos as a whole, Pollard disclosed that the majority of quartos were free of this taint of badness. Corruption could be limited to particular texts that were irregularly printed and were later rejected by the Folio editors.

Pollard had worked in close collaboration with Greg. In his preface he confessed: 'In some sections of this study Mr Greg and I have been fellow-hunters, communicating our results to each other at every stage.'[6] Greg had already published an old-spelling edition of *The Merry Wives of Windsor*.[7] Where Pollard's book had focused on the publishing context, Greg's edition of *Merry Wives* was a ground-breaking textual study, detailed to the point of speculation, in which he identified the actor of the Host of the Garter as the person who had reported and assembled the Quarto text. Greg's work in turn stimulated a number of other investigative studies published in the early decades of the century in which the case for memorial transmission was developed in relation to individual Quarto texts. Thus Q1 *Hamlet, Henry V*, and *Romeo and Juliet* were identified as 'bad' quartos, as were the first editions of *The First Part of the Contention* and *Richard Duke of York*. Quarto *The Taming of A Shrew* and *Pericles* were placed under the same general heading of 'bad' quartos, though *A Shrew* was usually also regarded as an independent non-Shakespearian version, and the case of *Pericles* was recognized as being complicated yet further by the issue of joint authorship.

Just what is at issue may be judged from the texts of Q1 and Q2 *Hamlet* 3.3.63–93 (see Appendix 1). It should be kept in mind that examples from other plays would show a different range of characteristics. After Q1 *The Merry Wives of Windsor*, Q1 *Hamlet* is perhaps the most clear-cut case of a text potentially or actually influenced by memorial transmission. The passage is well representative of *Hamlet*, and shows characteristics that have been identified, though often less emphatically and in different combinations, in other 'bad' quartos. These features include highly irregular metre, a low level of word-for-word correspondence with the more authorial text, a relationship with that text varying between fairly close paraphrase and complete verbal recasting in a different and coarsened language with distinct if less attuned imagery ('A looke fit for a murder and a rape, | A dull dead hanging looke, and a hell-bred eie, | To affright children and amaze the world'), relocation of lines within the passage, insertion of lines drawn from elsewhere in the text ('To liue in the incestuous pleasure of his bed', 'Hamlet, thou cleaues my heart in twaine'), and a distinct shortening in overall length. The passage is reasonably coherent and theatrically playable, and includes the staging detail of the Ghost appearing in his nightgown that is missing in Q2. But Q1 lacks the poetic texture and nuanced characterization of the longer and more familiar text. These are the characteristics that the theory of memorial reconstruction sought to explain.

The significance of memorial reconstruction in the period of the New Bibliography was twofold. First, it enabled the affected texts to be labelled as 'bad'—though the nature of that badness could never quite be declared homogeneous—and so assigned them to a marginal position in the editing of the plays in question. Second, it sustained the narrative of piracy by aligning the allegedly irregular circumstances of publication noted by Pollard with an activity on the part of actors that could readily be interpreted as theft. But by 1942, when Greg published *The Editorial Problem in Shakespeare*, this apparently strong convergence of textual analysis and book history had already begun to look vulnerable. Greg pointed out the limits of the evidence of the Stationers' Register:

absence of registration is not in itself evidence of piracy nor always accompanied by textual corruption; nor is simultaneous entrance and transfer proof of dishonest dealing ... On the other hand, some pieces that were quite regularly entered prove to have thoroughly bad texts.[8]

The suspected texts now included the Quartos of *King Lear* and *Richard III*. Both had been regularly entered in the Register and, though subjected to heavy annotation in the manner described in Chapter 4, were to be accepted as the foundations for the Folio texts. But both had nevertheless now emerged as 'presumably piratical and surreptitious'.[9]

A problem Greg recognized as early as his study of *The Merry Wives of Windsor* was that the effects of bad reporting cannot always be distinguished from those of adaptation. Shortening of a text, for instance, can be an effect of adaptation rather than poor memory. This instability of the boundary between the effects of memory and the effects of adaptation persistently plagued accounts of the 'bad' quartos, as did the difficulty in making all the textual data conform to any detailed fleshing-out of the hypothesis. But Greg and others were nevertheless able to argue persuasively that, if textual shortening is produced not by cutting but by rough, unShakespearian, and sometimes garbled paraphrase, and if the metricality of verse is sometimes severely damaged in the process, it is hard to see how a redactor working directly from a manuscript could produce such a text. A traumatic break in transmission seems to have happened. It is plausible to conclude that an effect of the limitations of memory is manifested.

In the mid-twentieth century this hypothesis of memorial reconstruction was tested against alternative postulates. A number of critics suggested that the affected quartos were put together from shorthand scripts taken by members of the theatre audience. This view is now discounted on the basis that early modern shorthand systems were inadequate to the task.[10] Another explanation is that they represent early authorial versions that were later filled out to become the plays we know from the longer quartos and Folio.[11] This view failed to gain wide acceptance, not least because features of language and metre, some of them demonstrable and quantifiable, lie well outside the range of Shakespeare's style at any point in his writing.[12] If Q1 *Hamlet* is an early draft, it represents a strange and otherwise unknown aspect of Shakespeare's writing. Moreover, the early draft hypothesis conflicts acutely with the signs of theatrical adaptation that numerous critics have observed as marking these as late texts in the process of transmission.

Kathleen O. Irace confirmed, for some texts more clearly than others, that the suspected reconstructions show a pattern of varying correspondence with their longer counterparts that had first been noted by Greg.[13] She produced a statistical analysis showing that where the actor was on stage his part was relatively well transmitted, and the parts of other actors were transmitted with intermediate reliability; the least accurate parts of the text were those where the actor or actors were offstage. The demonstration was more convincing for some texts than others. *The Merry Wives of Windsor* was a particularly clear example. Here the hypothesis of memorial reconstruction was considerably strengthened, for it is hard to think of any alternative way to account for the phenomenon.

The spirit of the 1990s was hostile to the New Bibliography, to its polarization of 'good' and 'bad', and to its optimistic drive to make the convoluted transmission of the text knowable. Paul Werstine's sharp, cynical, insightful, if ultimately inconclusive critiques set the tone, and proclaimed that the days of the New Bibliography were over.[14] Memorial reconstruction became a key instance in the crisis in theory and methodology, as the point where the work of the New Bibliographers was least empirical and so the Achilles heel of the whole movement. Where Werstine addressed the historical evolution of editorial theory, Laurie E. Maguire investigated the texts themselves, taking on board non-Shakespearian examples as well as the Shakespearian 'bad' quartos.[15] Maguire avoided the standard analytic method of comparing the suspect text with its longer counterpart, and carefully investigated the demonstrable effects of memory on textual transmission. By these means she established a more rigorous and narrowed approach to the question than other investigators. She found very few probable or possible cases of memorial reconstruction—though, given her self-imposed constraints and the scepticism that characterized the period, it is significant that *The Merry Wives of Windsor* still emerged as 'probably' memorial reconstruction, *The Taming of A Shrew* as 'part' memorial reconstruction, and Q1 *Hamlet* as 'possibly' one, a possibility that extended also to *Pericles*.[16] Maguire's work offered a strong critique of memorial reconstruction as a general explanation for 'bad' quartos, but the hypothesis survives her rigorous approach at least in vestigial form.

The 'bad' quartos were emerging in the 1990s as interesting more for their features of adaptation than for corruption, if only because the concept of corruption had itself fallen into disrepute. Every text was opened up for study as a potential or actual script for performance.[17] Andrew Gurr saw the 'good' quarto and Folio texts as representing a menu of 'maximal' performance possibilities from which shorter performance scripts would emerge; the 'bad' quartos, or at least the less corrupted examples such as *Henry V* and *Romeo and Juliet*, might bear a close relation to such 'minimal' stage versions.[18] As the century closed, editions of *Richard III* and *King Lear* for the Oxford series were in preparation that took the erstwhile 'doubtful' quartos as the primary text of choice.[19] But even in this environment memorial reconstruction of one kind or another could not be banished. It still continues to offer a compelling if problematic and partial explanation for a number of texts displaying distinctly unShakespearian features that have not been adequately explained by other theories.

AUTHORIAL AND THEATRICAL TEXTS

To Greg, Pollard's explanation of the 'good' quartos came to look as unsatisfactory as his account of the 'bad'. Pollard had read Heminge and Condell's claim that 'we have scarce received from him a blot in his papers' at face value, and so had argued that the manuscripts that became the printers' copy for the Folio were Shakespeare's original drafts. These had probably been submitted for licence to the Master of the Revels and adapted for use in the theatre as a prompt book.

The same explanation was extended to the 'good' quartos. The players would be prepared to surrender their prompt book to the printers for a few weeks for 'the superior convenience of a printed prompt-copy'.[20] Greg forcefully questioned several of Pollard's premisses.

Here the manuscript of *Sir Thomas More* became significant. A 1923 collection of essays edited by Pollard with major contributions from Greg advanced the case that Hand D was Shakespeare's.[21] Hand D's writing habits did not correspond with the account given by the Folio editors of Shakespeare's blot-free papers. 'Recent criticism', Greg notes, 'is inclined to discount their statement'.[22] Ironically, Pollard's own project on *Sir Thomas More* had undermined his earlier work on the quartos. Greg went on to draw an influential distinction, based on his study of other surviving dramatic manuscripts of the period, between 'foul papers' and 'fair copy'. This latter might be prepared by either the dramatist (or one of them in a collaboration) or a professional scribe. For Greg, the signs of textual cleanness combined with annotation for theatrical use are typical of Folio plays printed from manuscript, or with reference to manuscript. The 'good' quartos, in contrast, display features that suggest Shakespeare's rough draft, or 'foul papers'. These include difficulties resulting from hasty handwriting, undeleted first sketches of a phrase or passage that stood alongside its replacement, misplaced interlinear or marginal insertions, inconsistent forms and abbreviations of speech prefix, and imaginatively descriptive but theatrically redundant wording in stage directions.

Inconsistent speech prefixes are well attested in the Shakespearian passage of *Sir Thomas More*. One finds speech prefixes for 'Lincolne', 'Linco', 'Lin', and 'Linc'. A comparable case in a printed text is Q2 *Romeo and Juliet*, where Juliet is identified variously as '*Iuliet*', '*Iule*', '*Iuli*', '*Iul.*', and '*Iu*'. More striking are variations between the forms by which dramatic roles are identified. The character whom editions usually call Lady Capulet is a good case in point. She is not given a personal forename, and nowhere is she 'Lady Capulet', an editorial fabrication that combines 'Lady' as a term for a wife or the female head of a household with the family name to produce a misleading impression of an aristocrat (Capulet is never called 'Lord Capulet'). In stage directions she is variously '*Capulets Wife*', '*his wife*', '*Mother*', '*Lady*', and '*Lady of the house*'. There are similar variations in the speech prefixes, which vary between '*Ca. Wi.*', '*Capu. Wi.*', '*Wife.*', '*Wi.*', '*Moth.*', '*M.*', '*Old La.*', and '*La.*'. These designations place her in relation to different characters and show her in different social and personal capacities. Though her identity in the theatre would be settled on the person of a single actor, her identifiers in the script are, evidently, dependent on the situation she is in. Such inconsistencies are generally accepted as authorial in complexion. Some of them might survive in a playbook, but on the whole transcription produced more regular and so usable forms.

Q2 *Romeo and Juliet* also shows several cases of abandoned first drafts. In the following passage lines printed consecutively in Romeo's death-speech at 5.3.108–20 evidently represent two stages in the drafting of the script:

Depart againe, come lye thou in my arme,　　　　[First sketch]
Heer's to thy health, where ere thou tumblest in.
O true Appothecarie!
Thy drugs are quicke. Thus with a kisse I die.
Depart againe, here, here, will I remaine,　　[Elaborated version]
With wormes that are thy Chamber-maides: O here
Will I set vp my euerlasting rest:
And shake the yoke of inauspicious starres,
From this world wearied flesh, eyes looke your last:
Armes take your last embrace: And lips, O you
The doores of breath, seale with a righteous kisse
A datelesse bargaine to ingrossing death:
Come bitter conduct, come vnsauoury guide,
Thou desperate Pilot, now at once run on
The dashing Rocks, thy seasick weary barke:
Heeres to my Loue. O true Appothecary:
Thy drugs are quicke. Thus with a kisse I die.

Editors routinely remove the first four lines because they accept that they are a rough sketch superseded in the lines that come after. The raw process of composition seems to be witnessed.

Greg argued that such a document would be inadequate for the theatre company's purposes, and so would be copied out. When the company later relinquished a manuscript for publication during Shakespeare's lifetime, they would have retained the licensed prompt book and sent the back-up document instead.[23] Greg's account of 'foul papers' split up Pollard's large group of reliable texts, differentiating between the typical 'good' quarto and typical Folio texts. He accepted McKerrow's suggestion that there was a correspondence between signs of inconsistency and irregularity found in the 'good' quartos, such as *Love's Labour's Lost*, Q2 *Romeo and Juliet*, *The Merchant of Venice*, *1 Henry IV*, and *Much Ado about Nothing*, and similar signs in manuscript authorial drafts.[24] This enabled Greg to claim that, despite the difficulties in Pollard's argument, the grounds for optimism as regards the 'good' quartos were actually stronger than Pollard had realized, as they were especially close to an authorial draft.[25]

The term 'foul papers' was borrowed from its pragmatic use to describe various kinds of rough draft in the early modern period—sometimes, indeed, referring to drafts of plays, but not in recorded usage to refer to a completed draft. Greg elevated that term to a standard category in the description of dramatic manuscripts. His difficulty was that no extant manuscript fully conforms to the description. Nevertheless, it is self-evident that any 'fair copy' had an antecedent, that any transcript is a copy of something else. The passages written by the dramatists identified as Henry Chettle, Thomas Heywood, Shakespeare, and Thomas Dekker in *Sir Thomas More* and the entirety of a manuscript such as *The Captives* correspond with Greg's description of foul papers, except in so far as some (but not all) of them have been lightly annotated by a theatrical scribe, and the *Sir Thomas More* additions are not a complete draft.

Greg's insistence on establishing a category for which there is limited material evidence proved concerning to more recent critics such as Werstine. Yet Greg himself consistently showed awareness of the limits of categorization and recognized that each individual text displayed unique characteristics that were likely to place it in ambiguous relationship with the category to which it putatively belonged. In addition to the theatre-oriented manuscripts, Greg recognized another type, the 'literary' transcript prepared for a private reader such as a patron. He referred to dramatic manuscripts (specifically those used as Folio copy) as 'a misty mid region of Weir, a land of shadowy shapes and melting outlines, where not even the most patient inquiry and the most penetrating analysis can hope to arrive at any but tentative and proximate conclusions'.[26] This statement reflects his awareness of the diversity of feature in the extant dramatic manuscripts, as well as the complexities of transmission to print.

Mistiness notwithstanding, for Greg the foul papers and the tran-script of them that became the prompt book were the two key documents in the composition and preparation of the play for the theatre. Both would normally be held by the theatre company. In Fredson Bowers's influential development of Greg's work the number of categories swelled to thirteen—a formalization of the fluidity that was already acknowledged in Greg's simpler system made up of the binaries foul and fair, theatrical and literary, authorial and scribal.[27] Bowers suggested that there might have been a common expectation that the dramatist should deliver a fair copy in his own hand, and that this fair copy might itself have been transcribed. In this case the author's fair copy can be described as an intermediate manuscript.[28] Bowers points out the editorial implication. If the company's spare manuscript was at least sometimes an author's fair copy rather than foul papers, the editorial treatment of those texts may have been too liberal. Editors had assumed that the printer's copy would have been full of illegible readings, interlineations, side-notes, and the like, and emended accordingly, but these features would not be expected in the kind of copy Bowers postulates.[29]

The Oxford Shakespeare editors considered it clear enough that texts such as Q2 *Romeo and Juliet*, Q1 *2 Henry IV*, and even a text Bowers had proposed as 'intermediate', Q2 *Hamlet*, displayed the range of features to be expected of foul papers. But other 'good' quartos did not: for instance, Q1 *The Merchant of Venice* is described as 'Holograph (fair copy), or perhaps a scribal transcript of it', and *1 Henry IV* as a 'scribal transcript of authorial papers'.[30] Similarly, Folio *All's Well That Ends Well* is accounted 'Holograph (foul papers)', with the qualification that 'The foul papers may have been annotated by a book-keeper'.[31] The terminology developed by Pollard and Greg remained in place, but, in the spirit of Greg in his more permissive aspect, there was no expectation that texts will conform neatly to a fixed model.

The understanding that most of the Folio texts were in some way related to theatrical manuscripts remained in place throughout the century. Progress was made in identifying the nature of the copy: the edition used for quarto copy, and the nature of the intermixing of quarto and manuscript copy in plays.[32] Understanding of the involvement of scribes in supplying copy was advanced by Trevor

Howard-Hill's work identifying Ralph Crane as the copyist behind a number of Folio plays.[33] Scribal features were also identified in plays printed from evidently clean copy that had previously often been assumed to be holograph, both in quarto (*1 Henry IV*) and Folio (*Antony and Cleopatra, Coriolanus*).[34] Taylor confirmed that in printed texts act divisions relate to performance at the indoors Blackfriars theatre.[35] The expurgation of profanity similarly reflects modification of a text written before profanity was outlawed by the 1606 Act to Restrain Abuses of Players.[36]

One important conclusion reached in the work surrounding the Oxford Shakespeare was that the licensed prompt book was rarely if ever released to supply direct copy for the Folio compositors.[37] Accordingly, a premiss of Pollard's argument remained valid at the end of the century. That is to say, if few or none of Shakespeare's plays was printed directly from a playbook, the printed texts fall into two broad categories, pre-theatrical and post-theatrical. These roughly correspond to Pollard's good and bad. But they are broad categories indeed: the pre-theatrical might include authorial rough drafts, authorial fair copies, and manuscripts lightly annotated in anticipation of a new transcript; the post-theatrical covers scribal transcripts as well as later secondary theatrical adaptations and reconstructions. The Oxford Shakespeare placed theoretical emphasis on the document there referred to as the prompt book as the key point of reference, supplementing or even replacing the *desideratum* of the authorial draft. The theatre document offers promise of a convergence of different forms of non-exclusive authority: the dramatist (who, in the case of Shakespeare, is understood, as a member of the theatre company, to retain involvement after the notional transfer from author to company), the company itself (as agents of a collective form of 'publication' on the stage), and the licensing Master of the Revels (as a figure lending the official sanction of the state). Such a manuscript evidently lies behind many Folio texts, and yet typically seems to stand at more than one remove from it.

Some critics towards the end of the century found the lack of exact fit between the theorized models that map the territory and the materials to which they apply indicates that the misty land of Weir is unexplorable. For Werstine, the absence of a pure example of foul papers and doubts as to the historical evidence for memorial reconstruction dealt fatal blows to the edifice Pollard and Greg had built up. Werstine pointed to the survival in extant prompt books of features that had been thought typical of foul papers.[38] At a cursory reading Werstine here and elsewhere may seem to be saying that the New Bibliographers were wrong on all counts. His arguments do not stand up as such. They succeed in advancing the subtler proposition that there are no stable points of reference upon which to plot a categorization that can be applied to the lost copy for printed plays. His conclusion that New Bibliography presents 'narratives' rather than knowledge is well taken in the limited sense that applies to all scholarly reconstruction—for, as Edward Pechter has pointed out, Werstine and other 'newer bibliographers', though they programmatically discourage 'the construction of new meanings', nevertheless underpin their own narratives with unverifiable assumptions.[39]

COPY-TEXT AND VERSIONS

In another crucial intervention, the essay entitled 'The Rationale of Copy-Text', Greg urged a distinction between textual 'substantives' and 'accidentals'.[40] The 'substantives' are the words as signifiers and the 'accidentals' the spellings, punctuation, abbreviated speech prefixes, and other features of layout. Greg's innovation was to declare that editors should treat accidentals and substantives differently. He accepted, as McKerrow had argued, that it was impossible to restore Shakespeare's spelling and punctuation. But the editor working on an original-spelling edition needed some basis for the spellings in the text. On purely pragmatic grounds, therefore, Greg accepted that the copy-text should be the one that had the lowest level of scribal and compositorial interference with the accidentals, so being in this respect closest to Shakespeare's own practices. If, however, this principle were extended to the substantives, it would result in a 'slavish' adherence to the copy-text. Choice of copy-text for accidentals is a mere 'necessity'.[41] Despite his commitment to the old-spelling edition, Greg is almost disdainful towards the features of accidence. The essence of editing lies in establishing the substantives.

Greg's aim was to liberate the editor from the 'tyranny of the copy-text'.[42] The immediate intent was to provide a considered basis for selecting and adopting, for instance, justifiable Folio readings where a quarto was the copy-text. The procedure Greg advocated sharpened the distinction between the edition's basis in the copy-text as a document and its aspiration to recover the text that Shakespeare wrote, rejecting the former in favour of the latter. This gave the editor a freer hand in detecting and emending error in the copy, and so opened up a more eclectic approach to editing. The editing of substantives 'belongs to the general theory of textual criticism and lies altogether beyond the narrow principle of the copy-text'.[43]

This division between substantives and accidentals can be taken a long way, and sometimes has been. Taylor's edition of *Hamlet* for the original-spelling version of the Oxford *Complete Works* is based on two contrasting statements: 'Q2 is more likely to preserve Shakespeare's own incidentals [the Oxford Shakespeare alternative term to "accidentals"], and accordingly we have adopted Q2 as the copy-text for incidentals', and 'Since we believe that Shakespeare revised the play after completing the foul papers, and that the fruits of that revision survive in F, we have adopted F as the control-text for substantive variants.'[44] Like Folio *Richard II*, Folio *Hamlet* has been treated by various agents connected with the theatre, including Shakespeare. It is more developed as an authorial and theatrical text, more removed from the scene of writing where Shakespeare's hand monopolized or at least predominated. The Oxford response to this situation moves beyond Greg, in that, where Greg argues for editing each substantive variant on its merits, Taylor sets up a presumption in favour of the second text and introduces the distinguishing term 'control text'.

Whereas Taylor saw the Folio text as incorporating Shakespeare's revisions, the New Bibliographers did not think of Shakespeare as a revising author. They had a strong orientation towards the binaries of good and bad, not only as regards texts, but also as regards individual readings. Part of the intractability they found in plays such as *Hamlet, King Lear*, and *Othello* was that the two main substantive texts did not readily yield to a hierarchy of good and bad.[45] The two texts both had to be negotiated as good but imperfect testimonies to a single underlying version. Greg's 'Rationale' is acquisitive, reaching out to capture the most and the best in a single text. Taylor's development of it is based on partition, to the extent that material found only in Q2 is excluded, appearing only in an appendix. This includes a passage as substantial and as crucial to the play, in the Q2 version, as Hamlet's soliloquy 'How all occasions do inform against me'.

The theory of revision presents an image of Shakespeare as a writer who is dissatisfied with his first attempt rather than as a natural genius. It offers an image of the text as subject to instability and even indeterminacy. Yet the theory begins with a simple observation about the fixed material objects, the quarto and Folio texts of his plays. If two texts differ, those differences can be framed in terms of questions about how the texts were produced, rather than how they came to be deformed. Here, Shakespeare's relationship with the theatre companies to which he belonged becomes a pressing issue. How can Shakespeare the author be dissociated from companies that included Shakespeare the actor? If the Folio texts often relate to playbooks, on what basis could they be excluded from the editorial process? And finally, given the provenance of such texts, how else, other than in terms of authorial revision, are coherent variations in structure and verbal detail to be explained?

These questions began to be pursued with diligence and energy in work on *King Lear* surrounding the Oxford Shakespeare, an investigation that revitalized textual study in a way scarcely seen since the early work of Greg and Pollard.[46] The work of these scholars, revisionist in two senses of the word, inverted the New Bibliographers' presumption in favour of the pre-theatrical author's text. In the particular case of *King Lear*, they drew on Peter W. M. Blayney's investigation of the printing of Q1, which led to the conclusion that this text was badly set from a manuscript that was likely to be authorial, and so was not a 'doubtful' quarto or memorially transmitted text.[47] If, for instance in the play's opening scene, individual verbal variants had significant literary and theatrical import, if they contributed to an overall and connected strategy of revision, if as such these differences in detail related to larger cuts and additions, then the variants in question could scarcely be other than of an authorial complexion.[48] The minor and 'indifferent' variants inevitably resist critical investigation in such terms, but the further the argument for revision could be extended, the more it made sense to treat the 'indifferent' variants in the same way as the more fully characterized authorial variants, while remaining alert to the inevitable presence of errors of transmission in any text.

Such thinking underlay the Oxford Shakespeare presentation of two separate texts, printed under the Quarto and Folio titles of *The History of King Lear* and *The Tragedy of King Lear*. But the Oxford editors found this play different from other Shakespeare texts by virtue of the extent of revision rather than its presence. Authorial revision was seen to account for major changes in a number of plays—in particular *Hamlet*, *Troilus and Cressida*, and *Othello*—and for more localized variants in many other plays. In these cases the Oxford edition printed only one text, because, although there were good reasons for envisaging two versions, the more limited extent of variation made it impractical to offer separate texts.

Revision theory as it applies to Shakespeare shares something with the theory of memorial reconstruction. In most accounts, neither offers a complete explanation in itself. Both usually take on the adjunct of theatrical adaptation. If in the case of 'bad' quartos it had proven difficult to disentangle the corrupting effect of poor memory from the reconstitutive effect of adaptation, much the same proved true of the authorial and theatrical variant in, for instance, *King Lear*, or the cuts in Folio *Hamlet*. Indeed, the Oxford editors recognized that in the revised plays changes such as deletions and alterations to stage directions would not always necessarily have been directly effected by Shakespeare. In their thinking, the dramatist wrote so that the play in question could be performed, and the company's alterations would fulfil his intention to bring this about. There was, therefore, a complete difference between changes that were made by the theatre companies to which Shakespeare belonged and the undertakings of reconstructors thought to be responsible for 'bad' quartos, even if they were actors. Authorial authority devolved onto theatrical changes to the text in some circumstances, but not all.

This represented a radical change from earlier criticism, where the actors were almost always represented as agents of corruption. Stanley Wells in particular had brought onto the scene of editing a view of Shakespeare as a man of the theatre, and in the General Introduction to the *Textual Companion* Gary Taylor took this idea into rapprochement with Jerome McGann's writings on the socialization of the text.[49] Whereas McKerrow had defined the ideal state of the text as the author's fair copy before it had been altered in the theatre,[50] for Wells and Taylor the integrity of the play derives from authorially sanctioned theatre practice as well as direct authorial inscription.[51]

The Oxford Shakespeare treatment of *King Lear* found widespread assent, in that there have been few attempts to reject the presence of authorial revision. The textual landscape had changed decisively. For instance, in the case of a textual variant, editors now had to consider not simply which reading was correct, but whether the alternatives represent either two valid readings or one valid reading alongside one error. Editing in this environment is unstable. An example of a presumption in favour of revision combining with the recognition of error can be seen in Gary Taylor's editing of *The History of King Lear* (the Quarto-based version) at 21.34–6, where the edited text reads:

> Mine injurer's mean'st dog,
> Though he had bit me, should have stood that night
> Against my fire.

In the first quoted line the Quarto reads not 'injurer's' but 'iniurious'. It must be admitted that 'Mine injurious mean'st dog', though stylistically and metrically clumsy, is not entirely without sense. It could conceivably be preserved as being intelligible to the reader, though it is doubtful whether it could be preserved for its plausibility as a Shakespearian reading. The Folio supplies a noun such as would be expected. But it is not 'injurer's' but 'Enemies'. In adopting the reading 'injurer's' rather than Folio 'enemies', Taylor assumes that, whereas 'Enemies' is most unlikely to have been corrupted to 'iniurious', 'iniurious' is a relatively simple mistake for 'injurers' (perhaps written 'iniurors', and an example of Shakespeare's evident carelessness in forming minims as discussed in Chapter 1). Taylor's reading is underpinned by the assumption that Shakespeare revised the play, altering his original word 'injurer's' to 'Enemies', but also recognizes error in the Quarto text.

The two-text hypothesis was sometimes criticized for overemphasizing authorial revision.[52] These criticisms suggested either that the revision hypothesis had been exaggerated, or that the causation cannot be decided, or that the causation is irrelevant. Where Lear famously says 'Come, unbutton here' as he slips into insanity (3.4.102–3), the familiar reading is that of the Folio. As noted in Chapter 3, the Quarto unexpectedly reads 'come on bee true' in its uncorrected state, and merely 'come on' after the press had been stopped and a correction made. An editor will ask whether the reading is at fault in the 'corrected' or 'uncorrected' Quarto reading. The mechanics of transmission from the quartos to the Folio are complex in themselves. After considering them, an editor will decide whether either or both Quarto readings actually make(s) sense, whether that sense is adequate, and how the assumed reading in the manuscript can have led to the two settings in the Quarto. In the Quarto-based *History of King Lear* Taylor follows the uncorrected Quarto reading. One critic will accuse Taylor of failing to accept that the relationship between 'on bee true' and 'vnbuttone' indicates a misreading, 'on bee true' being an error.[53] Another editor, Jay L. Halio, following a logic similar to Taylor's treatment of 'iniurious', similarly finds that the Folio offers evidence of Quarto error and how to deal with it. He therefore emends his Quarto-based text to 'Come, unbutton'.[54] This lays Halio open to the opposite accusation, of collapsing textual difference towards the best single reading. But it is a persuasive solution in the light of the Folio. Any two-text *King Lear* is vulnerable to similar criticisms that pull in two opposing directions.

The most detailed critique of the revisionists for over-polarizing the textual differences addressed not *King Lear* but *Othello*. E. A. J. Honigmann was committed to putting in action Greg's advice to analyse every variant in the light of a thorough investigation of every cause of textual variation. In the case of *Othello*, he found many.[55] As a response to the revisionists Honigmann's study has two main points. First, he particularizes the agents of transmission, most notably by identifying the scribe behind the Folio text as Crane. This is persuasive textual scholarship, though our independent knowledge of Crane's work suggests that he cannot be held responsible for the major verbal variants. Second, Honigmann identifies both Folio and Quarto texts as independent derivatives. As a consequence, passages found only in the Folio are diagnosed not as additions to the Folio but as inept theatrical cuts in the Quarto. Honigmann's reading of these large-scale structural variants, including the presence of the 'Willow Song' in Folio but not Quarto, admits no simple linear development from Quarto to Folio by way of authorial revision, because the Quarto is itself a derivative and degenerate text. He still admits the presence of authorial revision in a number of verbal variants, but his hypothesis denies the possibility of revision being a general explanation of the textual differences. Both texts are flawed witnesses to underlying authorial texts, and the differences between those texts are limited. In the case of 'indifferent' variants, the presumption is pushed away from the author and back towards non-authorial transmitters of the text.

Honigmann refused to acknowledge a single overall copy-text for *Othello*. He instead identified the strengths and weaknesses of each text for each kind of feature (contractions and other syllabic variants, lineation, cuts, punctuation, and so on). In contrast, other textualists responded to the revision theory by rejecting even the limited eclecticism found in the Oxford Shakespeare *King Lear*. It is an undeniable and important consequence of the two-text *King Lear* that it drew attention to the separate integrities of the texts as they are printed. The argument that editors wrongfully replace a historical artefact (their copy-text) with their own approximate conceptualization of something else (the authorial text) has been expressed forcefully by various critics.[56] To a similar effect, the editorial theory of versions as it was developed in the first place with reference to writers other than Shakespeare often defines the term *version* as a discrete extant textualization.[57] Here too emendation can come to be seen as a falsification of a materialized text.

As compared with the conflated text, the differences between, for instance, an old-spelling edition based on the Folio and the printed document itself might seem relatively slight. Yet the distance in theory between the critical editors who work from the two-text position and the opponents of emendation is very considerable indeed. To the two-text critical editor the *version* is defined, not in the text as printed, but in something antecedent to it: As Peter Shillingsburg put it: 'A version has no substantial existence, but it is represented more or less well or completely by a single text.'[58] Emendation of that text is therefore defensible.

Both points of view have obvious limitations. The opponents of emendation fetishize the printed text as an object in itself, and in so doing they occlude both the process whereby it came into being and the very reason why it came into being. Their orientation to the material printed text is also, inevitably, an orientation against anything that might precede it, specifically the text as the author wrote it and, in the case of a play, the text as performed on stage. Though the adherents of the material artefact claim to adopt a historicist position, they can sometimes in practice isolate the printed book from all contingency. In one formulation, its 'identity' lies in its 'self-differentiation from the process of production and exchange'.[59] The proper reading text is accordingly a facsimile or reprint of an early printing that is detached from its basis in authorial and theatrical production. Critical editors, on the other hand, treat the printed text as evidence of something else that came before it. When they refer to manuscripts such as prompt books (or playbooks) and foul papers (or authorial drafts), they name documents that must have existed but that cannot be recovered in their full detail. This rejection of the textual artefact in favour of documents and readings that can only be postulated seems, from a materialist point of view, perversely idealist.

The purpose in referring to such documents is precisely to enable editors to address error. An extant document is completely sufficient unto itself. The text it contains can be described as incorrect at a given point only if there is, conceptually speaking, an alternative point of reference, whether that is posed in terms of a document (an antecedent, or perhaps even the same document before it was altered or damaged) or an intention (an author, or perhaps even an agent in the text's transmission). The purpose of emendation is to establish or reach towards something other than the document in hand. Whether this is appropriate will depend on the nature and purpose of the editorial act. In the case of Shakespeare it is relevant that the First Folio is a product of late Jacobean book production and as such differs radically from the original purpose in writing the play and its initial propagation as a stage work. This is symptomatic of the disjunction between text as written and text as printed that is the case with Shakespeare and most other dramatists working for the professional theatre in his time. Any approach to Shakespeare that is concerned *either* with the authorial figure *or* with the plays as scripts for performance will be ill served by an edition that perpetuates readings that post-date these stages in the text's history. In practice this means that the vast majority of readers would be misled by an edition that retains error on the basis that it belongs to a particular textualization in print.

A number of critics advanced a deconstructive reading of textual
instability and revision theory that stepped far beyond the attempt to
identify the text of Shakespeare as the text of a particular printing.
Jonathan Goldberg, for instance, declared that 'An examination of
the textual properties of Shakespearean texts ... will never produce a
proper, selfsame Shakespearean text', and indeed that 'we have no
originals, only copies. The historicity of the text means that there
is no text itself.'[60] This observation chimes surprisingly well with
what textual critics were advising throughout the century: 'it is very
doubtful whether, especially in the case of the earlier plays, there ever
existed any written "final form"'; 'we cannot be certain of any close
approach to the author's manuscript'; 'we cannot hope to achieve a
certainly correct text, not so much on account of the uncertainties of
transmission—though they are sometimes serious—as because the
author may never have produced a definitive text for us to recover';
'the written text of any such [theatrical] manuscript thus depended on
an unwritten para-text which always accompanied it'; 'the perfection
of permanence is unattainable if the text itself was never fixed'.[61] The
point of difference lies in whether the Shakespearian textual condition
allows any meaningful and coherent practice of editing. Goldberg
reifies the copy—potentially *any* existing text—and disallows the
attempt to reach beyond it.

The view is symptomatic of a wider critique of editorial practice,
and led to the emergence of a field of bibliographical study that is not
concerned with the text as such. In the closing years of the twentieth
century and after, scholars began to ask important questions about
Shakespeare as a published author in his own lifetime and after.[62]
This work steps back from the literary and theatrical aspects of the
plays, in order to place Shakespearian texts within a history of the
printed book.

By the end of the twentieth century it had become habitual to
dismiss the New Bibliography. To some critics, all that was left of
it were ruins of a former age. Its aspiration to move away from the
extant printed text in search of lost manuscripts was hopelessly idealist
in its intellectual foundation. This idealism, combined with a naive
positivism, led to binary categorizations that bore limited relation
to the fluidity of textual production in the early modern theatre.
The movement's dedication to recovering an authorial script isolated

Shakespeare from the contingencies of theatre and his involvement in collaborative playwriting. Its post-Romantic figuration of the author also diminished to the point of insignificance the possibility that Shakespeare revised his own works. Its technicalization of text now began to look like part of an outmoded masculinist culture that purveyed patriarchal attitudes and mystified subjective judgements with the aura of science.[63] The 'death of the author' proclaimed by Roland Barthes in 1968 seemed likely to lead to the death of the editor. An 'unediting' movement led by the anarchically brilliant interventions of Randall McLeod pressed towards the view that editions should be abandoned in the classroom and replaced with photofacsimiles.[64]

This is an impractical suggestion for most purposes, but the work of McLeod and others renewed the most fundamental questions as to what editing does and on what basis it proceeds. Shillingsburg influentially defined the different applications of editorial practice depending on what he termed the orientation of the editor: the *documentary*, 'founded on a sense of the textual integrity of historical moments and physical forms', the *aesthetic*, the *authorial*, the *sociological*, where authority 'resides in the institutional unit of author *and* publisher'[65]—or, to take account of the dramatist such as Shakespeare, the author and theatre company—and the *bibliographic*, which takes into account not only the text of a document but also its bibliographical coding as expressed in paper, font, binding, design, and layout. Shillingsburg suggests the inevitability of editing in the era after the New Bibliography. The question most relevant is not whether to edit, but how to edit.

Approaching the issue of editorial orientation from another direction entirely, Barbara Mowat argued that the editor should defer not to the author but to the needs of the reader.[66] The limitation of this approach is that potentially it licenses the editor to act merely according to convenience. It might be asked whether there is any real point where the reader is best served by a falsification of the author. As regards substantive readings, the answer is surely 'no'. Accidentals are another matter. It may be productive to synthesize Mowat's late-twentieth-century reader-oriented formulation with Greg's mid-century author-oriented 'Rationale'. Accordingly, matters of incidence and presentation would be ceded to the interests of the reader, while the substantives of the text as an utterance would be recognized as having integrity in terms of their origin. As we will see in Chapter 7, stage directions might profitably be positioned alongside spelling and punctuation as aspects of the text that an editor might approach from a user-oriented perspective.

At the end of the century some critics had begun to return to a view of Shakespeare as a poet. Lukas Erne suggested that the typically long Shakespeare text, beyond the utility of theatre, has instead a literary aspiration.[67] His and Gurr's views (as discussed in Chapter 2) destabilize the notion that Folio texts are close to the play as performed. It remains to be seen what the implications might be for practical editing. But for editorial theory Erne's title *Shakespeare as Literary Dramatist* is indicative of a new emphasis at the beginning of the twenty-first century, one that pares back the theatrical dimension and asserts on new grounds the presence of Shakespeare the author in the field of textual study. The upsurge in interest in Shakespeare's biography in the early twenty-first century points in the same direction. Nevertheless, any restatement of an authorial orientation would need to be carefully conscious that the author as invoked by the editor is a construct rather than a given entity, and to be conditioned by awareness of the nature of Shakespearian textual production in all its complex uncertainty. This implies a strong sense of struggle between the stubborn contingency of physical materials and the aspirational endeavour of the editor, a struggle that resists any pat resolution.

Emendation and Modernization

EMENDATION: DEPARTURE FROM THE BASE TEXT

Though it has been subject to few recent studies, textual emendation is common to critical editions of all kinds of text, and indeed can scarcely be avoided in any practice that aims to go further than reproduce a source text exactly as it stands. According to Greg's formulation, in one of the few discussions that attempt to rise above the particulars of individual readings, 'criticism must always proceed in relation to what we know, or what we surmise, respecting the history of the text'.[1] In other words, it will proceed by taking into account what is known in classical and biblical textual criticism as *recensio* or recension, the analysis of texts to establish how they relate to each other. Identification of error and proposals to emendation cannot, then, be based on critical judgement alone. Editing brings together a form of *criticism* and a form of more empirical *scholarship*. How one applies the correlation of criticism and textual study has always been subject to contention and debate, as is the breadth of scope that emendation can legitimately claim for itself, and as too is the weight of Greg's phrase 'what we surmise'.

Emendation seeks to correct error. The term 'error' need not refer to a Platonic and absolute concept of what is correct, but to the relationship between the text in question and an antecedent text that has been recognized as having a particular value. The correction of error in one document—typically an editor's base text—involves either reverting to a different surviving text, or accepting a postulate as to what a different text would have read. There is a crucial difference between emending to a reading that comes from an alternative text that has independent authority and emending without any recourse to such a text. Yet the alternative texts are themselves not all alike. In the case of editing Shakespeare, a substantive text is one that bears independent witness to a manuscript. The vital distinction between manuscripts and printed books is that manuscripts are products of writing, which includes original composition, whereas printed books are products of an art and technology of copying. It would be utterly incoherent to emend without reference to the alternative sources of authority, or without as firm a purchase as possible on the nature of these sources.

Alteration of the base text may also take into account deliberate changes that have taken the text away from its original form for reasons other than accidental error. In certain circumstances it may, for example, seek to undo the effect of censorship. Editors routinely restore the deposition scene in *Richard II*, which is entirely missing from their Q1 copy, on this basis. More contentiously, oaths and profanities deleted in the aftermath of the 1606 Act (see Chapter 2) can sometimes be restored. This can be executed either by reference to a collateral text such as Q1 *The Merry Wives of Windsor*, where the Folio is the editor's base text, or by inference from context. In *Measure for Measure*, for instance, in Angelo's 'heauen in my mouth, | As if I did but onely chew his name', 'heauen' is quite clearly an alteration of 'God'. There may be yet other reasons why an editor might choose to depart from the copy reading. As we have seen, an alternative text might incorporate Shakespeare's later alteration of the reading that came to be printed in the base text.

The editor's task is therefore to present something that in detail is somewhat different from the base text, and in essence is profoundly so. Emendation away from the base text is made on the premiss that it misrepresents an antecedent, a document or intention that has the stronger claim on our attention. To the charge that the pursuit of a prior text of this kind falls into an unjustifiable idealism, it can be replied that the more pernicious idealism would be to correct the errors in a document to no other criterion than an ideal version of itself.

Unfortunately, however, the principles of emendation become clouded once one begins to ask close questions about that antecedent. What exactly is it: a lost document, or a text as it may never have materially existed in the precise form envisaged? If it is a document, what is the nature of that document, how far is it regarded as the exclusive preserve of Shakespeare as author, how far can alterations by agents other than the author such as a theatre book-keeper be tolerated, how much can we know about this document, and how far would an editor accept all its features, including its errors and its alterations in later hands? If it cannot be rooted in a document, an editor might invoke the play as it might have existed in Shakespeare's mind, or as it might have been performed on the stage. These are problematic concepts, because they afford a release from the material chain of textual transmission and take us into realms of unverifiable conjecture.

In most editorial thinking, error usually manifests itself as a departure from the text as the author either intended or actually wrote it. The criterion of intention is deeply troublesome, as intentions are transitory, unstable, and unverifiable. Yet such projections are necessary. Setting aside all irregularities of punctuation and spelling, within ten lines Hand D in *Sir Thomas More*, which I take to be Shakespeare as author probably making the text in its first material form, wrote as follows:

| | to be thus vsd, this is the straingers case |
| all | and this your momtanish inhumanyty |

fayth a saies trewe letts vs do as we may be doon by

| all | weele be ruld by yo^u master moor yf youle stand our |
| | freind to procure our pardon |

moor	Submyt yo^u to theise noble gentlemen
	entreate their mediation to the kinge
	gyve vp yor sealf to forme obay the maiestrate
	and thers no doubt, but mercy may be found yf yo^u so seek y^t

The first 'all' in this passage is misplaced, and relates to the line beginning 'fayth a saies trewe'. As mentioned in Chapter 1, Shakespeare produced through a flaw of penmanship a word that looks like 'momtanish'. He wrote 'letts vs', evidently an uncorrected change of mind from 'letts' to 'lett vs'. Here again Hand C detected error and corrected it, incorrectly as judged by authorial intention, by deleting 'vs'. And Shakespeare arranged 'and thers no doubt, but mercy may be found yf yo^u so seek it' as a single verse-line. This arrangement is provoked by the shortage of space at the very foot of a page. The layout is determined by mechanical, non-literary factors. Accordingly, the text as physically realized, and as it would appear in a diplomatic text of the manuscript, conflicts with what the text is from a literary point of view that is concerned with the presentation of metre. In each case, it would be bizarre to claim that the text does not need correcting away from the materialized authorial text to a text that can be described only as the one that the author intended.[2]

The editor's base text, which in all other cases is more distant from Shakespeare and the theatre than the manuscript of *Sir Thomas More*, will always be flawed. The emended text, however, will always be insecurely grounded, even when the base text is an authorial manuscript. This unresolvable dilemma leads editors often to declare their reluctance to emend, while accepting the necessity of doing so. The practice acquires an aura of indefensibility. Where emendation is deemed necessary, editors are on their guard, and are inclined to protest too little or too much. And invocations of the author as the source of the correct reading sound either naive or apologetic.

Inevitably, however, the author, even where he or she is of unknown identity, retains a strong place in any conceptualization of text that attends to production as well as material outcome. He or she may be described as the primary originator of the text as a message that assumes a trajectory towards its recipients. The author, especially in the case of Shakespeare, need not be regarded as an isolated figure. Shakespeare inhabits a world of social and theatrical practice (see Chapter 1), a contextual world that can never be pared away from the authorial text. Seen thus, the text is not simply the isolated material document in which it is embedded. Its materiality lies also, and ultimately more significantly, in its function in a textual process whose nature is to convey meaning.

EMENDATION: COLLATERAL TEXTS

Shakespeare's plays show no sign of authorial correction in proof. But the Folio text of some plays includes a variously more or less complete, more or less extensive set of what appear to be revised authorial readings.[3] As we have seen in Chapter 4, the Folio text of most of these plays was set not directly from a manuscript. Instead, readings were tranferred from a manuscript onto the printed copy from which the compositor would work. Where this was done thoroughly, the aim of this annotation was presumably to reproduce as many variant readings found in the manuscript as possible. Yet the printed quarto remains the immediate compositor's copy, and so is the source for the Folio text wherever the reading is unaffected by annotation.

This more than residual dependence on the earlier printed edition limits the authority of a Folio text of this kind. A second limit lies in the degree of efficiency with which readings are taken up from the manuscript during the course of annotation, which at best never reaches 100 per cent. In Folio *Richard II* annotation was performed with about 50 per cent efficiency. This means that the Folio text not only retains a stratum of quarto features in its accidentals, but also gives only a partial impression of the substantive features of the new manuscript version. In this text the general pattern of annotation, with its variations in efficiency from one section of the text to another, is well evidenced, and can usefully inform an editor's approach to an individual reading. The tendency of much editorial practice has been to accept the Folio's act and scene division, incorporate its text of the deposition scene, make full use of its stage directions, yet shy away from its verbal variants. It is, therefore, worth insisting that the more distinctive verbal variants are probably authorial.[4]

Charles R. Forker, reviewing the most plausible readings in Folio *Richard II* as a group, came to the view that

A few of these may be defended as genuine improvements, and some scholars have believed them to represent authorial revisions or 'second thoughts'; but they have more commonly been attributed to a combination of sources including compositorial preferences or lapses of memory, substitutions made by players and recorded in the book-keeper's copy, and possibly even alterations made by an editor annotating copy for the printer.[5]

If this is true, it minimizes the extent to which an editor needs to consider accepting these readings. Here, then, is an example. Where in Q1 Richard II rebukes himself by saying, 'Awake thou coward Maiesty thou sleepest' (3.2.80), the Folio alters 'coward' to 'sluggard'. Forker simply asserts that the Folio's reading 'weakens the speech', and by this assertion dismisses the view that this particular reading might be an authorial revision. This would be a decisive consideration were it demonstrably true, but the opposite is the case.

The defence of 'sluggard' is as follows—and as we engage with this instance the practice of what Greg calls 'criticism' comes to the fore. The most distinctively Shakespearian locution will be exampled both as a word and as a usage in context elsewhere in Shakespeare's works, yet will exhibit the high level of particularity that we associate with his writing. We are looking, therefore, for neither a sealed wall nor a wide-open gap, but a distinctive, keylike aperture. *Sluggard*, and its use in the phrase 'sluggard majesty', fulfil this criterion. The word is within Shakespeare's usage: Shakespeare had elsewhere previously used *sluggard* twice. In one of these two earlier instances it appears, as here, as an adjectival qualifier of an abstract noun: 'The more to blame my sluggard negligence' (*The Rape of Lucrece*, l. 1278). These two lines appear in texts written by Shakespeare within two years of each other. Yet they afford the *Oxford English Dictionary*'s only examples of *sluggard* as an adjective before 1700. This is not to claim that Shakespeare is necessarily unique in this respect, but to highlight the distinctively Shakespearian quality of 'sluggard majesty'. Quite simply, it is far more Shakespearian than 'coward majesty'—which is not to say that Shakespeare did not write 'coward majesty', but that he may have considered 'sluggard' an improvement. The word is not only more unusual; it is more precise, as sluggards rather than cowards need awakening. And the meaning is reinforced in the alliteration between 'sluggard' and 'sleepest'. It can be claimed, then, that the Folio's reading strengthens the line, and strengthens it in a distinctively Shakespearian way.

This is one example in Forker's list of variants described as 'indifferent' where a difference can be determined. It illustrates how scepticism towards a reading in a collateral text can be deeply misguided. In this case an editor would be well advised to reject the 'combination of sources including compositorial preferences or lapses of memory, substitutions made by players and recorded in the book-keeper's copy, and possibly even alterations made by an editor annotating copy for the printer' in favour of accepting the validity of both readings, and the superiority of the Folio's altered text. The example influences our interpretation of other readings belonging to the putative group of variants where each reading is potentially valid. The more readings that deserve serious consideration from the Folio, the further the authority of Q1 as the editor's primary copy becomes compromised, and the less stable the editorial process becomes. The situation presents neither the purity of adherence to a single base text, nor the purity of adherence to two self-sufficient alternative versions. No one has suggested editing *Richard II* as a two-text play in the manner of *King Lear*, but the editorial dilemmas are similar.

Given a variant reading in a substantive text, an editor might ask the following initial question: How does the assumed history of transmission inform our understanding of the relationship between the readings? This might break down into subsidiary questions: Do the base text and a text of secondary authority—the collateral text—both present valid readings, or is one text in error? If error is posited, are there credible causes and mechanics of error, and do they conform to what we know about the transmission of the text in question? For instance, would the author's handwriting, or a known scribe's handwriting, readily be misread to produce the reading, or can it be associated with typical errors introduced by the compositor who set the passage?

Where the early texts printed after the first edition simply derive from the first edition as direct or indirect reprints, the corrections they contain have no authority in themselves even when they look plausible. Therefore the editor needs to be especially alert to the possibility that the base text reading might be defensible. As an example, in *Romeo and Juliet*, Q2, the editor's invariable base text, reads:

> loues heraulds should be thoughts,
> Which ten times faster glides then the Suns beames,

$$(2.4.4-5)$$

In the Fourth Folio of 1685 'glides' is altered to 'glide' to establish concord with 'thoughts'. But lack of agreement between subject and verb was common in Shakespeare's time. It took almost ninety years before any corrector or compositor found fault with Q2's reading. In this case the very absence of any alteration in the Jacobean, Caroline, and early Restoration Folios testifies to the acceptability of the apparent error in the period closer to Shakespeare's writing.

On the other hand, emendation in a derivative text might produce miscorrection even where the earliest text is incorrect. In *Antony and Cleopatra*, Caesar charges that Antony 'Hardly gaue audience | Or vouchsafe to thinke he had Partners' (1.4.7–8). The 1632 Second Folio recognizes that 'vouchsafe' can be justified neither as the infinitive nor as the present tense, and so emended to 'did vouchsafe'. Editors now usually reject this reading in favour of Samuel Johnson's 'vouchsaf'd'. This supposes a misreading of 'd' at the end of a word for 'e', an easy error in reading Shakespeare's handwriting that is more plausible than omission of the entire word 'did'. It may be noted in passing that problems of metre and lineation make this example more complex, but the present point about the unreliability of readings from derivative early editions holds true.

CONJECTURAL EMENDATION

Emendations initiated by editors without the testimony of an early text are sometimes called conjectural emendations.[6] Their plausibility will depend on the authority not only of the base text but also of a collateral text if there is one: if the two agree in a reading that is supposed to be an error, can this be explained, and if they disagree, how can both readings be wrong? If the collateral text is as a whole effective in either affirming the base text or offering alternative readings to it, the scope for later editorial emendation is reduced.

Therefore most editorial emendation replaces the function of a good collateral text where none is available. Editors are constrained by the lack of independent evidence and may feel that they are duty-bound to intervene little. As A. E. Housman noted, for any editor single texts 'are the easiest, and for a fool they are the safest'.[7] This kind of safety lies in small numbers: the editor can make a virtue of inaction and so avoid exercising choice and judgement. But some measure of intervention will be required. The extent to which error is identified and emended depends properly on the assumed reliability of the base text and editors' general assumptions as to the nature of the edition being produced. It will also depend unavoidably on the conservatism or liberalism, skill or folly, of their scholarly persona.[8]

There will be further questions, once error is identified, as to exactly how it should be put right. In *Coriolanus*, Volumnia chides her son by pointing out:

> You might haue beene enough the man you are,
> With striuing lesse to be so: Lesser had bin
> The things of your dispositions, if
> You had not shew'd them how ye were dispos'd
> Ere they lack'd power to crosse you.

> (F; 3.2.20–3)

Editors recognize that the reading 'things' is wrong. The context shows that Volumnia is talking about the things that prevent Coriolanus from achieving his wishes, not the 'things of' his dispositions, whatever they might be. Moreover, the line is metrically defective in that it has only nine syllables; the disruption of the iambic pattern falls precisely on the word that fails to provide sense, 'things'. In some situations an irregularity in metre can suggest corruption even where the sense appears good; here, however, the conjunction of metrical irregularity and defect of sense gives a far clearer indication of error. In these circumstances an editor would be relinquishing his or her function if the text were not emended. The difficulty here is that there is no secondary substantive text to which to refer, and several alternative emendations have been adopted at different times. These include 'things that thwart your dispositions' (Nicholas Rowe, 1709), 'thwartings of your dispositions' (Lewis Theobald, 1733), 'taxings of your dispositions' (Charles J. Sisson, 1954), and 'crossings of your dispositions' (G. R. Hibbard, New Penguin, 1967). All these restore both metre and sense, but of course at best only one of them can be correct. Rowe's emendation, the earliest, has the disadvantage that it supposes not only omission of 'that thwart' in the Folio but also addition of 'of'. Theobald resolved this problem, but produced a word that is much longer than 'things'; one would have to suppose that the middle of the word was illegible or apparently deleted in the manuscript. 'Taxings' is designed to offer a word that could more easily be read as 'things', bearing in mind the graphic similarity of 'x' and 'h' in early modern 'secretary' hand.

One celebrated and widely debated emendation involves a rejection of a collateral reading, but nevertheless takes limited cognisance of it.

It is Theobald's 'a' babled of green fields' (that is, he babbled of green fields) in Mistress Quickly's account of the death of Falstaff (*Henry V*, 2.3.16). The Folio reads 'a Table of greene fields'. There have been ingenious attempts to find sense in the Folio, but none of them has been convincing, and most commentators have agreed with Alexander Pope (1723–5) and Theobald that the Folio's reading is '*Nonsense*'. Theobald's particular daring was to reject the emendation 'talked', which at least begins with the same letter as 'Table' and is supported by the ('bad') Quarto, which has the paraphrase 'And talk of floures'. But, as Taylor notes, the palaeographical argument is inconclusive; Q_1 persistently substitutes highly particularized words with more banal synonyms, and its substitution of 'floures' for 'greene fields' in itself hints at the vulnerability of its reading 'talk'. In these circumstances there is scope for 'a purely aesthetic decision'.[9]

A more conservative interpretation of this principle would be that Q_1 as a textual witness should be followed, at least to the extent of accepting 'talk' and emending it grammatically to 'talked'. Taylor's negotiation of Q_1 allows a greater space for the editorial conjecture. The relative claims of bibliography (founded on scholarship) and aesthetics (founded on criticism) upon the practice of emendation came into focus in A. E. Housman's attack on what he saw as the mechanical approach to textual emendation brought in by the early New Bibliography.[10] A good emendation should be both explicable in bibliographical terms and convincing in literary terms. If it does not fulfil both criteria, one might suspect that something is wrong, but in the real world choices have to be made as to which criterion takes precedence and the extent to which it can override the other. In the *Coriolanus* example, 'taxings' is probably the best word from a palaeographical point of view, but has been criticized as inferior to 'thwartings' in literary terms. The second-series Arden editor, Philip Brockbank, comments that the latter word is 'rhetorically potent' and that dispositions 'are more cogently thwarted than taxed', and allows these considerations to prevail over those of palaeography. In defence of the possibility, nevertheless, of misreading, he cites John Dover Wilson's suggestion that a copy spelling 'thwarthings', unusual in itself, might lead to eye-skip from the first 'th' to the second, an explanation that smacks of over-ingenuity.

The subjective judgements that Taylor characterizes as aesthetic lead us to another of Shillingsburg's categories of editorial orientation. It is the one that has found least favour in its own right, but that nevertheless persistently finds a role in evaluating readings. The 'aesthetic' cannot be disregarded, for an emendation founded entirely on bibliographical and palaeographical reasoning without reference to the effect of the emendation on the literary quality of the text might produce a reading that is not only displeasing but also, in the case of a major writer, less likely to be correct on that very account. However, the term as used in current textual editing should not be taken to refer to an absolute standard of beauty, nor even to the aesthetic standards that prevail at any one time. Edmond Malone noted over two hundred years ago that 'the question is not, which regulation [i.e. emendation] renders the passage most elegant and spirited, but what was the poet's idea'.[11] The terms 'elegant and spirited' capture something of the passing Enlightenment age. But, if Malone's words suggest a shift from what M. H. Abrams encapsulates as the 'mirror' of Augustan aesthetics to the 'lamp' of the Romantics, it also differentiates between two polarities of editing.[12] 'Elegant and spirited' refers to aesthetic accomplishment of a particular kind; 'the poet's idea' makes no immediate appeal to the aesthetic but refers instead, or at least in the first instance, to authorial intention. The aesthetic judgement that is most likely to produce an effective outcome in terms of editorial practice is therefore one grounded not on the editor's personal sense of literary beauty, but on an awareness of literary qualities specific to the period, the author, and even, it should be added, the text. If 'thwartings' is rhetorically potent in the context of the stylistically rugged *Coriolanus*, it might be positively ugly in another literary environment.

Decades before Malone, Alexander Pope's edition of 1723–5 had emended in a spirit that later became notorious by altering Shakespeare's language to conform to Augustan sensibilities of metre and decorum. In more recent discussions Pope has often been invoked as a model of the dangers of editing according to a particular and misplaced aesthetic. In contrast, editors of the later eighteenth century such as Capell and Malone sought to reach closer to the authorial text by investigating the language of Shakespeare's time, the cultural environment in which he wrote, the specific words he invented, and the usages that he adopted. To these editors, a historical approach is directed towards an archaeological excavation of the author, but it need not serve this agenda exclusively. One might think of progressive proximities by which to scrutinize the reading in question, beginning with the English language in general and proceeding through the language of the period (as in the case of lack of agreement between subject and verb), and usages in the drama or a genre within it as a particular index of spoken and literary language (as with colloquialisms, 'Senecan' rhetoric, features of parody). Below the level of authorial usages are linguistic features specific to a group of plays (for instance, the prevalence of feminine endings in Shakespeare's late plays), or to the text in question (for instance, a pattern of imagery), or even to a dramatic role (malapropism, repetition, distinctive oaths, and other mannerisms). When the matter is put this way, the author has no special privilege. It is probable nevertheless that, with the writer of a distinctive, large, and largely determined corpus of work that has been closely analysed such as is Shakespeare, the author will remain the most important single point of reference.

'WIFE' OR 'WISE': MATERIALITY, AESTHETICS, AND POLITICS

In the closing years of the twentieth century a line in *The Tempest* became a test site for current ideas about editorial procedure. Whether emendation is involved in either proposed reading is in itself a moot point. The issue, more familiar when interpreting handwriting than print, concerns identifying the reading that stands in the text in the first instance. The word is 'wise'; or the word is 'wife'.[13] At question at the quite literally microcosmic level is whether the third letter is an 'f' with a damaged crossbar or a long 's'. At question on the larger scale of debate is the interface between critical editing and sexual politics.

The passage reads:

> So rare a wondered father and a wife/wise
> Makes this place paradise.

(*The Tempest*, 4.1.123–4)

In 1978 Jeanne Addison Roberts argued that some copies of the Folio show evidence of a breaking cross-bar; therefore, although most copies seem to read 'wise', the reading that the compositor originally set was 'wife'.[14] In his 1987 edition, Stephen Orgel accepted the reading 'wife'; he regarded Roberts's bibliographical demonstration as conclusive and found no need to discuss the literary merits, demerits, or implications of either reading.

In what she took to be the earliest printings, Roberts had claimed to see no more than 'what appear to be fragments of a broken crossbar'. The ambiguity of the typographical evidence even in these copies leaves open the possibility that, if indeed the typepiece was a damaged 'f' at the earliest point in the printing of which we have evidence, then it could have been misidentified as an 's' by the compositor who set it; indeed it could have been deposited in the compositor's 's' box when type had been distributed after the printing of earlier text. In other words, the essential character of the typepiece as originally manufactured is not inevitably the determining consideration; the compositor's momentary perception of its identity, established primarily by the box in which he found it, is the factor that matters in tracing the transmission from a reading in the printer's copy to the printed text itself.

There are grounds, then, for discussing the aesthetic and authorial dimensions of the alternative readings. For instance, might the line-endings 'wise … paradise' constitute a Shakespearian rhyme, even though 'Make this place paradise' is an incomplete verse-line? The answer is 'yes', for the rhyme is found in the same sequence elsewhere in Shakespeare:

> If by me broke, what fool is not so wise
> To lose an oath to win a paradise?
>
> (*Love's Labour's Lost*, 4.3.69–70)

Such literary considerations compete with more political issues. Valerie Wayne argues that the reading 'wise' exiles the female presence from Ferdinand's Utopia. In the discursive scene sketched out by Wayne, 'wise' is revealed as the product of unfounded bias in a male editorial tradition; 'wife' is the suppressed reading whose time perhaps 'has not yet arrived … in some quarters', but, by the same token, it is on the way, and seems to have the forward movement of history on its side.[15] From this point of view, the important changes lie not in our knowledge of textual transmission but in our ideology. There is something persuasive about this suggestion, though the assumption that editorial readings should be deliberately selected on grounds of sexual politics is contentious to say the least.

The trouble is that an approach to editing driven by interpretation is susceptible to reversal, for a critical argument can be advanced that works in just the opposite direction. It is perfectly true that 'wise' creates a Utopia that excludes women. But that may be the point, a point that would be consistent with the picture painted repeatedly in recent criticism of Prospero as an anxiously patriarchal figure. The function of the masque is on the face of it to celebrate the betrothal of Miranda and Ferdinand, but what is new to this scene, and in the process of negotiation, is the dynastic bonding between 'father' and son-in-law. To that extent it arguably puts Miranda into eclipse. At this point in the play, it is not Miranda who is on display, as she is when Ferdinand first meets her and again when she is revealed playing chess with him—by which time Ferdinand too has been subsumed within Prospero's emotive–political spectacle. Instead, every (other) single word of the exchange between Prospero and Ferdinand is about the actual display of the masque. Ferdinand's admiration is for the 'majestic vision', and it is in response to it that he is prompted to admire the new wondered father who has made it. In much the same way, Prospero specifically addresses Ferdinand and not Miranda when explaining why the revels now are ended: 'You do look, my son, in a moved sort': more male bonding. The absence of Prospero's wife has been noted in recent criticism, and Stephen Orgel relates it to the 'wife' / 'wise' crux.[16] The masque, as an artwork, is an offspring that needs no wife. Even as it celebrates marriage, heterosexuality, and geniture, it offers a fantasy in which the woman is a means to the end of the patriarchal bonding between men.

To put the issue provocatively, it might be argued that 'wife' is a more sentimental reading, and the effacement of Miranda in 'wise' a more politically knowing one. But let us not forget the technical issue. Wayne's advocacy for 'wife' was made in knowledge that, since Orgel's edition appeared, Roberts's conclusion has been questioned by Peter Blayney. She quotes Blayney as saying: 'As a typographer I cannot agree that what resembles a crossbar in Folger copies 6 and 73

[Roberts's 'two clear examples' in copies of the Folio] is in fact part of the type at all, or that the marks in the supposedly intermediate copies were impressed by the remnants of a crossbar.' Though he postpones full resolution of the matter to 'a much more thorough discussion', his view is unequivocal. Wayne counters by disparaging Blayney's gender, his specialism, and his reliance on an electron microscope; for us to defer to 'the scientific discourse of technology' that 'is usually gendered as male' is 'no more mandatory than deferring to the weight of masculinist editorial tradition'. At this juncture the strength of Roberts's analysis is not that she was a trained bibliographer who followed standard specialist procedure in the analysis of typography by examining the maximum quantity of evidence gathered from multiple copies of the Folio. Her limitation becomes her advantage: that she simply used the 'naked human eye'—naked as in lacking gendered technology and scientific discourse; naked as in truthful, and universally 'human'.

Other textual critics have considered Blayney's examination decisive in its implication for the edited text. This is most notable in Vaughan and Vaughan's Arden edition, where the editors would by temperament prefer to read 'wife' but accept the authority of what is, in view of Blayney's work, the Folio reading.[17] Their discussion addresses not only the effect of the reading adopted but also that of the rejected word. In this they show both a respect for the textual evidence as it now stands and a commendably undogmatic way of annotating what remains a controversial reading.

MODERNIZATION

Modernization arises because of Shakespeare's specific historical position in the early modern period. His language is not as linguistically distinct as Chaucer's Middle English or the Old English of *Beowulf*. The lexis and grammar are largely comprehensible to the modern reader. However, spelling and punctuation were particularly unstable during the period, and are recurrently confusing to the modern reader. Especially given the currency of Shakespeare in the classroom and on the stage, the spellings and punctuation of the early texts, far from refining our understanding of the texts, for the most part present an obstacle. The aim articulated in Stanley Wells's studies of the practice is to be consistent as regards spellings, and clear, logical, and unelaborate as regards punctuation.[18] This practice obliges the editor to make W. W. Greg's distinction, discussed in Chapter 5, between 'accidentals' and 'substantives'. Substantives are preserved except in the exceptional case of emendation; accidentals are routinely altered.

The case in favour of modernization is especially cogent as the spelling and punctuation in the early printed texts of Shakespeare's plays demonstrably are for the most part those of the printers' compositors, and bear limited relation to the features that one would find in the underlying manuscripts. Early modern compositors freely altered spelling and punctuation to conform to their sense of both house style and meaning. Indeed, Joseph Moxon's 1683–4 manual of printing makes a specific distinction in the compositor's treatment of spellings and punctuation. The rule is that 'a compositor is strictly to follow his copy'. But, he adds, it is 'a custom which among them is looked upon as a task and duty incumbent on the compositor, viz. to discern and emend the bad spelling and pointing of his copy, if it be English'.[19] The practice of altering the spelling and punctuation of copy in the period is well testified.[20] An example from 1656 of a passage as it appeared in the compositor's manuscript copy and in the print he set from it is:

This yeare the said Sr John Savage caused, *The Popish Plais of Chester*, to be played the Sonday, Monday, teusday & Wensday after Midsomer Day. In Contempt of an Inhibition & the Primats Letters from York, & from ye Erle of Huntington.

This year the said Sir *John Savage* caused *The Popish Playes of Chester*, to be played the Sunday, Munday, Tuesday and Wednesday after *Mid-sommer-day*, in contempt of an Inhibition and the Primats Letters from *York*, and from the Earl of *Huntington*.[21]

This treatment of copy corresponds to Moxon's later prescription. Practices of spelling, punctuation, capitalization, and abbreviation are all altered. But in the absence of any agreed system of spelling the compositor could himself generate what today look like irregular spellings. In the word *plays*, the change of 'i' to 'y' is probably a standardization, but 'e' is almost certainly added to help the compositor to justify the type-line (that is, to fill it out to the right-hand margin), for the line ends in the following word '*of*' after a series of widely spaced words. To a modern eye perhaps the most distinctively irregular form in the print is '*Mid-sommer-day*', which does not reflect copy. From such cases of surviving printer's copy, it can be inferred that the earliest surviving texts of Shakespeare have already both abandoned the forms in their copy-text and established a new text founded on this distinction between meaning and form, or, in Greg's terms, substantives and accidentals. Such an inference is confirmed by a comparison between the pointing in the Hand D section of *Sir Thomas More* and the punctuation in Shakespeare quartos and the Folio. It is often supposed that the Folio's punctuation provides a significant guide to Shakespeare's intentions as regards rhetorical pointing, but this is clearly not the case.

Punctuation, though formally falling in the area of accidence, is critical as a guide to meaning. Capitalization too might have significance. When Sir Thomas More says to himself, to quote the manuscript, 'but moore. the more thou hast ...', a modernizing editor will alter to 'But More, the more thou hast ...'. The meaning is affirmed by alterations to the misleading lower-case 'm' and the erratic full stop as well as spelling. Of course, the distinction between the role Sir Thomas More and the comparative adjective *more* is crucial. Matters that are accidental in terms of form—spellings and punctuation—have substantive, or at least 'semi-substantive' status.

On grounds such as these, the distinction between accidentals and substantives has been much criticized for its lack of rigour. It makes an unavoidable fudge between a distinction of form—'words' versus 'spellings and punctuation'—and a distinction of significance—matters of 'substance' or meaning versus matters of 'accidence' that are not intrinsic to meaning. The term 'semi-substantive' drives a hole through the wall between matters of substance and matters of accidence that is particularly troublesome to an editorial practice that offers to treat the features that fall under the two headings differently. Yet the hole is not as large as it might seem. Punctuation that is seriously misleading to the modern reader is not necessarily wrong by the light of the text in which it appears. An editor of *Sir Thomas More* producing a text in original spelling and punctuation would usually preserve the pointing and non-capitalization in the line quoted. The modernizing editor will therefore be justified in regarding his or her treatment of the text as modernization, not emendation.

When it comes to the words themselves, the aim of modernization is not to translate. It does not seek to normalize features of syntax or archaic but distinct words such as 'betwixt'. Modernization is usually a straightforward activity. There is nothing controversial or puzzling about the relationship between the early modern form 'booke' and the modern form 'book'. This is not to say that the word *book* has the same meanings in both periods: in Shakespeare's time it could mean specifically 'playbook', while today it can refer to bets on a horse race. Such variability in signification will only rarely detain us. The word is a relatively stable lexical item (as we would now establish from its entry in a dictionary), fundamentally the same in both periods. That is to say that, although words are never absolutely stable, in the case of 'book(e)' it would be impossible to make a case for treating the different forms of the word as separate words.

There are, nevertheless, repeated difficulties relating to the lack of exact equivalence between early modern and current usage, and it is in dealing with these words that modernization becomes a more thought-provoking practice. Some regular old spellings are at first sight unexpected, and would more obviously be interpreted to represent the word that is spelt the same way today: 'I' for 'ay', 'one' for 'on', 'then' for 'than', 'here' for 'hear', 'sonne' for 'sun', 'course' for 'corpse', and so on. Usually the required modernization is clear from the context, but not always. Consider the following exchange in *Richard III*:

> QUEEN Say then, who dost thou mean shall be her king?
> KING RICHARD Even he that makes her queen; who should be else?
> QUEEN What, thou?
> KING RICHARD Ay, even I. What think you of it, madam?
>
> (4.4.240–3)[22]

This modernized text resolves an ambiguity inherent in the ambiguities of early modern spelling. Q1 reads 'I euen I'.[23] Should Richard's second reply instead read 'I, even I'? The decision is finely balanced. It is probable that there is a kind of wordplay present, whereby the simple affirmation 'ay' overlaps with the affirmation of self in the first-person pronoun. The famous opening lines of *Richard III* involve a much more distinct wordplay on 'sun'/'son'. It is arguable that Q1 and the Folio, if taken at face value, give what looks to us like the secondary sense:

> Now is the winter of our discontent,
> Made glorious summer by this sonne of Yorke:
>
> (Q1)
>
> Now is the Winter of our Discontent,
> Made glorious Summer by this Son of Yorke:
>
> (F)

The seasonal metaphor, but not the idea of family relationships, is put in place in advance of the word printed 'sonne' or 'Son'. To follow the logic set up by 'winter' and 'summer', 'sun' is the reading that should be printed in a modern-spelling text.

In both examples from *Richard III* there is a choice of primary meaning for the purposes of print that becomes less critical when the lines are spoken aloud on stage: it takes a carefully weighted delivery to bring out the ambiguity. But this does not apply to 'then'/'than' or 'one'/'on', where the different modernizations mean different things, are now pronounced differently, and cannot coexist. When Richard calls his horse 'white Surrey' (Q1 and F) he is naming it *not* after the English county *but* after the Middle Eastern region that is now the state of Syria. It seems important, then, that in the text and in spoken delivery the reading should be 'White Syrie', though this straightforward modernization was not introduced in any edition before the twenty-first century.

The examples considered so far involve etymologically distinct words. There is a strong boundary in signification, even in the case of a pun, which indeed depends on an awareness of logically separable and conflicting meanings. A different situation arises with forms that are related to each other, where the discrimination we usually observe between variant spellings and distinct words is insecure. This occurs in part because of the sheer variety of early modern spellings, in part because words have histories of changing signification, in part because there were no systematic dictionaries to give formal definition to words as distinct lexical items. The lack of codification is not simply an inconvenience to the modern scholar attempting to understand early modern language; it represents a fundamental instability in the word itself. In cases such as 'charnel'/'carnal', 'ingenuous'/'ingenious', 'metal'/'mettle', 'human'/'humane', 'perilous'/'parlous', and 'wreck'/'wrack', editors face an intractable uncertainty as to whether they are looking at alternative spellings of single words that have subsequently taken on separate forms and meanings, or what would have been already recognized in the period as alternative words. Stanley Wells's work aims to introduce greater consistency in modernization practice. It has led to a greater acceptance that in such cases the early modern form printed in the original text does not dictate that a modern-spelling edition should itself print a misleading modern form.

One basis on which some editors have chosen to preserve individual old spellings has been in order to indicate distinctive pronunciations. Wells demonstrated that early spellings are unreliable as a guide to pronunciation. Moreover, historical shifts in pronunciation render the whole enterprise problematic. There are nevertheless situations in which Wells suggests that an old form might be preserved. One is to indicate a rhyme, as of 'mouth' with 'drouth' rather than 'drought', or 'enter' with 'venter' rather than 'venture'.

Before Wells's work, proper names were particularly liable to be preserved in antiquated forms such as 'Bristow' for 'Bristol', 'Saint Albons' for 'St Albans', 'Callice' for 'Calais', 'Rice up Thomas' for 'Rhys ap-Thomas', and so on. Older forms that still have a residual presence in current use, such as 'Pomfret' for 'Pontefract' and 'Brecknock' for 'Brecon', present a special problem. The example of 'Callice' also raises the issue of foreign words that might be considered to have a distinct Anglicized form.

Language can be a political issue in this respect. Critical examples are found in plays that concern themselves with English identity in relation to Wales, a nation invaded or subsumed. These are the names traditionally presented, in line with the early texts, as Glendower and Fluellen. Would it not be following normal modernization to print instead the forms that would be given in standard modern historical studies, Glyndŵr and Llewellen? This would recognize the characters on their own terms as Welshmen, emphasizing their linguistic and political separation from the English. One line of response would say that Glendower and Fluellen are strongly sanctioned by stage tradition; these are the names that identify the roles and always have done. Another response would say that the erosion of Welsh identity and nationhood is all to the point, both in the usages of the speakers in the play and in the linguistic practices of the Tudor period. The Anglicized forms are therefore both accurate and telling. A reply to this second point would make reference to the first: the traditional Anglicizations give no visibility to the issue, as the usages of Shakespeare and early modern England operate within much the same ideological horizon as does dominant modern cultural practice. So the political thrust of the argument against modernization is neutralized by the blandness it produces. The Welsh forms have the advantage of making the issue visible, in a way that might be compared with the (unscripted) use of the Welsh language in *1 Henry IV*, 3.1. They do not necessarily falsify the text, for, unless the Anglicization can be shown to be at some level conscious, it cannot be asserted that it is meaningful.

To return to the general principles underlying these individual decisions, it is undeniable that the distinction between form and meaning is arbitrary, and that features of the text removed through modernization have the potential, to some extent, to signify. The meaning of a modernized text has been imbued with a certain amount of definitude and limit. The justification is clear: modernization aims to remove kinds of miscommunication and non-communication that are not inherent to the text but have accrued through the passage of time. Its practice may never be perfect. But modernization is necessary if the text is to be realized as an active part of today's landscape of reading. The option seems better than leaving it ossified in a form a little richer in potential meaning but a lot poorer in meaning achieved.

Versification and Stage Directions

VERSIFICATION

Owing to the troubled interface between play manuscript and print in the early modern period, and to the intermixing of verse and prose within plays, establishing the verse in plays presents challenges to the editor in ways that are not typical of non-dramatic poetry. Distinguishing between verse and prose, and affirming line endings, are as subjective and delicate tasks as any in editing. Like the editorial regulation of stage directions, this area of intervention has a marked effect on the text. More is at issue than the formalities of presentation, for metre is the vital pulse of poetic language. Some practitioners, such as the theatre director Peter Hall, have urged that actors should emphasize the verse line-ends in performance. Even if one rejects this strong view, the layout of verse on the page offers an important guide to rhythms of verse and their modulation with and against the flow of semantically oriented speech.

The writing, copying, and printing of dramatic verse was usually sensitive to metre. Past participles were often presented in spellings that showed whether they were syllabic or not. The distinction is well illustrated in the opening lines of *Richard III* as printed in Q1:

> Now is the winter of our discontent,
> Made glorious summer by this sonne of Yorke:
> And all the cloudes that lowrd vpon our house,
> In the deepe bosome of the Ocean buried.
> Now are our browes bound with victorious wreathes,
> Our bruised armes hung vp for monuments,
> Our sterne alarmes changd to merry meetings,

> Our dreadful marches to delightfull measures.
> Grim-visagde warre, hath smoothde his wrinkled front,
> And now in steed of mounting barbed steedes,
> To fright the soules of fearefull aduersaries.
> He capers nimbly in a Ladies chamber,

Here 'lowrd', 'changd', 'visagde', and 'smoothde' are spelt in ways that correctly indicate monosyllables, whereas the spellings 'bruised', 'barbed', and perhaps 'buried' indicate that the final '-ed' is pronounced.[1] Apostrophes are not necessary, though they are regularly used in some texts, and occasionally in others, including *Richard III*:

> *Q. M.* Foule shame vpon you, you haue all mou'd mine,
> *Ri.* Were you well seru'd you would be taught your duty.
>
> So deare I lou'd the man, that I must weepe

In this text, apostrophes in past participles are almost entirely reserved for words where the preceding letter is a 'u' equivalent to modern 'v', to avoid the ambiguity of potential forms such as 'moud' or 'loud'. It is no coincidence that the one line in the Hand D section of *Sir Thomas More* that otherwise misleadingly is written with a final '-ed' has the 'u'-for-'v' immediately before it:

> graunt them remoued and graunt that this yor [y] noyce

The texts therefore usually reflect an awareness of metre, though the conventions for marking it do not correspond exactly to those in use now. Words such as 'even', 'marvel', 'spirit', and 'heaven' commonly counted as monosyllables. Spellings such as 'ene' and 'heau'n' sometimes affirm the pronunciation, but are not required. In more regular use are spellings such as 'nere' and 'ere' for monosyllabic forms of 'never' and 'even'.

Modern readers grow familiar with syllabic past participles because they are often printed with an accent—'bruisèd', 'barbèd'—though the convention is not followed in some editions, such as the Arden Shakespeare. Readers may be less attuned to metrical variables that editors do not mark. For instance, stress could fall in unexpected patterns. Prefixed words such as 'advertise', 'demonstrate', and 'precedent' could take the main stress on the second syllable, as could 'aspect'. Contrariwise, words such as 'congealed' and 'detest' could be stressed

on the first syllable. Only occasionally editors will recognize a particularly unexpected pronunciation and mark the word accordingly, as
with trisyllabic 'statuës' or 'statuas' in *Richard III*, 3.7.25, and *The First
Part of the Contention*, 3.2.80.

In prose these distinctions scarcely matter, as there is no metrical
pattern against which to gauge the pronunciation of the individual
word. The basic distinction between verse and prose was formally
observed in play manuscripts, and so must have mattered from the
point of view of dramatic writing and, presumably, performance.
But the method of distinguishing does not exactly correspond to the
markers familiar to modern readers. In manuscripts, the right-hand
section of the page was not usually needed for verse but was fully
utilized for prose. If in this respect the verse/prose distinction was
clear, in another respect it lacked a now-familiar marker. The opening
words of verse-lines were not usually capitalized. Manuscripts contrast
with printed books of the period, which usually adopted capitalization,
though passages of verse-lines beginning with lower-case letters are
found intermittently in Q1 *Merchant of Venice*, in this instance partially
preserving this feature of the copy manuscript. In print, capitalization
was more necessary because the typical compositor's measure afforded
less width than the manuscript page. Verse-lines took up a greater
proportion of the space, so were less differentiated by layout.

Scribes and even dramatists sometimes wrote a part-line of verse
continuously with the previous line. An apposite example has already
been quoted in Chapter 6 from *Sir Thomas More*:

> and thers no doubt, but mercy may be found yf yo^u so seek y^t

The example quoted is interesting, as noted above, because it shows
a discrepancy between the actualities of writing and the implied
metre, notwithstanding Hand D's habit of writing in clearly defined
pentameters. In a printed book Hand D's line would need to be split
between two type-lines. The normal measure (that is, the maximum
width of the type as established by the set width of the compositor's
typesetting stick) would in any common format be too narrow. A
hypothetical compositor might have preserved the single line by
setting up a turn-line:

> And thers no doubt, but mercy may be found yf
>   (you so seek it.

Or he might have set the line as prose:

> and thers no doubt, but mercy may be found yf you
> so seek it.

Or he might have guessed where the verse line-break should fall, using punctuation or syntax as a guide:

> And thers no doubt, but mercy may be found
> Yf you so seek it.

> And thers no doubt,
> But mercy may be found yf you so seek it.[2]

Errors based on such rationalizations are common in printed texts of the period. This provides one illustration of how the lineation in such texts might stand in need of correction. The question it poses is how the editor should respond to such situations when faced not with the manuscript but only with the book printed from it.

It is common enough to find variations in lineation between two substantive texts. In *Richard III* at 1.1.42–5, Q1 reads:

> Brother, good dayes, what meanes this armed gard
> That waites vpon your grace?
>   *Clar.* His Maiesty tendering my persons safety hath ap-
>   pointed
> This conduct to conuay me to the tower.

The Folio, instead, has:

> Brother, good day: What meanes this armed guard
> That waites vpon your Grace?
>   *Cla.* His Maiesty tendring my persons safety,
> Hath appointed this Conduct, to conuey me to th' Tower

Editors follow neither text. They recognize that the words 'His majesty' complete the verse-line that begins 'That waits upon your grace'. They then follow Q1 in dividing after 'appointed'. One can deduce that the mistake in Q1 arises from following a manuscript in which 'His ... appointed' was written as a single line, as the awkward line-break in 'appointed' and the inelegant use of space suggest a determinedly conservative treatment of copy within the limits imposed by the measure. Folio Compositor B, in contrast, was probably willing to take his own initiative. He probably found no correction marked into the printed copy, and improvised to improve the layout on the page, so taking the lineation further away from that required by metre. It is possible that the manuscript indirectly underlying the Folio shared the same layout as the copy for Q1. This would be the same arrangement witnessed directly in the last line of the Hand D section of *Sir Thomas More*.[3]

In the course of printing, lineation was repeatedly misunderstood or rationalized. Sometimes the copy itself might have been written in a large handwriting so that the right-hand line-end of verse persistently spilt over towards the edge of the paper, making the distinction between verse and prose hard to detect. For whatever reason, some printed texts, such as George Chapman's comedy *An Humorous Day's Mirth*, are almost entirely set in prose, where most passages can be resolved into good iambic pentameter. The situation is not found to this consistency and extreme in Shakespeare, though *Pericles* contains gross examples of verse printed as prose and prose printed as verse.

Most of Mercutio's 'Queen Mab' speech in *Romeo and Juliet* is incorrectly set as prose in the editor's usual base text, Q2. The speech should certainly be verse throughout. But the editor does not have to rely entirely on a purely critical view that the verse has been mis-set. It can be seen in this example that there is a bibliographical basis for the conclusion. The printer's casting-off calculation has gone astray. The speech reverts to verse at the exact point where it continues on a new page. The page-break, as an aspect of the book's design that has no relation to the manuscript, is the determining factor. The casting-off probably failed to take into account lines added in the margin of the manuscript. A further bibliographical reason for affirming that the speech should all be verse without resort to syllable-counting is that it is printed as orthodox verse in the collateral text Q1.

Those who seek to emend the lineation in the Shakespeare quartos and Folio need to do so with some understanding of scribal and compositorial practices that might have affected it. Paul Werstine has examined the work of Folio compositors when they worked from printed copy that is known and surviving. He establishes incontrovertible evidence that they occasionally made alterations. Different compositors were susceptible to different kinds of change; for instance, Compositor A was inclined to rearrange verse in irregular lines.[4] This is an especially striking conclusion, as it would have been much more straightforward for compositors to adhere to printed copy, as in the cases Werstine examined, than to the lost manuscripts that were the copy for many of the Folio plays where lineation difficulties are most intractable. Werstine refutes a strand of criticism that rejects editorial relineation in favour of the supposed expressive power of irregular lineation, especially in the late plays. These views are exemplified for him in G. B. Harrison, but they are prevalent in much recent editing as well.

Werstine's analysis should be taken into account by all who are inclined to endorse the irregularities in F's lineation. He gives this example from *Coriolanus*:

> *Titus Lartius.* Oh Generall:
> Here is the Steed, wee the Caparison:
> Hadst thou beheld—
> *Martius.* Pray now, no more:
> My Mother, who ha's a Charter to extoll her Bloud,
> When she do's prayse me, grieues me:
> I haue done as you haue done, that's what I can,
> Induc'd as you haue beene, that's for my Countrey:
>
> (*Coriolanus*, 1.10.11–17)

Werstine's discussion decisively supports the relineation accepted by most editors:

> LARTIUS   O general,
> Here is the steed, we the caparison.
> Hadst thou beheld—
> MARTIUS   Pray now, no more. My mother
> Who has a charter to extol her blood,
> When she does praise me, grieves me. I have done
> As you have done, that's what I can; induced
> As you have been, that's for my country.

In some circumstances it is possible to show that the compositor was forced to make adjustments because the lines in his copy would not fit the width of the Folio column, but this does not apply here.

Folio Compositor A has followed a practice witnessed elsewhere in his work of adjusting the lineation to make the line-breaks coincide with the strong punctuation. In doing so, he has damaged the metre severely.

More specifically, he has disrupted a highly typical feature of Shakespeare's late metrical art, which is to establish a counterpoint between syntax and metre by lightening the end-stopping and placing major caesuras mid-line:

> *Ar.* To euery Article. |
> I boorded the Kings ship: | now on the Beake,
> Now in the Waste, the Decke, in euery Cabyn,
> I flam'd amazement, | sometime I'ld diuide
> And burne in many places; | on the Top- mast,
> The Yards and Bore-spritt, would I flame distinctly, |
> Then meete, and ioyne. | *Ioues* Lightning, the precursers
> O'th dreadfull Thunder-claps more momentarie
> And sight out- running were not; | the fire, and cracks
> Of sulphurous roaring, the most mighty *Neptune*
> Seeme to besiege, and make his bold waues tremble,
> Yea, his dread Trident shake. |
>
> (*The Tempest*, 1.2.196–207)

This passage is correctly printed in the Folio. The major syntactical breaks, here marked with vertical bar, occur mostly mid-line. Indeed, the one vertical bar marked at the end of a full verse-line, after 'distinctly', is the most doubtful of all, as the phrase 'Then meete, and ioyne' remains governed by the modal 'would I'.

Another situation in which the work of the compositor needs to be taken into account is where he was trying to gain or lose space in order to keep to a casting-off mark. The presentation of verse as prose in the Queen Mab speech is one example. In setting Acts 4 and 5 of *2 Henry IV* Folio Compositor B was aware of the need to use up as much space as possible. He did so by expedients such as splitting single verse-lines in two. This can be demonstrated convincingly in two ways. First, comparison can be made with the earlier text in Q1. Second, Charlton Hinman's bibliographical analysis of the Folio has shown that an initial space shortage was solved by adding in an extra sheet to quire gg, with the result that the compositor now had more space than he needed. The experienced Compositor B's free-handed resourcefulness in dealing with such difficulties is even more clearly evident here than in his more localized alteration in Clarence's speech in *Richard III*. It emerges again when he was confronted with another superfluity of space in *Timon of Athens*. The following passage (4.3.11–16) is manifestly prose, eked out into rough verse-lines to waste space:

> *Painter.* Nothing else:
> You shall see him a Palme in Athens againe,
> And flourish with the highest:
> Therefore, 'tis not amisse, we tender our loues
> To him, in this suppos'd distresse of his:
> It will shew honestly in vs,
> And is very likely, to loade our purposes
> With what they trauaile for,
> If it be a iust and true report, that goes
> Of his hauing.

An understanding of the various licences Shakespeare accepted highlights those lines that remain outside Shakespeare's usage, even in his late plays, where variants on the standard iambic pentameter are more common. To take the passage from *Coriolanus* quoted above, the succession after Martius' 'Pray now, no more' of lines with thirteen and seven syllables is outside Shakespeare's usage. In 'My Mother, who ha's a Charter to extoll her Bloud', the hexameter with an added syllable at the caesura is possible in late Shakespeare, but the irregular caesura itself occurs at an unusually early point in the line, compounding the irregularity in relation to Shakespearian norms. Though Shakespeare's sense of metre cannot be reduced to absolute rules, the information that can be brought to bear from studies of metre, as with bibliographical studies, offers a useful corrective to Harrison's postulate of a late Shakespeare who sometimes tipped over from iambic pentameter into something more like modern free verse. Shakespeare identifiably avoids both the extreme metrical freedoms found in modern verse and the iambic polish of Pope.

Editors have paid special attention to a feature of Shakespeare's metre that is illustrated in the passage quoted above from *Coriolanus*: his division of a line of verse between speakers. A typical edition will introduce indents that had no place in Shakespeare's text before George Steevens began the practice in his Variorum edition of 1793:

> Hadst thou beheld—
> MARTIUS   Pray now, no more. My mother

Once these indentations are established, it becomes possible for the purposes of line-numbering to count the quoted text as one verse-line rather than two printed lines. Most pairings are readily identified, even in passages of sustained part-lines:

> O thou shalt finde.
>   *Tim.* A Foole of thee: depart.
>   *Ape.* I loue thee better now, then ere I did.
>   *Tim.* I hate thee worse.
>   *Ape.* Why?
>   *Tim.* Thou flatter'st misery.
>   *Ape.* I flatter not, but say thou art a Caytiffe.
>   *Tim.* Why do'st thou seeke me out?
>   *Ape.* To vex thee.
>   *Tim.* Alwayes a Villaines Office, or a Fooles.
> Dost please thy selfe in't?
>   *Ape.* I.
>   *Tim.* What, a Knaue too?

By consensus, this emerges as:

> O, thou shalt find—
> TIMON   —a fool of thee. Depart.
> APEMANTUS   I love thee better now than e'er I did.
> TIMON   I hate thee worse.
> APEMANTUS   Why?
> TIMON   Thou flatter'st misery.
> APEMANTUS I flatter not, but say thou art a caitiff.
> TIMON Why dost thou seek me out?
> APEMANTUS   To vex thee.
> TIMON Always a villain's office, or a fool's.
>   Dost please thyself in't?
> APEMANTUS   Ay.
> TIMON   What, a knave too?

> (*Timon of Athens*, 4.3.233–9)

As can be seen, two of these lines consist of three part-lines, but the fragmented nature of the verse offers no obstacle to reconstructing the lineation.

More vexatious is the following passage:

> *Cla.* What (but to speake of) would offend againe.
> *Luc.* What, is't murder?
> *Cla.* No.
> *Luc.* Lecherie?
> *Cla.* Call it so.
> *Pro.* Away, Sir, you must goe.
> *Cla.* One word, good friend:
> Lucio, a word with you.
> *Luc.* A hundred:
> If they'll doe you any good: Is *Lechery* so look'd after?
>
> (*Measure for Measure*, 1.2.127–32)

Difficulties in determining the exact metre can be examined in the putative verse-line 'What is't murder? No. Lechery? Call it so.' These speeches used to be, and sometimes still are, regarded as prose, but J. W. Lever's presentation of them in his 1963 Arden edition as a line of verse is illuminating. If the contraction is right, Lucio's hasty 'is't' might be regarded as a purposeful crushing of regular metre. Stress on the first, third, and fifth syllables ('What', 'mur-', and 'No') irregularly inverts the iambic pattern. But the reversed initial stress followed by iambic feet of 'What is it murder? No' would be relatively acceptable.

The problems in interpreting the metrical pattern continue. As generally used, 'lechery' might count as either two or three syllables. It might be understood here as a disyllable that establishes two irregular but metrically identical and rhyming part-lines. If this is accepted, the exchange is followed by another part-line, now of regular metre, but with the same rhyme:

> What is't murder? No.
> Lech'ry? Call it so.
> Away, sir, you must go.

To print the passage thus is not to suggest a proper editorial resolution, but to highlight one dimension of its metricality.

Whether the Provost's 'go' can actually stand as a rhyme word at the end of a line (pairing with either 'No' or 'so' but not, ultimately, both) depends on the resolution of Claudio's following speech. The Folio divides that speech into two part-lines, indicating, if the division is reliable, that the second part-line 'Lucio, a word with you' pairs up with Lucio's 'A hundred'. But this gives two ametrical lines. The first has a reversed stress throughout if 'Lucio' is scanned as three syllables, or a missing final syllable if 'Lucio' counts as two. The second line consists of fifteen syllables:

> Lucio, a word with you.
> LUCIO   A hundred,
> If they'll do you any good. Is lechery so looked after?

It is more likely that the valid verse-line is 'A hundred, if they'll do you any good', and that the compositor, faced with Lucio's speech written on a single manuscript line, divided after the wrong syntactic break. In that case, 'go' can stand as a rhyme word, as the following words spoken by Claudio, 'One word, good friend. Lucio, a word with you' would make a verse-line. But the Folio's splitting of Claudio's speech into two lines would be puzzling if it were a mistake. An alternative explanation, accepted by some editors, is that Lucio's last speech should be prose; but this involves identifying error in two successive speeches.[5]

This passage exemplifies in concentrated form some of the issues of verse lineation. Such matters are often passed over quietly, for there is little scope for confidence, and the rules or norms governing Shakespeare's metre are not readily explicable and understood. What can be said here is that the verse patterning in the passage runs against pentameter norms. It can almost go unsaid, and must be taken as an absolute premiss, that it was within Shakespeare's competence as a writer to construct this exchange in regular pentameter. The irregularity of metre and rhyme is purposeful. It provides good clues as to the pacing of the first exchange between Lucio and Claudio in delivery. Lucio, we might infer, expects something more than 'No' (to be more accurate, his speech generates such an expectation in the listener), but Claudio will not be drawn. Shakespeare is writing at the point where verse and prose begin to blur, but it seems clear that the exchange exploits the underlying rhythmicality of verse.

STAGE DIRECTIONS

Stage directions—a term that here and in the following discussion encompasses speech prefixes—invite the reader to envisage the written dialogue as dramatic action played out in the theatre. Although performers rarely accept them uncritically as prescriptions as to what they should do, they nevertheless offer an important point of departure for the stage realization of a play. Yet the directions presented in modern editions are often read uncritically or misunderstood. In many cases they do not derive from any early text, but have been introduced by editors. The reasons why editors intervene in this way, and how they do so, will be explored in the remainder of the present chapter.

Stage directions lead a double life. In one capacity they are text. They are words that signify. They are written and printed like all other text. In *Sir Thomas More*, the act of inscribing the stage direction 'Enter the L. maier Surrey | Shrewsbury' is in kind the same as the act of inscribing the speech that follows, 'hold in the king*e*s name hold'. The same is true of the subsequent textual transmission of a play: stage directions, like dialogue, are susceptible to revision and to error. On the other hand, stage directions stand apart from the text of the play in that they are not part of the performed script in the particular sense of the words the actors speak. They do not belong to the semiotic system of the dialogue. Instead, they provide an index towards a different semiotic system, that of stage action. To speak of them as providing an index is to draw attention to the fact that their realization is not in language, the medium they themselves inhabit as words.

Indeed, the semiotician Marco de Marinis in his analysis of performance points out that stage directions are not even expressed in a notational language. Whereas a musical note, or a choreographed dance movement, or a word in a dramatic script can be realized in a performance in a precise form that can be accounted more or less accurate as a performance of the notation, stage directions do not formally notate the actions they anticipate.[6] It might be argued that formulae such as 'enter', 'exit', 'above', 'severally', and 'flourish', call for standard action such as 'kneels', 'sits', and 'fight', conventionalized physical descriptions such as 'mad', 'singing', 'aloof', 'like a …', and calls for stock properties such as swords, drums, beards, caps, and beds do indeed constitute a notational system. This is especially the case in so far as early modern staging practices were more governed by convention than later, more naturalist forms of theatre. In other words there will be some anachronism in *our* sense that 'mad' might be realized on stage in many different ways if early modern actors responded to such calls with a more generic and formulaic understanding of how madness is performed; therefore to call this apparently question-begging word non-notational might be misleading. But, if this is admitted, the degree of notational efficacy in stage directions is nevertheless limited. Even a semi-technical formulation such as 'Exeunt severally' does not tell us *who* leaves by *which* exit route, and a given performance based on this script would not allow its audience to know whether the script read 'Exeunt severally' or 'Exeunt at several doors' or 'Exeunt' or 'Exit' (which was often used as a plural), or indeed had no direction at all.[7]

But more to the point is de Marinis's insistence that a process of 'transcoding' stands between stage direction and stage action: the signified is not the signified of the word, but the signified of the action it signifies in performance, which is a different means of expression. The editing of stage directions needs to take account of their double existence as words on the page and as inscription that invites transcoding into compliant action. To take an extreme example, from the first point of view Samuel Beckett's wordless drama *Actes sans paroles* consists entirely of words—namely, a script consisting wholly of stage directions; whereas from the second point of view it conforms to its title in being wordless.

This duality would apply to an actively functional theatre document such as a modern prompt book, at least up to the point that words were supplemented or replaced with diagrams and formulaic abbreviations. But there is another, different, distinction to be observed within word-based printings such as the modern edition. The script can be apprehended and used either as a dramatic text anticipating performance or as a literary text. We now usually understand that Shakespeare's plays *originated* as (primarily) dramatic texts and *became* (primarily) literary texts. Hence, even in our literary readings, we find it appropriate to recuperate an understanding of the script's dramatic aspect. To this end, editorial stage directions help by establishing a more fully realized account of stage action than the base text acknowledges. They do so by modifying and complementing stage directions that are deemed insufficient—not because they belong to the antipathetic world of print, or even because they necessarily come from 'pre-theatrical' or 'post-theatrical' versions of the script, but because early modern sets of stage directions do not comply with a modern reader's sense of what is coherent and adequate.

We have seen in Chapter 1 an extreme example of deficiency in the original stage directions: the absence of an entry for the protagonist More in Shakespeare's contribution to *Sir Thomas More*. It is more usual for minor roles to lack an exit, or for re-entrances not to be stipulated. Directions for properties and for actions such as kneeling are few, and speech directions such as 'aside' are rare. Calls for music and other sound effects such as thunder will be generously included in some texts but almost absent from others. Consistency is the exception, not the rule. In such a situation it is scarcely meaningful to speak of a criterion for correctness in the stage directions of a play of Shakespeare's time as explicitly written.

The criterion for what is explicitly supplied in an edition is the need to alert the reader to the stage action. In this respect the affinities of editing stage directions lie with the practice of modernizing spelling and punctuation. Even if editorial stage directions are correct in that they articulate the requirements of early modern staging in appropriate language, they are inescapably modern: they are explicit where the early text was silent, following criteria of consistency that the early text did not observe. They also differ crucially from the original stage directions in their relation to the original performances they invoke or, by anticipation, re-create. The original stage directions are written prior to performance, and they are elements in a real historic process of determination of what *will* happen.[8] Editorial stage directions are *post hoc* rationalizations that account for what *must have* or *might have* happened. They are, therefore, ontologically distinct from the original stage directions, and logically require a rigorous differentiation on the page.[9]

As with modernization, the endeavour to clarify for the reader must be subject to constraints. In recent editorial practice it has been accepted that the action in editorial stage directions should be framed within the staging conventions and vocabulary of the early modern theatre. Entrances are by doors; beds or thrones are thrust out to bring them on stage; action may make use of the trapdoor in the middle of the stage, and so on. Modern practice offers an advance on that of earlier editors, who had often casually allowed assumptions based on the proscenium-arch theatre to influence the wording of stage directions and conceptualization of stage action. So the editor's endeavours on behalf of the reader should not lead to a dehistoricizing of the play's theatrical dimension. And, because the early modern stage was without scenery, the editorial tradition of inserting location notes at the beginning of each scene has died away over the past few decades. Locations that used to be identified in the text from the eighteenth century on, such as 'A plain near Actium', were not capable of being realized on the early Modern stage. A succession of notes specifying such locations interrupts the fluidity of place and action that typifies the theatre of Shakespeare's time. This is especially so where there is a sequence of short scenes as in parts of *Antony and Cleopatra*, or a fluidity of location within a single scene, as in *Julius Caesar*, 3.1, which begins in a public place and moves onwards without interruption into the Senate.

The editor's awareness of the general conditions of the early modern theatre combines with an alertness to the idiosyncratic and the particular in the wording of original stage directions. Editors recognize and usually preserve this verbally distinctive aspect. Expressive detail such as '*on the walls*' (*King John*, 4.3.0.1), or '*within the Forest of Gaultres*' (*2 Henry IV*, 4.1.0.1), or '*The King takes place under the cloth of state*' (*All Is True*, 2.4.0.14–15), or '*They all shout and wave their swords, take him up in their arms, and cast up their caps*' (*Coriolanus*, 1.7.75.1–3), or '*Leonatus Posthumus following like a poor soldier*' (*Cymbeline*, 5.2.0.3), says something valuable about the writer's conceptualization of the action. It might be said to be part of the play's literary as well as dramatic fabric.

Wording that is usually understood to have been supplied by Shakespeare often allows for more than one possible staging. In one stage direction in *Romeo and Juliet* one finds the phrases '*three or four*' and '*clubs or partisans*' (1.1.69.1–2). These are called permissive stage directions. Further examples from the same play, '*with his train*' (1.1.77), '*five or six*' (1.4.0.1–3), '*all the guests and gentlewomen*'

(1.5.15.1–2), 'and all' (3.1.140.2), and 'three or four' (4.4.13) all belong to the same category, because they do not specify how many actors need to enter, let alone identify the roles that they play. As W. W. Greg put it: 'An author shows his hand most clearly in indefinite directions and in what may be called permissive or petitory directions, neither of which could originate with or commend themselves to the book-keeper.'[10] A dramatist might leave it to the theatre company to work out exactly what could be afforded. Formulations such as '*as many as may be spared*' are typical of a dramatist seeking to maximize effect while being unsure of the exact resources of the theatre company at moments in the future. In the case of *Romeo*, Shakespeare seems to have wanted the stage to have been as busy as possible at a number of moments, but to have been aware that he was stretching the resources of the company. This is nowhere more so than in the sequence of 1.4 and 1.5, which in some editions are treated as a single scene. In 1.5 the staging requires Capulet and his wife, his cousin, Juliet, the Nurse, Tybalt, his page, Romeo, Benvolio, Mercutio, and at least three servingmen, all of whom have speaking parts, as well as an unspecified number of guests including one called Petruccio, and musicians. It is not clear whether the five or six extra masquers of 1.4 are the same as or distinct from the torchbearers, nor whether they have opportunity to leave the stage before the party of guests arrives at Capulet's feast. The requirement for an extra 'five or six' masquers combines ambition with an awareness that the limits of practical performance may have been reached.

The editorial task may be relatively straightforward in responding to such cases, but becomes more taxing when a second substantive text removes or alters the descriptive or permissive details. Consider the following variants between Quarto and Folio in Shakespeare plays:

Richard II, 4.1.0.1–3

Q1   *Enter Bullingbroke with the Lords to parliament.*
F   *Enter as to the Parliament, Bullingbroke, Aumerle,*
      Northumberland, Percie, Fitz-Water, Surrey, Carlile,
      Abbot of Westminster.

2 Henry IV, 2.1.0.1–3

Q1   *Enter Hostesse of the Tauerne, and an Officer or two.*
F   *Enter Hostesse, with two Officers, Fang, and Snare.*

Hamlet, 2.1.0.1

Q2   *Enter Polonius, with his man or two.*
F   *Enter Polonius, and Reynaldo.*

These texts fall within a pattern, discernible in a range of evidence, that the Quarto in question was printed from a manuscript close to Shakespeare's hand and the Folio text in question from, or with reference to, a theatrical manuscript or a copy of such a manuscript. In each case, the permissive aspect of the direction is removed in F. The entry in *Richard II* specifies who the lords are. The permissive 'or two' in the Quarto directions from *2 Henry IV* and *Hamlet* is resolved in favour of the theatrically more economical solution in each case, and the figure is identified by name.

In all three plays the Quarto and Folio stage directions repeatedly differ in this kind of way. This is true too of the two longer quartos of *Romeo* and *Hamlet*. It is in the generally unreliable, or at least radically different, first quartos that one finds '*Enter Iuliet somewhat fast, and embraceth Romeo.*' and '*Enter Ofelia playing on a Lute, and her haire downe singing.*' The question then arises: how much attention should an editor pay to the stage directions in texts other than the edition's base text?

The answer will depend, at least to some extent, on the editor's understanding of the provenance of the texts and general policy towards readings in the collateral text. If, for example, the edition aspires to represent the play in a state as close as possible to the finished theatrical form, and if the Folio brings us closer to that form, both its dialogue variants and its stage direction variants will come to the editor's close attention, and the Folio stage directions might be accepted where they give revised or fuller or more precise details of the staging. But if, let us say, an editor is following Q2 *Hamlet* as a separate version from the Folio, the use of the Folio's stage directions might be limited to remedying only those deficiencies in Q2 that present themselves irrespective of the existence of the Folio. Many editors have accepted the directions quoted from Q1 *Romeo* and Q1 *Hamlet*, on the understanding that the texts are *corrupted* versions of Shakespeare's play and therefore testify, albeit imperfectly, to the same underlying text. But if these texts are also considered to be *different* versions adapted for the theatre from the longer authorial texts, the stage directions might be misleading in relation to the longer versions from which the editor is working.

A collateral text can, at the very least, provide information that relates to staging where the base text is inadequate. In Q1 *Richard II*, the scene 1.4 begins '*Enter the King with Bushie, &c at one dore, and the Lord Aumerle at another*'; the Folio alters this to '*Enter King, Aumerle, Greene, and Bagot*'. Q1 is wrong in naming Bushy, because later in the scene, after l. 52, in both texts Bushy enters with news. In Q1 we evidently see Shakespeare's evolving intentions leading to a specific inconsistency that represents a real obstacle to staging. In the Folio we see the issue resolved.

But in this case there are two complications to note. First, the dialogue in the Folio reflects the intention expressed in the opening direction of the other text, Q1. At 1.4.23, the Folio has Richard name 'Ourselfe, and *Bushy*: heere *Bagot* and *Greene*'. 'Heere' presumably relates to Bushy, notwithstanding the punctuation, and so indicates, in accordance with Q1 but not the Folio, that Bushy is present on stage. The reading is independent of the quartos, for Q1 has the short line 'Our selfe and Bushie', which itself looks like an improvised correction. So, although in the Folio the staging is resolved in the stage directions by way of reference to the manuscript, a difficulty lingers in the dialogue. It is in conflict with the corrected stage direction, for, according to that direction, Bushy is not 'here'. Most editors resign themselves to following the Sixth Quarto of 1634, which reads 'Ourselfe, and *Bushy, Bagot* here and *Greene,*'— an elegant and persuasive reading, but an unauthoritative one. This crux evidently illustrates that even a theatrical manuscript in which the staging had been more fully worked out could retain inconsistencies. Although stage directions are *sui generis* as the object of editing, problems relating to staging are to be found in the dialogue too. We see here the consequences of editing to establish a theatrical coherence that is necessary to make the play stageable. A working solution must have been achieved in performance, but in this case is absent in both the early authoritative texts.

The second complication relates to Q1's stipulation as to the doors that are used for the entry. The Folio makes no such stipulation. Does this mean that Q1's separate entries are rejected in the Folio? The opening lines of the scene read (in both texts, but to quote the Folio):

'*Rich*. We did obserue. Cosine *Aumerle*, | How far brought you high Herford on his way?'. Taking the Folio in isolation, one would assume that 'We did obserue' is addressed to Aumerle, and that all the roles enter together in mid-conversation. But if one takes an overview of the relation between Q1 and the Folio, one would argue, on the contrary, that the Folio's concentration on identifying roles and its rejection of other information is typical of its stage directions. The absent detail about the grouping of characters found in Q1 therefore reflects the nature of the Folio's stage directions rather than the nature of the staging. On this basis, editors usually maximize their capture of staging information from both Q1 and the Folio *Richard II*, therefore engaging in a particularly active kind of conflation.

As already suggested, the scope that should be afforded for pure-ly editorial interventions has been widely debated. If a character kneels, is it interfering pedantry or logical common sense for an editor to stipulate where he or she rises up again? Should asides, which are rarely printed in the early editions, be marked rigor-ously or left to the reader's interpretative discretion? How much detail of costume should be read in from the dialogue of a scene and stipulated when the character first enters? How clear should an editor seek to be about stage groupings? Such questions could be multiplied.

Editors who need to intervene, or choose to do so, have to determine the form of words in which the direction is expressed. At 1.2.87–90 in *Richard III*, we find the following dialogue:

> RICHARD DUKE OF GLOUCESTER   Vouchsafe to wear this ring.
> LADY ANNE   To take is not to give.
> RICHARD DUKE OF GLOUCESTER
>   Look how this ring encompasseth thy finger,
>   Even so thy breast encloseth my poor heart.

A conservative editor will let the text speak for itself in such an instance, but an editorial stage direction will undoubtedly clarify the action. Once an editor has decided that an intervention is justified, the question arises as to the precise nature of the symbolically expressive exchange. Should the direction stipulate that Richard gives the ring or that Anne takes it? Is 'To take' an active or passive action, to take hold of or to receive? Does the action take place before or after Anne's line?

Such questions are critical, for, as the play unfolds, it emerges that to take is indeed to give: Anne not only gives her hand in marriage but loses her life as a result.

Stanley Wells, in establishing procedures for the Oxford Shakespeare as it re-emerged in the 1980s, argued that an editor needed to be more active in releasing the implicit visual and aural semiotics of the text in terms appropriate to the early modern theatre.[11] To achieve this end, the editor must have the courage to risk being wrong—or rather risk putting determinacy on the indeterminate—rather than leave the visual and aural semiotics unaddressed. The practice in the Oxford Complete Works was not to mark off all editorial stage directions in brackets. Instead, it reserved brackets for contentious alterations and additions. The editors recognized that what should happen was perhaps in some cases 'never clearly determined even by the author'.[12] This statement recognizes the uncertainties surrounding stage action, the likelihood of authorial imprecision, and different possible outcomes on the stage. An attempt is made to reconcile the realm of the uncertain with the fixity of print by creating a special, typographically marked realm for the uncertain. Alan C. Dessen has drawn attention to the danger nevertheless of the editor making 'a plausible but iffy decision that may in turn close down equally valid or theatrically interesting options of which the reader is no longer aware'.[13] His 'no longer' reverses the premiss of the Oxford Shakespeare by making the assumption that readers *are* aware of interesting options when there is no stage direction. Wells and Taylor understand that many if not most readers are inexperienced in translating the script of a play into imagined theatrical action. For them—in the context of an edition without the luxury of commentary notes to discuss staging issues—the better procedure is to offer a plausible solution. The brackets are designed to highlight the problem in staging and invite the reader to consider possible alternatives to the words enclosed within them.

Editors are far more justified in providing stage directions if they clearly signal that the directions do not belong to the original text. The obvious and conventional way of doing so is to place the editorial direction in brackets:[14]

Sc. 1   *Enter Poet* [*at one door*], *Painter,* [*carrying a picture, at another door; followed by*] *Jeweller, Merchant, and Mercer, at several doors*

POET Good day, sir.
PAINTER   I am glad you're well.
POET I have not seen you long. How goes the world?
PAINTER It wears, sir, as it grows.
POET   Ay, that's well known.
  But what particular rarity, what strange,
  Which manifold record not matches?—See,
  Magic of bounty, all these spirits thy power
  Hath conjured to attend.
          [*Merchant and Jeweller meet. Mercer passes over the*
          stage, and exits]
                          I know the merchant.
PAINTER I know them both. Th' other's a jeweller.
MERCHANT   [*to Jeweller*] O, 'tis a worthy lord!
JEWELLER   Nay, that's most fixed.

This is the opening of *Timon of Athens* as printed in the Oxford
Middleton *Collected Works* (2007). The one direction in the underlying
Folio version of this passage is at the beginning of the scene, which
reads as does the edited text once the words in square brackets
are subtracted: '*Enter Poet, Painter, Ieweller, Merchant, and Mercer,*
at seuerall doores'. In the Oxford Shakespeare edition, the words
'*carrying a picture*' are regarded as non-contentious, and are therefore
not bracketed. In contrast, in the Middleton edition the added
stage directions are all bracketed, so the Folio direction can here be
reconstructed simply by omitting the words placed in brackets.

Brackets allow the editor a single act of textual differentiation.
This act can be defined in different ways. Most Shakespeare editions
place added asides and speech directions such as '*to Jeweller*' in round
brackets. There are many subtle but significant variations in current
editorial usage of brackets in stage directions, sometimes guided by
series guidelines (which themselves evolve), sometimes as an element
in the editor's individual practice, sometimes as a response to the
particular circumstances of a given text. And in earlier practice, square
brackets were often used as part of the typographical offsetting of stage
directions in dialogue, or to indicate the editorial status of location
notes at the head of a scene. As noted in Chapter 5, John Dover
Wilson's Cambridge series employed quotation marks to identify
wording taken from the base text. It is important, therefore, for the
reader to choose an edition that records changes to stage directions,

to be alert to the technique being used in a particular edition or series, and to keep an eye on the added information given in the collation line or textual notes.

It would be easier to establish a regular and self-explanatory practice if stage directions could be separated into two categories, those present in the base text and those added by the editor. Unfortunately this is far from the case. An editor may need to correct error, to reword so that, for example, unspecified '*other lords*' are named, to move a stage direction to another location, to split a stage direction in two, and so on. The altered direction may be purely editorial, but it may come from a collateral text—typically, as in examples considered above, the Folio, where the base text is a quarto. It may alternatively be suggested by but altered from a collateral text. In *The Merry Wives of Windsor* the base text F is lacking in mid-scene stage directions, and so the generally defective Quarto is an important source of staging information. Because Q1 is shortened and reorganized, it can offer only a single exit direction where the fuller Folio text requires two. '*Exit Mis. Page, & Sir Iohn.*' underpins editors' two separate directions: '*Exit Sir John*' at 4.2.75 and Mistress Page's '*Exit*' at 4.2.100. The typographical device of brackets is a crude instrument to cope with all these situations.

To summarize, editing stage directions and speech prefixes is fundamentally different in kind from editing dialogue. They belong to a distinct semiotic system that is verbal in immediate form but extra-verbal in referent. Editors regulate that system so that, from a modern reader's perspective, the text functions effectively as a script for performance. The major interventions of this kind are usually signalled with brackets, but the precise use of these brackets is variable. So too is the extent to which editors are willing to intervene, and the degree of theatrical awareness they bring to the editorial process. There will perhaps always be something unsatisfactory about the editing of stage directions, because it occupies a hinterland between purely textual editing and choices that are otherwise associated with theatre practice. Carefully edited stage directions certainly help readers to visualize the action, but it is essential that readers should be enabled (and willing) to understand the nature of the editorial intervention, and be guided to consider other possible solutions.

Texts for Readers

We have seen in the previous chapters how the text assumes the form it does in manuscripts, in early printed books, and in modern editions. At the other end of the process that the text enacts lies the reader, as implied addressee, as bearer of cultural value, and as actualization of the market in which the book as a commodity circulates. For the main purpose of this study, it is the book as a material object that actualizes the text, from the publication of play quartos in Shakespeare's time to the preparation of critical editions today. Most readers still experience Shakespeare through the medium of print, and use modern-spelling editions. The present study has therefore made extensive reference to the intellectual foundations, procedures, and problems entailed in critical editing, to enable its readers to understand the ways in which it both does and does not represent the text of Shakespeare. But it has also identified what might be called the realm of the reader within the edited text. Modern spelling and punctuation, and enhanced stage directions, are two areas where editing addresses the readers' interests rather than the actual foundations of the text. In the present chapter this realm will be enlarged by briefly considering questions of design, coverage, and medium.

An edition might be defined as a mediation of a text to a reader. The phrase raises major issues not only about the 'text', as it has been addressed throughout this book, but also the nature of the communication that the editor seeks to enable. Beyond the text of the play, the modern critical edition includes some or all of a number of elements: a record of the foundation of the text (typically a collation line or textual notes); a commentary explaining and contextualizing words and expressions, justifying textual decisions, and perhaps exploring the theatrical dimension of the script, an introduction dealing with text, critical reception, theatre history, and other matters, appendices of supplementary information such as extracts from source material, and visual illustrations. The basic form will follow the guidelines for the series to which the edition belongs. But there remains scope for each editor to shape his or her edition in ways that no other editor would follow, to an extent that is often apparently belied by the shoe-horning of the material into the series format. The editor too is an author, and intends certain outcomes.

The page layout of series such as the Oxford, Cambridge, and Arden is carefully designed to offer a clear reading text alongside a large volume of compacted commentary. Editors nevertheless need to concentrate on how to select, prioritize, and sometimes disperse the information they include. A good critical edition is a highly crafted and highly efficient conveyor of a wide variety of information, in which the predigested and lumpy intellectual content that is the editor's raw material has been filtered with a view to the interests of the reader and harmonized through the imperatives of design and presentation.

The leading series have a similar page layout. The text is placed in the upper part of the page and has a generous and clear design conducive to unfettered continuous reading. The collation line appears as a single bank of type in a small typeface, and the commentary is printed in a larger but still compact typeface in two columns. The layout is not inevitable, and it is subject to some variation. For instance, the Arden 3 series places the collation line at the foot of the page rather than between text and commentary, and the present writer's Oxford edition of *Richard III* separates out the potentially tangled textual documentation by presenting separate collation lines for the Quarto and Folio texts.[1] But the basic common features that have been described are shared because they are effective in establishing separation between the different elements on the page, and in confining the specific reading experience appropriate to each of those elements to one area of the page.

The collation line has been denounced as a 'band of terror' whose effect on the reader is to intimidate, and whose function is to imbue the edition with an air of scholarly authority.[2] When it comes to charm, its high level of codification is a distinct disadvantage. But arguably it is no more codified and restrictive than footnotes in an article or monograph and other forms of scholarly documentation. And it serves a similar purpose in demonstrating the foundations of the text—scholarly in one case, textual in the other. Both acknowledge the ways in which the text that is given to the reader, potentially presenting itself as though a text without origin, needs to acknowledge its relationship to the material that existed before it. In other words, like a footnote, a collation note is a record both of origin and of change. It would be easier on the reader to displace or entirely remove such information, but this would belie the nature of the text he or she was reading, and it would make the very textuality of text invisible.

The naive view would be that in the above paragraphs we have left text behind and turned to the edition as the container of that text. But, as we have already seen in reviewing the early modern book, an encounter with a text is never disembodied. Assuming that the words are the same, a passage of Shakespeare is ontologically different in different physical manifestations such as an early modern quarto inspected in a research library, a photographic reproduction of that quarto in book form, a modern critical edition in paperback, a quotation used as background in a theatre poster, a printout of a file marked with tabs for digital coding, an online digitized set of images of the quarto, or an online edited text panelled with a source text or film-script adaptation. The physical form will not be merely a channel through which the text passes indifferently. In each case the reader's experience of the text will be constituted in relation to the physical form of the text. If the bibliographical codes are not intrinsic to the text as originated by the author, and can be hypothetically but only hypothetically pared away from specific manifestations of the kinds mentioned, they are nevertheless absolutely intrinsic to the text as encountered by the reader.

These matters may be approached by considering one aspect of the Shakespearian text, its instability, and its potential for being realized in either one or more than one versions. If we assert the instability of Shakespeare, we are asserting not a fact but a way of thinking. For centuries the hermeneutics of corruption enabled critics to posit an underlying text that was stable. The increased awareness in recent years that the text of Shakespeare is not self-evident and stable is, of course, sympathetic to postmodern perspectives. It has also been given a strong impetus by the emergence of electronic forms of editing that have highlighted different possibilities for presentation. High-quality digital images of the Shakespeare quartos and folios that far surpass their black-and-white pre-digital print equivalents are now freely available online (see Further Reading). Students of Shakespeare can readily access the documentary foundations of the editorial process, rendering the process itself unprecedentedly open to scrutiny.

Even today, print editions offer a view of the text as determinate and, for the most part, unitary. That is what print does best. Once the paper is inked and bound, it is, to most practical purposes, fixed. The model of the unitary text can prevail even where the editors are committed to a two-text model, as is the case in the Oxford *Complete Works*, where the two texts of *King Lear* are printed as if they were two separate plays. Here the conventions of reading appropriate to the book, and endorsed by an understanding of how and why a play is read, prevail over the strictly necessary constraints of print. For, if anything, the two-page opening that meets the eye of a book-reader is actually more conducive to parallel-text presentation than to single-text presentation. Pedagogic, aesthetic, and critical assumptions that have come into being during the era of print determine that the readers of the pioneering two-text edition encounter only one text at a time.

René Weis's 1993 edition of *King Lear* and the same play in the Norton Shakespeare of 1997 are rare instances of two texts of a Shakespeare play appearing in parallel in a fully edited form designed for literary reading. In both, the Quarto-based 'History of King Lear' appears on the left-hand page of each opening, the Folio-based 'Tragedy' on the right. Elsewhere, parallel text has been reserved as a special format usually for purposes of textual documentation rather than reading; it commonly signifies a state of uneditedness. An example is Greg's edition of *Doctor Faustus*, where two alternative texts are adjusted in position so that passages can be read opposite their equivalents in the opposing version but are otherwise taken letter-for-letter from the two copy-texts.[3] Kristian Smidt adopts a similar presentation in order to demonstrate the Quarto and Folio texts of *Richard III*.[4] Here the act of collocation—presenting two physically separate texts alongside each other—can serve as a preliminary to an act of conflation—the establishment of a critically edited text that, though based on one base text, recognizes its limitations and accepts readings from the second text where deemed necessary.

Potentially at least, parallel text can be used not only to correlate different early texts of the same work, but also different states or stages within an editorial process. Stephen Booth's famous edition of Shakespeare's Sonnets prints a facsimile of the Quarto on the left-hand page and a fully edited and modernized text opposite it on the right-hand side.[5] In this case there is a straightforward relationship between copy and edited text, as there is rarely a second substantive text to take into account, so the reader can immediately appreciate the relationship between the Quarto and the edited text—a relationship that centres on normalization of typography, modernization of words, and clarification of punctuation. This combination of photofacsimile and edited text effectively answers the criticism that critical editing occludes the material on which it is based, and so it can offer a highly attractive solution to some of the difficulties inherent in presenting the text. But it comes at a price: not only the literal cost of added facsimile pages, but also a loss in utility. A typical quarto page has about thirty-two lines of type, all of it the play's text, whereas a typical page in a critical edition has anything between about three and about twenty lines of text. The reason for the extreme variation in the volume of text per page is that the need for textual documentation and commentary varies considerably. As with all forms of footnoting from the Renaissance onwards, the more apparatus is printed on a page, the less text. If the layout of the base text determines the amount of edited text on the page, there is a limited and fixed space available for commentary.

The problem is not insuperable. Editions such as the New Penguin routinely place textual documentation and commentary in appendices, leaving a plain-text presentation of the play itself. This presentation can be combined with parallel-text photofacsimile, as indeed is the case with the Booth edition of the Sonnets. Yet most general editors reject the Penguin approach on the grounds that readers will find it more convenient to have the commentary on the same page as the text. The book form presses towards a binary choice: the plain text might be elaborated *either* with a commentary and textual notes, as in the Arden, Oxford, and Cambridge series, *or* with a facing photofacsimile, as in Booth's edition of the Sonnets, but it is impractical to do both unless the apparatus is limited and some pages are allowed aesthetically unpleasing areas of white space. Such choices are highly characteristic of the constraints of the print medium.

A case has been made for more open and 'friendly' forms of presentation that break open the efficient formality of the standard edition. Steven Urkowitz advocates jaunty magazine-style editions of Shakespeare with 'space for treats'—in other words, areas of the page that can be used more whimsically, for instance to enlarge on the theatrical potential of a given passage or to comment on the differences between different texts. Such an edition would, he argues, open up new possibilities for thinking about the play. Urkowitz believes that a more extensive amount of textual discussion than is customary can be a source of intellectual provocation and enjoyment if it is attractively and casually packaged. He proposes to introduce 'a collaborative, generative model of playing and play-making'.[6] Such an edition would be unmistakably marked with the personality of its editor, and would be attractive or not accordingly. It would have particular kinds of use-value, for instance, in opening up new performance possibilities by presenting text from alternative versions. Its free-style design, with an abundance of space that could be used as need be, would allow these alternative passages of text to be presented in their entirety, a liberation both from the volume and constraints of parallel-text format and from the fragmented congestion of the collation line. This liberation would be achieved, most fundamentally, by a change in format to a larger page-size.

A good example of a series that goes some way at least in the direction Urkowitz defines is the Cambridge Schools Shakespeare series. This assigns the right-hand page to text and the left-hand page to summary of the action, illustration, points for discussion, and a basic glossarial commentary. The text is taken from the New Cambridge Shakespeare, and so can be presented on the understanding that the foundation and documentation of the text have safely been dealt with elsewhere. There is no critical introduction, but an appendix offers 'Ideas and Activities' that relate to the play as a whole. The series achieves integrity as a pedagogical resource, meeting specific aims at the expense of excluding much that would be expected of a standard critical edition.

As the discussion to this point has suggested, there is an intricate relation between form and content, on the one hand, and use and readership, on the other, in the printed Shakespeare edition. One point is clear: no single format can meet all needs. From some points of view the Arden–Oxford–Cambridge model is excessive in its documentation and claim to rigour; from other perspectives it subordinates or entirely omits certain kinds of significant textual information.[7] In fact the precocious compaction of these editions is a sign that they are catering to many needs. On the one hand, they aim at markets extending not only to undergraduates but even to advanced school students. (They are in common use on the British schools' A-Level syllabus.) On the other hand, they offer themselves as the most meticulous and scholarly editions available.

Urkowitz's idea that the scholarly edition might be unpacked can most fully be realized in the medium of electronic text. Here the discipline and constraint of the printed page immediately disappear. We may think of the various components of the page—most usually text, commentary, and collation—as equivalent to separate electronic files; and indeed in current book production this is exactly how they originate. Once the files are electronically linked, they can be displayed on-screen in any combination. The number of components or files in view at any one moment may be no greater than is possible with the printed book. But the most immediate asset of the electronic text is the malleability of the on-screen view. The hierarchy of material is not rigidly set; it is generated according to need. And, because of the efficiency of electronic data storage, vast realms of documentation can be captured. For the user, the data can be kept out of sight until required, and then either displayed alone or collocated with any other material.

The possibilities are endless. An electronic edition might include facsimiles and transcripts of the substantive texts—but why not follow the prompt of the British Library Shakespeare Quartos website and include the non-substantive texts as well? In the case of a complex manuscript such as *Sir Thomas More*, it would be possible to demonstrate the progress from manuscript to edited text stage by stage: the reorganization of the pages into a single sequence, the omission of text deleted in the manuscript, the treatment of passages where the Original Text overlaps with the revisions, the different interpretations of semi-legible words, the readings for which we are dependent on transcriptions made before the damage incurred in the later nineteenth century and the twentieth century, the various alternative readings that are editorially conjectured where the manuscript was damaged before it was first transcribed, the emendations of error, different realizations of the text according to different editorial principles (for instance, an author-based approach versus a collective theatre-based approach), the process of modernization, different possibilities for editorial stage directions, and so on. For other plays one might include adaptations, prompt books, and film scripts. The edition could incorporate not only static images, as in the illustrations in a print edition, but also moving images and sound, hence film clips or, potentially, entire films.[8]

An electronic edition can aim to include a large array of data and cater for a wide and sometimes unpredicted range of scholarly and pedagogic purposes. Specific forms of study encouraged by the medium include searching, task-oriented study of passages, comparison of texts, and accessing of performance archive material. A major electronic project can be developed only stage-by-stage over many years. Fortunately, the medium lends itself to dynamic development: publication is not a one-off event but an ongoing process, and can be funded not by a single payment but by subscription. If an edition is going to succeed in attracting initial funding and later subscriptions, it will need to be credible as a scholarly project, with the rigorous quality control over the editorial processes that would be found in print projects, but also over issues specific to electronic scale, such as sound selection of content in relation to purpose, coherent forms of linking to enable effective navigation, fully articulated systems of file-labelling to enable different varieties of electronic searching, robust forms of encoding to ensure compatibility with different systems and longevity, and a secure place of archival deposit that will deal with issues relating to both public access and, again, the longer-term durability of the resource.

The procedures for such an edition are therefore going to include some version of the established procedures for establishing the text found in print editions, but will focus also on the particular circumstances of the electronic medium. Typographical effects that are directly mimicked by the editor of a print edition will be determined, in their on-screen virtual equivalents, by systems of text coding such as those developed by the Text Encoding Initiative.[9] The following is part of the simplified coding adopted for Shakespeare Internet Editions, which is the leading project of its kind at the time of writing:[10]

<TITLEHEAD> </TITLEHEAD>

Title page material in quartos; initial heading in Folio.

<LD> </LD>

Literary Division (e.g. Act, Scene.).

<S> </S> Speech.

Includes the speech prefix and any included stage directions (</S> may appear at the end of a hung word).

<SP> </SP> Speaker Prefix.

norm=Name *Normalized form of the name; must be included in every instance of a speech prefix, but not in the course of a speech.

*Example: <SP norm=Hamlet>Ham.</SP>.

<SD> </SD> Stage Direction.

Each line of a split direction in the right hand margin should be tagged separately; directions different in kind should also be tagged separately.

*t =[type] entrance | exit | setting | sound | delivery | whoto | action | other

Example: <SD t= exit> *Exeunt.*</SD> <SD t=sound>*Alarum*</SD>.

Of course there will be single instructions that include more than one kind of direction, in which case you should choose what you judge to be the most important: <SD t=entrance> *Enter Macbeths Wife alone with a Letter.*</SD>.

<VERSEQUOTE> </VERSEQUOTE>

*Verse quotation (e.g. song).

source= When the verse is a quotation from another source, the source should be recorded (as in Pistol's quotations from earlier plays).

<PROSEQUOTE> </PROSEQUOTE>

*Prose quotation (e.g. quoted letter).

source= (As for verse.)

<MODE> </MODE>

*Indicator of verse or prose.

*t=[mode] prose | verse | uncertain

Example: <MODE t=prose> ... </MODE>. Note that you may choose to use a type of "uncertain" where it is not clear that the section is either verse or prose.

<FOREIGN> </FOREIGN>

Language when not English. Used for the content of speeches only, not Latin stage directions, literary divisions etc.

lang= Type. Example <FOREIGN lang=French>Diable!</FOR-EIGN>.

Each pair of mark-up codes encloses the affected text, with the forward slash identifying the code that ends the section. The refinement of 't=' enables editors to specify a sub-type, as in the example of stage directions, which can be divided into eight categories. The mark-ups illustrated here are concerned with identifying the formal function of text, whether distinguishing between dialogue and non-spoken elements such as stage directions, or marking differentiations within the dialogue. In addition to these mark-ups, there are further ones to deal exclusively with printing elements such as special typographical sorts. From these codes, software will generate an on-screen presentation in which the coding is hidden but used to generate features of layout. The aim of the coding is to enable the presentation, but not to determine detail such as the choice of font. It also creates a supporting framework for selective searching and manipulation of the text.

The development of the electronic edition of each play in Internet Shakespeare Editions is in the hands of a single editor or pair of editors, as with print editions. Despite these aims, it might be alleged that Internet Shakespeare Editions is compromised in its commitment to the print medium as well. Conventional edited texts will be published in print by Broadview Press. Perhaps it is useful for the project to signal that the two media can both find a place in the overall integrated project. Perhaps this symbiosis of media represents a more mature stage of development than the earlier Utopian vision of electronic text inexorably sweeping aside the older technology. Certainly it draws attention to the relatively conservative structure of Internet Shakespeare Editions even before the print series was attached to it. The project's emphasis on quality of editorial input and effectiveness of output will lead to selective, limited, and carefully structured editions centred on a text edited in a similar way to print editions. Indeed, the editorial guidelines are based on those devised by David Bevington for the Revels series of print editions of non-Shakespeare plays. As is declared on the website: 'Much about the editions will be the same as those prepared for print: the same high standards of scholarship, the same activities involved in arriving at the modern text, and the same kinds of supporting discussions on the text.' An Internet Shakespeare Edition may still aspire to conform to Jerome J. McGann's description of a critical edition as having the 'ultimate goal of critical self-consciousness', a phrase that usefully suggests a line that might be drawn between an edition and a database.[11]

This is certainly not to say that Shakespeare Internet Editions is simply an online version of a print edition. The files will be capable of being manipulated by the user, and there is considerable scope for and expectation of additional files, along with links to external websites. What emerges is that, despite the rapid changes in patterns of reading and research that have taken place since computers became the primary mode of scholarly communication, the aesthetics and pedagogy of studying a Shakespeare play are sufficiently robust for the readable and therefore conventionally edited text to retain its centrality.

The current interface of technologies is unlike anything seen since the coming of the printing press. It may well be that the book and the culture of the book are in their final days, and that structures of reading experience and literary appreciation will reorient themselves to the new media to the extent that the notion of reading a whole play and the kinds of response expected of such a reading will become obsolescent. Certainly, an electronic edition or archive is not a significatorily neutral alternative to print. The medium pushes towards redefining the act of reading as cross-referential, reconfigurable, discontinuous, and unrepeatable. Almost certainly, it will become more incumbent on editors of electronic projects to be explicit about the nature of the electronic edifice they construct and the way in which it determines a specific set of experiences of the work.[12]

At the level of linguistic code, the text of Shakespeare will almost certainly be preserved. But our ways of reading Shakespeare will evolve in conjunction with the developing textual economy of the digital age. What Shakespeare means to his readers will depend on the modes in which he is read. There is nothing dystopian or fatalistic in such a statement, for readers will make choices about how they read that will help shape the directions that technology takes.[13] It is not inevitable that the modes of reading associated with complete electronic projects will put an end to the reading of Shakespeare's plays as literary and dramatic works. Perhaps the utility of the fully articulated electronic edition is not to enable and therefore transform reading, but to enable activities that supplement reading. In that case the book-model edition may retain its place.

It might survive the end of the book itself if that were to happen. The book is vulnerable in two important respects: as a textual unit it is intrinsically more expensive than an equivalent electronic product, and ecologically it is inefficient. A book makes significant demands on labour, transport, and trees. But these comments refer to the book as a material object, which is not necessarily coterminous with book-originated ways of reading. Books may be replaced with portable, light, robust, and preferably size-adjustable electronic text-readers with a screen as clear and easy on the eye as paper. It may even be that such a text-reader or ebook will accommodate editions that foster that most bookish of qualities, a critical self-consciousness.

A Passage from Hamlet *in Q1 and Q2*

From *The Tragicall Historie of Hamlet Prince of Denmarke* (Q1; 1603)

Looke you now, here is your husband,
With a face like *Vulcan*.
A looke fit for a murder and a rape,
A dull dead hanging looke, and a hell-bred eie,
To affright children and amaze the world:
And this same haue you left to change with this.
What Diuell thus hath cosoned you at hob-man blinde?
A! haue you eyes and can you looke on him
That slew my father, and your deere husband,
To liue in the incestuous pleasure of his bed?
   Queene O Hamlet, speake no more.
   Ham. To leaue him that bare a Monarkes minde,
For a king of clowts, of very shreads.
   Queene. Sweete Hamlet cease.
   Ham. Nay but still to persist and dwell in sinne,
To sweate vnder the yoke of infamie,
To make increase of shame, to steale damnation.
   Queene Hamlet, no more.
   Ham. Why appetite with you is in the waine,
Your blood runnes backeward now from whence it came,
Who le chide hote blood within a Virgins heart,
When lust shall dwell within a matrons breast?
   Queene Hamlet, thou cleaues my heart in twaine.
   Ham. O throw away the worser part of it, and keepe the better.
         Enter the ghost in his night gowne.

From *The Tragicall Historie of Hamlet, Prince of Denmarke* (Q2; 1604–5)

Heere is your husband like a mildewed eare,
Blasting his wholesome brother, haue you eyes,
Could you on this faire mountaine leaue to feede,
And batten on this Moore; ha, haue you eyes?
You cannot call it loue, for at your age
The heyday in the blood is tame, it's humble,
And waits vppon the iudgement, and what iudgement
Would step from this to this, sence sure you haue
Els could you not haue motion, but sure that sence
Is appoplext, for madnesse would not erre
Nor sence to extacie was nere so thral'd
But it reseru'd some quantity of choice
To serue in such a difference, what deuill wast
That thus hath cosund you at hodman blind;
Eyes without feeling, feeling without sight,
Eares without hands, or eyes, smelling sance all,
Or but a sickly part of one true sence
Could not so mope: ô shame where is thy blush?
Rebellious hell,
If thou canst mutine in a Matrons bones,
To flaming youth let vertue be as wax
And melt in her owne fire, proclaime no shame
When the compulsiue ardure giues the charge,
Since frost it selfe as actiuely doth burne,
And reason pardons will.
　　Ger. O *Hamlet* speake no more,
Thou turnst my very eyes into my soule,
And there I see such blacke and greeued spots
As will leaue there their tin'ct.
　　Ham. Nay but to liue
In the ranck sweat of an inseemed bed
Stewed in corruption, honying, and making loue
Ouer the nasty stie.
　　Ger. O speake to me no more,
These words like daggers enter in my eares,
No more sweete *Hamlet.*
　　Ham. A murtherer and a villaine,
A slaue that is not twentith part the kyth
Of your precedent Lord, a vice of Kings,
A cut-purse of the Empire and the rule,
That from a shelfe the precious Diadem stole
And put it in his pocket.
　　Ger. No more.
　　　　　　　Enter Ghost.
　　Ham. A King of sheds and patches,

Shakespeare in Early Editions and Manuscripts

I. QUARTOS AND OCTAVOS BY YEAR OF PUBLICATION, 1592–1640

1592	*Arden of Faversham Q1*
1593	*Venus and Adonis Q1*
1594	*Titus Andronicus* Q1, *The First Part of the Contention (2 Henry VI)* Q1, *The Rape of Lucrece* Q1, *Venus and Adonis* Q2
1595	*Richard Duke of York (3 Henry VI)* O1, *Venus and Adonis* Q3
1596	*Edward III* Q1, *Venus and Adonis* Q4
1597	*Richard II* Q1, *Richard III* Q1, *Romeo and Juliet* Q1
1598	*1 Henry IV* Q1/0 and Q2/1, *Love's Labour's Lost* Q1, *The Rape of Lucrece* Q2, *Richard II* Q2 and Q3, *Richard III* Q2
1599	*The Passionate Pilgrim* O1 and O2, *Arden of Faversham* Q2, *Venus and Adonis* Q5 and Q6, *Edward III* Q2, *Romeo and Juliet* Q2, *1 Henry IV* Q3/2
1600	*Henry V* Q1, *2 Henry IV* Q1, *Much Ado About Nothing* Q1, *A Midsummer Night's Dream* Q1, *The Merchant of Venice* Q1, *Titus Andronicus* Q2, *The First Part of the Contention (2 Henry VI)* Q2, *The Rape of Lucrece* Q3 and Q4, *Richard Duke of York* Q2
1601	'The Phoenix and the Turtle', appended to Robert Chester, *Love's Martyr* Q1
1602	*The Merry Wives of Windsor* Q1, *Venus and Adonis* Q7, *Richard III* Q3, *Henry V* Q2
1603	*Hamlet* Q1
1604	*1 Henry IV* Q4/3
1604–5	*Hamlet* Q2

1605	*Richard III* Q4
1607	*The Rape of Lucrece* Q5
c. 1607	*Venus and Adonis* Q8
1608	*King Lear* Q1, *Richard II* Q4, *1 Henry IV* Q5/4
c.1608	*Venus and Adonis* Q9
1609	*Troilus and Cressida* Q1, *Pericles* Q1 and Q2, *Sonnets* Q1, *Romeo and Juliet* Q3
c. 1610	*Venus and Adonis* Q10
1611	*Titus Andronicus* Q3, *The Phoenix and the Turtle* Q2, *Hamlet* Q3, *Pericles* Q3
1612	*Richard III* Q5, *The Passionate Pilgrim* O3
1613	*1 Henry IV* Q6/5
1615	*Richard II* Q5
1616	*The Rape of Lucrece* Q6
1617	*Venus and Adonis* Q11
1619	*The Whole Contention* (*The First Part of the Contention* Q3 and *Richard Duke of York* Q3), *Henry V* Q3, *A Midsummer Night's Dream* Q2, *The Merchant of Venice* Q2, *The Merry Wives of Windsor* Q2, *King Lear* Q2, *Pericles* Q4
1620	*Venus and Adonis* Q12
c. 1621–2	*Romeo and Juliet* Q4, *Hamlet* Q4
1622	*Othello* Q1, *Richard III* Q6, *1 Henry IV* Q7/6
1624	*The Rape of Lucrece* Q7
1627	*Venus and Adonis* Q13
1629	*Richard III* Q7
1630	*Venus and Adonis* Q14, *The Merry Wives of Windsor* Q3, *Pericles* Q5, *Othello* Q2
c. 1630–6	*Venus and Adonis* Q15
1631	*Love's Labour's Lost* Q2
1632	*The Rape of Lucrece* Q8, *1 Henry IV* Q8/7
1633	*Arden of Faversham* Q3
1634	*The Two Noble Kinsmen* Q1, *Richard II* Q6, *Richard III* Q8
1635	*Pericles* Q6
1636	*Venus and Adonis* Q16
1637	*Romeo and Juliet* Q5, *The Merchant of Venice* Q3, *Hamlet* Q5
1639	*1 Henry IV* Q9/8
1640	*Poems*

2. WORKS BY TITLE: DATES OF COMPOSITION AND DETAILS OF PUBLICATION

This is a listing by title, with date of composition, followed by a bibliography of first editions and other substantive editions, and a summary of reprints. It includes works currently thought to be wholly or partly by Shakespeare, with the exception of the non-dramatic oddments brought together under the heading 'Poems Attributed to Shakespeare in the Seventeenth Century' in Colin Burrow (ed.), *Complete Poems and Sonnets* (Oxford, 2002). It does not include apocryphal works such as *A Yorkshire Tragedy*, nor texts that are related to Shakespeare's works but that are linguistically unShakespearian, such as *The Taming of A Shrew* (1594) and *The Troublesome Reign of King John* (1591), nor passages quoted in compilations such as *England's Helicon*.

The format of editions is quarto unless otherwise noted. Where works were excluded from the Folio (F), a note is made to that effect. In the notes of entries in the Stationers' Register (SR), only significant variants of the printed title page are recorded. Unless otherwise noted, where there is an SR entry the stationer(s) to whom the title was assigned or transferred issued the immediately following edition. Similarly, unless otherwise noted, reprints were issued by the previous stationer to have been named, and were generally set from the immediately preceding quarto or octavo edition. Details of printers are given only for first and other substantive editions.

Transcripts of titles, provided for the first edition and later substantive editions, follow the spellings and punctuation of the originals. However, capitals are normalized to lower case where allowable, and variant typefaces such as italic are normalized to roman. In the originals there is usually a printed ornament between the title etc. and the imprint. Plays were originally printed without act divisions unless otherwise noted.

For reprints, brief bibliographical notes, details of changes of publisher, and altered title-page information about performance details and author attribution are added in brackets.

All Is True (1613)

Now attributed to Shakespeare and John Fletcher.

First published in F as *Henry VIII*.

All's Well That Ends Well (1604–5)   First published in F.

Antony and Cleopatra (1606)

    SR: Entered 20 May 1608 to Edward Blount, with allowance.

First published in F.

Arden of Faversham (1587–92)

Sometimes attributed partly to Shakespeare.

> *SR: Entered 3 April 1592 to Edward White, with allowance.*

Q1 1592. 'The lamentable and trve tragedie of M. Arden of Feversham in Kent. Who was most wickedlye murdered, by the meanes of his disloyall and wanton wyfe, who for the loue she bare to one Mosbie, hyred two desperat ruffins Blackwill and Shakbag, to kill him. Wherin is shewed the great mallice and discimulation of a wicked woman, the vnsatiable desire of filthie lust and the shamefull end of all murderers. Imprinted at London for Edward White, dwelling at the lyttle north dore of Paules church at the signe of the gun. 1592.' Printed by Peter Short.

> *SR: entry of 18 December 1592 records Stationers' Court order that copies of an edition printed by Abel Jeffes be confiscated. No copies survive.*

Q2 1599 (Edward White).

> *SR: Transferred 24 June 1624 from the widow of White (junior) to Edward Allde.*

Q3 1633 (Elizabeth Allde; variant title pages 'Printed by Eliz. Allde dwelling neere Christs-Church' and 'Printed by Eliz. Allde, and are to be sold by Stephen Pemel at the signe of the black bull on London Bridge').
Not in F.

As You Like It (1599–1600)

> *SR: 'staied' 4 August 1600.*

First published in F.

Comedy of Errors (1594)   First published in F.

1 Contention (*2 Henry VI*) (1591)

> *SR: Entered 12 March 1594 to Thomas Millington.*

Q1 1594. 'The first part of the contention betwixt the two famous houses of Yorke and Lancaster, with the death of the good Duke Humphrey: and the banishment and death of the Duke of Suffolke, and the tragicall end of the proud Cardinall of Winchester, with the notable rebellion of Iacke Cade: and the Duke of Yorkes first claime vnto the crowne. London Printed by Thomas Creed, for Thomas Millington, and are to be sold at his shop vnder Saint Peters church in Cornwall. 1594.' Variant text of Folio *2 Henry VI*.
Q2 1600.

> *SR: Transferred 19 April 1602 to Thomas Pavier.*

Q3 1619, with *Richard Duke of York*, as 'The whole contention betweene the two famous houses, Lancaster and Yorke' (Thomas Pavier, undated, printed from Q1, 'written by William Shake-speare, Gent.').

> *SR: Transferred 4 August 1626 from widow of Pavier to Edward Brewster and Robert Bird as part of 'Paviers right in Shakesperes plaies or any of them'.*

Coriolanus (1608)   First published in F.

Cymbeline (1610)   First published in F.

Edward III (1595)

Usually now attributed to Shakespeare and others.

> *SR: Entered 1 December 1595 to Cuthbert Burby: 'Edward the Third and the Blacke Prince their warres with Kinge John of Fraunce'.*

Q1 1596. 'The raigne of King Edward the third: As it hath bin sundrie times plaied about the citie of London. London, printed for Cuthbert Burby. 1596.' Printed by Thomas Scarlet.

Q2 1599.

> *Transferred in SR: 16 October 1609 from the widow of Burby to William Welby; 2 March 1618 to Thomas Snodham; 23 February 1626 from the widow of Snodham to William Stansby; 4 March 1639 from Stansby deceased, with the consent of his widow, to Richard Bishop.*

Not in F.

Hamlet (1600–1)

> *SR: Entered 26 July 1602 to James Roberts, with allowance: 'a booke called the Revenge of Hamlett Prince Denmarke as yt was latelie Acted by the Lo: Chamberleyn his servantes'.*

Q1 1603. 'The tragicall historie of Hamlet Prince of Denmarke by William Shake-speare. As it hath beene diuerse times acted by his highnesse seruants in the cittie of London: as also in the two vniuersities of Cambridge and Oxford, and else-where At London printed for N.L. and Iohn Trundell. 1603.' 'N.L.' = Nicholas Ling. Short and heavily variant text on Q2 and F.

Q2 1604–5. 'The tragicall historie of Hamlet, Prince of Denmarke. By William Shakespeare. Newly imprinted and enlarged to almost as much againe as it was, according to the true and perfect coppie. At London, printed by I.R. for N.L. and are to be sold at his shoppe vnder Saint Dunstons church in Fleetstreet. 1604.' Variant title page dated '1605'. 'I.R.' = James Roberts. 'N.L.' = Nicholas Ling. A longer and evidently more authorial text than Q1.

> *SR: Transferred 19 November 1607 from Ling to John Smethwick.*

Q3 1611. Q4 undated; *c.* 1621–2 (printed from Q3). Q5 1637.

1 Henry IV (1596–7)

> *SR: Entered 25 February 1598 to Andrew Wise, with allowance: 'The historye of Henry the iiijth wth his battaile at Shrewsburye against Henry Hottspurre of the Northe wth the conceipted mirthe of Sr Iohn Falstoff'.*

Q1/0 [1598]. An undated edition known only by a single sheet (C) of a single copy. Printed by an unidentified printer, presumably for Andrew Wise. Identified as Q1 in the Oxford *Complete Works*, Q0 elsewhere.

Q2/1 1598. 'The history of Henrie the Fovrth; with the battell at Shrewsburie, betweene the King and Lord Henry Percy, surnamed Henrie Hotspur of the North. With the humorous conceits of Sir Iohn Falstalffe. At London, printed by P.S. for Andrew Wise, dwelling in Paules churchyard, at the signe of the angell. 1598.' 'P.S.' = Peter Short.

Q3/2 1599 ('Newly corrected by W. Shake-speare').

> *SR: Transferred 25 June 1603 to Matthew Law.*

Q4/3 1604. Q5/4 1608. Q6/5 1613. Q7/6 1622. Q8/7 1632 (John Norton). Q9/8 1639.

2 Henry IV (1597–8)

> *SR: Entered 23 August 1600 to Andrew Wise and William Aspley: 'the second p[ar]te of the History of Kinge Henry the iiijth wth the humo^{r}s of Sr Iohn Fallstaffe: Wrytten by m^r Shakespere'.*

Q1 1600. 'The second part of Henrie the fourth, continuing to his death, and coronation of Henrie the fift. With the humours of sir Iohn Fallstaffe, and swaggering Pistoll. As it hath been sundrie times publikely acted by the right honourable, the Lord Chamberlaine his seruants. Written by William Shakespeare. London Printed by V.S. for Andrew Wise, and William Aspley. 1600.' 'V.S.' = Valentine Simmes. First issue lacks scene 3.1. Expanded sheet E in second issue, printed after *Much Ado About Nothing*, includes 3.1.

Henry V (1598–9)

> *SR: 'staied' 4 August 1600.*

Q1 1600. 'The cronicle history of Henry the fift, with his battell fought at Agin Court in France. Togither with Auntient Pistoll. As it hath bene sundry times playd by the right honorable the Lord Chamberlaine his seruants. London Printed by Thomas Creede, for Tho. Millington, and Iohn Busby. And are to be sold at his house in Carter Lane, next the powle head. 1600.' Variant on later and subsequently standard F. Lacks Chorus speeches.

> *SR: Transferred 14 August 1600 to Thomas Pavier.*

Q2 1602. Q3 '1608' (actually 1619; printed from Q1).

> *SR: Possibly transferred 4 August 1626 from widow of Pavier to Edward Brewster and Robert Bird as part of 'Paviers right in Shakesperes plaies or any of them'.*

1 Henry VI (1592; rev. 1594?)

Usually now attributed to Shakespeare, Thomas Nashe, and others.
First published in F.

2 and 3 Henry VI: See *1 Contention* and *Richard Duke of York*.

Henry VIII: See *All Is True*.

Julius Caesar (1599)	First published in F.
King John (1596)	First published in F.

King Lear (1605–6; rev. 1610)

> *SR: Entered 26 November 1607 to Nathaniel Butter and John Busby, with allowance.*

Q1 1608. 'M. William Shak-speare: his true chronicle historie of the life and death of King Lear and his three daughters. With the vnfortunate life of Edgar, sonne and heire to the Earle of Gloster, and his sullen and assumed humor of Tom of Bedlam: as it was played before the Kings maiestie at Whitehall vpon S. Stephans night in Christmas hollidayes. By his maiesties seruants playing vsually at the Gloabe on the Bancke-side. London, printed for Nathaniel Butter, and are to be sold at his shop in Pauls church-yard at the signe of the pide bull neere St. Austins Gate. 1608.' Printed by Nicholas Okes.

Q2 'Printed for Nathaniel Butter. 1608' (actually published by Thomas Pavier, 1619).

Love's Labour's Lost (1594–5)

Q1 1598. 'A pleasant conceited comedie called, loues labors lost. As it was presented before her Highnes this last Christmas. Newly corrected and augmented By W. Shakespere. Imprinted at London by W.W. for Cutbert Burby. 1598.' 'W.W.' = William White. Sometimes thought to replace an earlier edition (Q0), now lost.

> *SR: Transferred 22 January 1607 from Burby to Nicholas Ling, 'by direccon of A Court'. Transferred 19 November 1607 to John Smethwick.*

Q2 1631 (changes details of players to 'Acted by his Maiesties seruants at the Blacke-Friers and the Globe'; 'Written by William Shakespeare').

'Lover's Complaint' (1603–4): See *Sonnets* and *Poems*.

Shakespeare's authorship has been questioned. Not in F.

Macbeth (1606; rev. 1616)

Revision now attributed to Thomas Middleton. First published in F.

Measure for Measure (1603–4; rev. 1621)

Revision now attributed to Thomas Middleton. First published in F.

Merchant of Venice (1596–7)

> SR: *Entered 22 July 1598 to James Roberts, subject to licence from the Lord Chamberlain: 'a booke of the Marchaunt of Venyce or otherwise called the Iewe of Venyce'. SR 28 October 1600, transferred to Thomas Heyes.*

Q1 1600. 'The most excellent historie of the merchant of Venice. With the extreame crueltie of Shylocke the Iewe towards the sayd merchant, in cutting a iust pound of his flesh: and the obtayning of Portia by the choyse of three chests. As it hath beene diuers times acted by the Lord Chamberlaine his seruants. Written by William Shakespeare. At London, printed by I.R. for Thomas Heyes, and are to be sold in Paules church-yard, at the signe of the greene dragon. 1600.' 'I.R.' = James Roberts.

Q2 'Printed by J. Roberts, 1600' (actually published by Thomas Pavier, 1619; lacks details of players).

> SR: *Transferred 8 July 1619 from Heyes, deceased, to Laurence Heyes.*

Q3 1637 (printed from Q1).

Merry Wives of Windsor (1597–8)

> SR: *Entered 18 January 1602 to John Busby: 'a booke called. An excellent & pleasant conceited cõmedie of Sʳ Io. Faulstof and the merry Wyves of Windesor'. SR 18 January 1602, transferred to Arthur Johnson.*

Q1 1602. 'A most pleasaunt and excellent conceited comedie, of Syr Iohn Falstaffe, and the merrie wiues of Windsor. Entermixed with sundrie variable and pleasing humors, of Syr Hugh the Welch knight, Iustice Shallow, and his wise cousin M. Slender. With the swaggering vaine of Auncient Pistoll, and Corporall Nym. By William Shakespeare. As it hath bene diuers times acted by the right honorable my Lord Chamberlaines seruants. Both before her maiestie, and else-where. London Printed by T.C. for Arthur Iohnson, and are to be sold at his shop in Powles church-yard, at the signe of the flower de leuse and the crowne. 1602.' 'T.C.' = Thomas Creede. Short and heavily variant text on later and subsequently standard F.

Q2 1619 (as published by Arthur Johnson, actually published by Thomas Pavier; lacks performance details; 'Written by W. Shakespeare').

SR: Transferred 29 January 1630 from Johnson to Richard Meighen.

Q3 1630 (printed from F).

Midsummer Night's Dream (1595)

SR: Entered 8 October 1600 to Thomas Fisher, with allowance.

Q1 1600. 'A midsommer nights dreame. As it hath beene sundry times publikely acted, by the right honourable, the Lord Chamberlaine his seruants. Written by William Shakespeare. Imprinted at London, for Thomas Fisher, and are to be soulde at his shoppe, at the signe of the white hart, in Fleetestreete. 1600.' Printed by Richard Bradock.

Q2 'Printed by Iames Roberts, 1600' (actually published by Thomas Pavier, 1619).

Much Ado About Nothing (1598)

SR: 'staied' 4 August 1600: 'the cōmedie of Muche A doo about Nothinge/A booke'. SR: Entered 23 August 1600 to Andrew Wise and William Aspley: 'Muche a Doo about Nothinge'.

Q1 1600. 'Much adoe about nothing. As it hath been sundrie times publikely acted by the right honourable, the Lord Chamberlain his seruants. Written by William Shakespeare. London Printed by V.S. for Andrew Wise, and William Aspley. 1600.' 'V.S.' = Valentine Simmes.

Othello (1603–4)

SR: Entered 6 October 1621 to Thomas Walkley, with allowance.

Q1 1622. 'The tragedy of Othello, the Moore of Venice. As it hath beene diuerse times acted at the Globe, and at the Black-friers, by his maiesties seruants. Written by William Shakespeare. London, printed by N.O. for Thomas Walkely, and are to be sold at his shop, at the eagle and child, in Brittans Bursse. 1622.' 'N.O.' = Nicholas Okes. Printed with act divisions.

SR: Transferred 1 March 1628 to Richard Hawkins.

Q2 1630 (printed from Q1, with reference to F).

Passionate Pilgrim (1593–9)

A collection of poems including variants of Sonnets 138 and 144 and three sonnet passages from *Love's Labour's Lost*. Others are doubtfully ascribed to Shakespeare, or are demonstrably not by Shakespeare.

O1 [1599?] (octavo). Printed by Thomas Judson, for William Jaggard? Single extant copy lacks title page.

O2 1599 (octavo). 'The passionate pilgrime. By W. Shakespeare. At London Printed for W. Iaggard, and are to be sold by W. Leake, at the greyhound in Paules churchyard. 1599.' Printed by Thomas Judson.

O3 1612 (octavo). Expanded edition, 'where-unto is added two loue-epistles, the first from Paris to Hellen, and Hellens answere backe againe to Paris'. Added material from Thomas Heywood, *Troia Brittanica*. Variant title pages, with and without Shakespeare's name.

Not in F. See also *Poems*.

Pericles (1607)

Usually now attributed to Shakespeare and George Wilkins.

> *SR: Entered 20 May 1608 to Edward Blount, with allowance.*

Q1 1609. 'The late, and much admired play, called Pericles, Prince of Tyre. With the true relation of the whole historie, aduentures, and fortunes of the said prince: as also, the no lesse strange, and worthy accidents, in the birth and life, of his daughter Mariana. As it hath been diuers and sundry times acted by his maiesties seruants, at the Globe on the Banck-side. By William Shakespeare. Imprinted at London for Henry Gosson, and are to be sold at the signe of the sun in Pater-noster row, &c. 1609.' Printed by William White.

Q2 1609. Q3 1611 (printed and perhaps published by 'S.S.' = Simon Stafford). Q4 1619 (Thomas Pavier; lacks Qq1-3's performance details).

> *SR: Transferred 4 August 1626 from widow of Pavier to Edward Brewster and Robert Bird as part of 'Paviers right in Shakesperes plaies or any of them'.*

Q5 1630 (Robert Bird)

> *SR: Transferred 8 November 1630 from Bird to Richard Cotes.*

Q6 1635 (printed probably from Q4).
Not in F.

'Phoenix and Turtle' (1590–1601), appended to Robert Chester, *Love's Martyr*

Q1 1601. 'Loves martyr: or, Rosalins complaint. Allegorically shadowing the truth of loue, in the constant fate of the phoenix and turtle. A poeme enterlaced with much varietie and raritie; now first translated out of the venerable Italian Torquato Caeliano, by Robert Chester. With the true legend of famous King Arthur, the last of the nine worthies, being the first essay of a new Brytish poet: collected out of diuerse authenticall records. To these are added some new compositions, of seuerall moderne writers whose names are subscribed to their seuerall workes, vpon the first subiect: viz. the phoenix and turtle. Mar:—Mutare dominum non potest liber notus. London Imprinted for E.B. 1601.' Printed by Richard Field. Published by Edward Blount. Poem untitled but in section headed 'Diverse poeticall essaies on the former subiect; viz: the Turtle and Phoenix'; ascribed to 'William Shake-speare'.

Q2 1611. 'The anuals of Great Brittaine ...' (sheets of Q1 reissued with a new title page; published by Matthew Lownes).

Not in F. See also *Poems*.

Poems (1590–1604; 1640 edition)

Contains reprints of all but eight of the sonnets (with alterations), 'A Lover's Complaint', all poems in *The Passionate Pilgrim*, 'The Phoenix and Turtle', and poems by various other authors.

O1 1640 (octavo). 'Poems: written by Wil. Shake-speare. Gent. Printed at London by Tho. Cotes, and are to be sold by Iohn Benson, dwelling in St. Dunstans church-yard. 1640.'

Rape of Lucrece (1593–4)

> SR: *Entered 9 May 1594 to John Harrison: 'The Ravyshement of Lucrece'.*

Q1 1594. 'Lvcrece. London. Printed by Richard Field, for Iohn Harrison, and are to be sold at the signe of the white greyhound in Paules churh-yard. 1594.' Dedication signed 'William Shakespeare'. Head title 'The rape of Lvcrece'.

Q2 1598 (octavo). Q3 1600 (octavo). Q4 1600 (octavo). Q5 1607 (octavo).

> SR: *Transferred 1 March 1614 to Roger Jackson.*

Q6 1616 (octavo). Q7 1624 (octavo).

> SR: *Transferred 29 June 1630 to John Harrison.*

Q8 1632 (octavo).
Not in F.

Richard Duke of York (*3 Henry VI*) (1591)

Sometimes suspected to have non-Shakespearian passages.

O1 1595 (octavo). 'The true tragedie of Richard Duke of Yorke, and the death of good King Henrie the Sixt, with the whole contention betweene the two houses Lancaster and Yorke, as it was sundrie times acted by the right honourable the Earl of Pembrooke his seruants. Printed at London by P.S. for Thomas Millington, and are to be sold at his shoppe vnder Saint Peters church in Cornwal. 1595.' Variant text of Folio *3 Henry VI*. Thomas Millington. 'P.S.' = Peter Short.

Q2 1600.

SR: Transferred 19 April 1602 to Thomas Pavier.

Q3 1619 (printed from O1; lacks performance details): see *1 Contention.*

SR: Transferred 4 August 1626 from widow of Pavier to Edward Brewster and Robert Bird as part of 'Paviers right in Shakesperes plaies or any of them'.

Richard II (1595)

SR: Entered 29 August 1597 to Andrew Wise.

Q1 1597. 'The tragedie of King Richard the second. As it hath beene publikely acted by the right honourable the Lorde Chamberlaine his seruants. London Printed by Valentine Simmes for Androw Wise, and are to be sold at his shop in Paules church yard at the signe of the angel. 1597.' Lacks the 'deposition scene' (4.1.145–308).
Q2 1598 ('By William Shake-speare'). Q3 1598.

SR: Transferred 25 June 1603 to Matthew Law.

Q4 1608 (contains first printing of the deposition scene; variant title advertises the addition and revises players to 'the Kinges Maiesties seruantes, at the Globe'). Q5 1615. Q6 1634 (John Norton; printed from F2).

Richard III (1592–3)

SR: Entered 20 October 1597 to Andrew Wise, with allowance: 'the tragedie of kinge Richard the Third wth the death of the duke of Clarence'.

Q1 1597. 'The tragedy of King Richard the third. Containing, his treacherous plots against his brother Clarence: the pittiefull murther of his iunocent nephewes: his tyrannicall vsurpation: with the whole course of his detested life, and most deserued death. As it hath beene lately acted by the right honourable the Lord Chamberlaine his seruants. At London Printed by Valentine Sims, for Andrew Wise, dwelling in Paules church-yard, at the signe of the angel. 1597.' Actually printed by Valentine Simmes and Peter Short.
Q2 1598 ('By William Shake-speare'). Q3 1602.

SR: Transferred 25 June 1603 to Matthew Law.

Q4 1605 ('and are to be sold by Matthew Lawe'). Q5 1612 (printed from Q3 and Q4; revises players to 'the Kings Maiesties seruants'). Q6 1622. Q7 1629. Q8 1634 (John Norton).

Romeo and Juliet (1595)

Q1 1597. 'An excellent conceited tragedie of Romeo and Iuliet. As it hath been often (with great applause) plaid publiquely, by the right honourable the L. of Hunsdon his seruants. London, printed by Iohn Danter. 1597.' Actually printed by John Danter and Edward Allde. Presumably published by Danter. Variant on later and subsequently standard Q2.

Q2 1599. 'The most excellent and lamentable tragedie, of Romeo and Iuliet. Newly corrected, augmented, and amended: as it hath bene sundry times publiquely acted, by the right honourable the Lord Chamberlaine his seruants. London, printed by Thomas Creede, for Cuthbert Burby, and are to be sold at his shop neare the Exchange. 1599.' From MS, supplemented by Q1 for one substantial passage and perhaps locally elsewhere. A longer and evidently more authorial text than Q1.

> SR: *Transferred 22 January 1607 from Burby to Nicholas Ling. Transferred 19 November 1607 to John Smethwick.*

Q3 1609 (revises players to 'the Kings Maiesties seruants at the Globe'). Q4 undated (*c*. 1621–2; variant title adds 'Written by W. Shake-speare'). Q5 1637.

Sir Thomas More (rev. 1603–4)

Not printed. See '4: Works in Manuscript'.

Sonnets (1593–1603)

Also contains 'A Lover's Complaint'.

> SR: *Entered 20 May 1609 to Thomas Thorpe.*

Q1 1609. 'Shake-speares sonnets. Never before imprinted. At London By G. Eld for T.T. and are to be solde by Iohn Wright, dwelling at Christ church gate. 1609.' 'T.T.' = Thomas Thorpe. Issue with variant title page: '… and are to be solde by William Aspley. 1609'.

Individual sonnets in seventeenth-century manuscripts are listed in Peter Beal, *Index of British Literary Manuscripts*, 2 vols. (London, 1980–93). The manuscript texts include significantly variant versions of Sonnets 2 and 106. See *Textual Companion* 444–5, and *Sonnets*, ed. Katherine Duncan-Jones (London, 1997), 453–66.

Not in F. See also *Passionate Pilgrim* and *Poems*.

### *Taming of the Shrew* (1590–1)	First published in F.
### *Tempest* (1611)	First published in F.

Timon of Athens (1606)

Now attributed to Shakespeare and Thomas Middleton.
First published in F.

Titus Andronicus (1592–3)

Now attributed to Shakespeare and George Peele.

SR: Entered 6 February 1594 to John Danter: 'a Noble Roman Historye of Tytus Andronicus'.

Q<u>1</u> 1594. 'The most lamentable Romaine tragedie of Titus Andronicus: as it was plaide by the right honourable the Earle of Darbie, Earle of Pembroke, and Earle of Sussex their seruants. London, printed by Iohn Danter, and are to be sold by Edward White & Thomas Millington, at the little north doore of Paules at the signe of the gunne. 1594.' Quartos lack the 'fly scene' (3.2).

Q<u>2</u> 1600 (Edward White; adds 'the Lorde Chamberlaine theyr seruants' to the players).

SR: Transferred 19 April 1602 from Millington to Thomas Pavier.

Q<u>3</u> 1611 (octavo in 4s; Edward White; 'As it hath sundry times beene plaide by the Kings Maiesties Seruants').

SR: Possibly transferred 4 August 1626 from widow of Pavier to Edward Brewster and Robert Bird as part of 'Paviers right in Shakesperes plaies or any of them'.

Troilus and Cressida (1602)

SR: Entered 7 February 1603 to James Roberts, 'to print when he hath gotten sufficient aucthority'. Re-entered 28 January 1609 to Richard Bonian and Henry Walley, with allowance.

Q<u>1</u> 1609 (first issue). 'The historie of Troylus and Cresseida. As it was acted by the Kings maiesties seruants at the Globe. Written by William Shakespeare. London Imprinted by G. Eld for R. Bonian and H. Walley, and are to be sold at the spred eagle in Paules church-yeard, ouer against the great north doore. 1609.' Compare SR: 'as yt is acted by my Lord Chamberlens men'.

Q<u>1</u> 1609 (second issue). 'The famous historie of Troylus and Cresseid. Excellently expressing the beginning of their loues, with the conceited wooing of Pandarus Prince of Licia. Written by William Shakespeare. London Imprinted by G. Eld for R. Bonian and H. Walley, and are to be sold at the spred eagle in Paules church-yeard, ouer against the great north doore. 1609.' The title page is followed by an epistle declaring that the play had been 'neuer stal'd with the Stage'. See Chapter 3.

Twelfth Night (1601) First published in F.

Two Gentlemen of Verona (1590–1) First published in F.

Two Noble Kinsmen (1613–14)

Q<u>1</u>'s attribution to John Fletcher and Shakespeare is generally accepted. Not in F.

SR: *Entered 8 April 1634 to John Waterson, with allowance: 'a tragicomedy called the two noble kinsmen, by Jo. Fletcher and Wm. Shakespeare'.*

Q1 1634. 'The two noble kinsmen: Presented at the Blackfriers by the Kings maiesties servants, with great applause: written by the memorable worthies of their time; Mr. John Fletcher, and Mr. William Shakspeare. Gent. Printed at London by Tho. Cotes, for Iohn Waterson: and are to be sold at the signe of the crowne in Pauls church-yard. 1634'. Printed with act divisions.

Venus and Adonis (1592–3)

SR: *Entered 18 April 1593 to Richard Field.*

Q1 1593. 'Venvs and Adonis *Vilia miretur vulgus: mihi flauus Apollo / Pocula Castalia plena ministret aqua.* London Imprinted by Richard Field, and are to be sold at the signe of the white greyhound in Paules church-yard. 1593.' The sign identifies the bookseller as John Harrison.

SR: *Transferred 25 June 1594 to John Harrison.*

Q2 1594 (imprint as Q1 except for date; added dedication signed 'William Shakespeare'). Q3 (octavo) 1595? (single extant copy lacks Sheet A, including title page). Q4 1596 (octavo).

SR: *Transferred 25 June 1596 to William Leake.*

Q5 (octavo) 1599. Q6 (octavo) 1599. Q7 (octavo) 1602. Q8 (octavo) '1602' (*Short-Title Catalogue* (*STC*; 1976–86) suggests actual publication date 1607). Q9 (octavo) '1602' (*STC* suggests actual publication date 1608). Q10 (octavo) '1602' (*STC* suggests actual publication date 1610; only the title page of a single copy survives).

SR: *Transferred 16 February 1617 to William Barrett.*

Q11 1617 (octavo).

SR: *Transferred 8 March 1620 to John Parker.*

Q12 1620 (octavo). Q13 (octavo) 1627 (Edinburgh: John Wreittoun; printed from Q8).

SR: *Transferred 7 May 1626 to John Haviland and John Wright.*

Q14 1630 (octavo; John Haviland). Q15 1630–6? (octavo; single extant copy lacks title page).
Q16 1636 (16mo in 8s; John Haviland).
Not in F.

Winter's Tale (1609)   First published in F.

3. THE 1623 FIRST FOLIO

[*SR: Entered 2 May 1594, to Peter Short, 'a plesant conceyted historie called The Taming of a Shrowe.'*]

SR: Entered 8 November 1623 to Edward Blount and Isaac Jaggard 'Mr William Shakspeers Comedyes Histories, & Tragedyes soe manie of the said Copies as are not formerly entred to other men': The Tempest, The Two Gentlemen of Verona, Measure for Measure, The Comedy of Errors, As You Like It, All's Well That Ends Well, Twelfth Night, The Winter's Tale, '3 part of Hen 6^t' (error for 1 Henry VI?), Henry VIII, Coriolanus, Timon of Athens, Julius Caesar, Macbeth, Antony and Cleopatra, Cymbeline. Omits King John.

'Mr. William Shakespeares comedies, histories, & tragedies. Published according to the true originall copies. London Printed by Isaac Iaggard, and Ed. Blount. 1623.' Actually printed by William and Isaac Jaggard. Colophon identifies publishers: 'Printed at the charges of W. Jaggard, Ed. Blount, I. Smithweeke, and W. Aspley, 1623.' William Jaggard had died by 1623, and his interest was inherited by Isaac.

Titles as given below are normalized in typography and lower-case initials as for the quartos, but otherwise printed as in the head title at the beginning of each play. The more significant variants in running titles and the Catalogue are noted. Plays were printed with act divisions unless otherwise noted.

Notes on the nature of manuscript copy are necessarily conjectural.

Comedies

'The tempest.' Text followed by 'The scene, an vn-inhabited island' and list of 'Names of the actors'. From MS transcribed by Ralph Crane.

'The two gentlemen of Verona.' Text followed by list of 'The names of all the actors.' From MS expurgated and transcribed by Ralph Crane.

'The merry wiues of Windsor.' From MS expurgated and transcribed by Ralph Crane.

'Measvre, for measure.' Text followed by 'The scene Vienna' and list of 'The names of all the actors'. From MS expurgated, thought to have been adapted for revival, and transcribed by Ralph Crane.

'The comedie of errors.' From MS transcribed by Ralph Crane.

'Much adoe about nothing.' From Q1, with reference to a theatre MS.

'Loues labour's lost.' From Q0 or Q1, lightly annotated from a theatre MS.

'A midsommer nights dreame.' From Q2, lightly annotated from a theatre MS.

'The merchant of Venice.' From Q1, probably lightly annotated from a theatre MS.

'As you like it.' From MS.

'The taming of the shrew.' From (theatrical?) MS.

'All's well, that ends well.' 'All is …' in Catalogue. From MS.

'Twelfe night, or what you will.' From MS.

'The winters tale.' Text followed by list of 'The names of the actors'. From MS transcribed by Ralph Crane.

Histories

'The life and death of King Iohn.' From expurgated MS.

'The life and death of King Richard the second.' From Q3, annotated from an expurgated theatre MS, and supplemented with a new text of the deposition scene from the same source.

'The first part of Henry the fourth, with the life and death of Henry sirnamed Hot-spvrre.' To 'fourth' only in Catalogue and running titles. From Q6/5, annotated probably from a transcript of a theatre MS.

'The second part of Henry the fourth, containing his death: and the coronation of King Henry the fift.' To 'fourth' only in Catalogue and running titles. The end of the play is printed on an anomalous four-sheet quire, which includes the epilogue and 'The actors names'. From a transcript of a revised and expurgated theatre MS showing minor influence from Q1.

'The life of Henry the fift.' From authorial MS.

'The first part of Henry the sixt.' From collaborative authorial MS.

'The second part of Henry the sixt, with the death of the good Duke Hvmfrey.' To 'Sixt' only in Catalogue and running titles. Lacks act divisions. From MS, supplemented with Q3 for some passages.

'The third part of Henry the sixt, with the death of the Duke of Yorke.' To 'Sixt' only in Catalogue and running titles. Lacks act divisions. From MS, with reference to Q3.

'The tragedy of Richard the third: with the landing of Earle Richmond, and the battell at Bosworth Field.' Running title 'The Life and Death of Richard the Third'. Catalogue similarly. From Q3 and Q6, heavily annotated from a MS.

'The famous history of the life of King Henry the eight.' 'Famous history of the' omitted in Catalogue and running titles. Also known as *All Is True*. From MS.

Between Histories and Tragedies

'The tragedie of Troylus and Cressida.' Running titles 'The tragedie of Troilus and Cressida' ($\chi 2$ and $\chi 2^v$) and 'Troylus and Cressida' (thereafter). Lacks act divisions. The first two leaves, unsigned but conventionally identified as $\chi 2$ and $\chi 2$, were originally printed to follow *Romeo and Juliet*, this being the position originally intended for *Troilus and Cressida*. The recto of $\chi 1$, the leaf whose verso prints the beginning of the play, is found in two states: (*a*) with the last page of *Romeo*, (*b*) with the Prologue to *Troilus and Cressida*. The rest of the play after the first two leaves was printed when other work on F was complete. The play is not included in the Catalogue, which had already been printed. From Q1, with thorough annotation from a MS.

Tragedies

'The tragedy of Coriolanus.' From MS.

'The lamentable tragedy of Titus Andronicus.' 'Titus Andronicus' in Catalogue. 'Lamentable' omitted in running titles. From Q3, with light annotation and addition of the 'fly scene' (3.2) from a theatre MS.

'The tragedie of Romeo and Ivliet.' 'Romeo and Juliet' in Catalogue. Lacks act divisions. From Q3, perhaps with light annotation from MS.

'The life of Tymon of Athens.' 'Timon of Athens' in Catalogue and running titles. Text followed by list of 'The actors names'. Lacks act divisions. From collaborative authorial MS. Introduced to replace *Troilus and Cressida*, which was originally assigned to this position.

'The tragedie of Ivlivs Caesar.' 'The life and death of Julius Caesar' in Catalogue. From MS.

'The tragedie of Macbeth.' From MS, thought to have been adapted for revival.

'The tragedie of Hamlet, Prince of Denmarke.' 'Prince of Denmarke' omitted in Catalogue and running titles. From a revised MS, with possible reference to Q3.

'The tragedie of King Lear.' 'King Lear' in Catalogue. From Q2, heavily annotated from a revised MS.

'The tragedie of Othello, the moor of Venice.' 'The tragedie of' omitted in Catalogue. Text followed by list of 'The names of the actors.' From MS, a revised text transcribed probably by Ralph Crane, with probable influence from Q1.

'The tragedie of Anthonie, and Cleopatra.' Catalogue 'Antony and Cleopater'. Lacks act divisions. From MS.

'The tragedie of Cymbeline.' 'Cymbeline King of Britain.' in Catalogue. From MS.

The Second Folio

SR: The sixteen titles entered in 1623 transferred on 16 November 1630 from Edward Blount to Robert Allott.

F2: 1632.

4. WORKS IN MANUSCRIPT

Sir Thomas More

Play in manuscript (British Library Harleian 7368). Original text in the hand of Anthony Munday, a fair copy transcribed probably mid- to late-1590s, with censorship annotations particularly by Edmund Tilney (Master of the Revels). Revisions on separate interleaved leaves and pasted-in part-leaves, composed probably 1603–4, in hands identified as Henry Chettle, Thomas Dekker, Thomas Heywood, and Shakespeare, with transcriptions and annotations by a theatre scribe ('Hand C'). Original Text now usually attributed to Munday and Chettle.

Henry IV (**The Dering Manuscript**)

Play in manuscript (Folger V.d.34). A 1623 conflation based mainly on *1 Henry IV* (Q7/6) and partly on *2 Henry IV* (Q1). In the hand of a scribe identified, from the payment of 4 shillings for the task by Sir Edward Dering (1598–1644), as 'Mr Carington' (perhaps Samuel Carington, rector of Wotton, Kent). Revised in Dering's hand.

Sonnets: See '2. Works by Title'.

Glossary of Key Terms

accidentals In 'The Rationale of Copy-Text' W. W. Greg distinguished between 'accidental' and '*substantive*' readings. 'Substantives' are words as conveyors of meaning; 'accidentals' are other more incidental features of the text such as spelling and punctuation. The distinction is far from absolute.

allowance The official authorization required for printing a potentially controversial book. Controlled by the ecclesiastical authorities, though from 1610 for plays this authority was devolved to the Master of the Revels. Distinct from the licence issued by the Stationers' Company: see *Stationers' Register*.

authority (*a*) In editing, the reliability of a text as a witness to an underlying text that is the object of editorial recovery. (*b*) In the study of printed books, equivalent to *allowance*.

autograph Manuscript written in the author's own hand. The 'Hand D' section of *Sir Thomas More* is the one probable example of an autograph manuscript of Shakespeare's dramatic writing or poetry.

'bad' quarto A heavily altered and usually shortened text printed in *quarto*. The alterations have been frequently ascribed to *memorial reconstruction* in combination with theatrical adaptation. The term is now contentious for its polarization of texts according to a quasi-moral evaluation. Alternatives such as 'suspect' or 'short' have not won wide acceptance, partly because there is no agreement as to the contents and viability of the category itself.

base text The early text on which a modern edition is primarily based. Favoured in recent editions in the Arden Shakespeare series as an alternative to *copy-text* or *control text*. The former has reduced meaning for modern-spelling editions and is sometimes paradoxically and pejoratively associated with a form of editing that characteristically departs from copy.

cancel   When a serious error in the setting and printing of a sheet was discovered, it could be rectified by reprinting either the whole sheet or individual
leaves (or conjugate pairs of leaves). If individual leaves were replaced, the
new printing needed to be pasted onto the stub of the original. The rejected printing is technically called the 'cancellandum', and its replacement the
'cancellans'. A cancelled sheet in the 1623 Folio occurs at the beginning of
Troilus and Cressida (see Chapter 3). In Q1 *2 Henry IV* an entire scene (3.1)
was omitted by accident; when the mistake was discovered, the scene was
included by cancelling the third and fourth leaves of the original sheet E, and
replacing them with a new sheet of four leaves. As the first two leaves of the
original printing were retained, the cancellation expanded the book by two
leaves.

casting-off   A calculation made before the stationer began printing a text
from manuscript to determine the number of sheets of paper that would be
required for a single copy, and hence the total paper stock that would be
consumed in printing the edition as a whole.

catchword   At the foot of each page in the right-hand corner the compositor
would set the first word of the following page (occasionally two short words
such as 'I am' or a speech prefix and the following word, occasionally part of a
longer word such as 'Lamen-' for 'Lamenting').

chain line   Parallel lines in paper formed by the wires of the mould on which
the paper was manufactured. The direction of chain lines is a guide to *format*,
and the distance between them can help to identify the stock of paper.

collateral text   A substantive text other than the base text used in preparing
an edition.

collation line   A record of variant readings, as usually printed between
the text and commentary, or below the commentary, in modern editions
of Shakespeare. In some usage, such as recent Arden practice, the term is
replaced by 'textual notes'. The formatting of a collation note varies from
one edition or series to another in detail, but for recording an emendation is
usually as follows: (*a*) line reference, (*b*) lemma (the reading in the edited text
that the note is about), (*c*) a closing square bracket, (*d*) the short identifier or
siglum for the text that is the authority for the reading (codified in forms such
as 'F' for Folio, 'Q2' for Second Quarto, 'Qq' for a run of quartos, and so on),
(*e*) a semi-colon, (f) the first alternative reading followed by the identifier of
the text (or texts) in which it first appeared, (*g*) further entries in the same
form as (*f*) as necessary, each separated by a semi-colon:

191 With all] F; Withall Q2; In all Q1

Sometimes this formula is elaborated by adding in brackets the exact reading in the early text or texts where the difference, though noteworthy, is merely one of spelling, and so the authority of the source text is unaffected:

416 valenced] Q2 (valenct), Q1 (vallenced); valiant F

Other editions dating from Nicholas Rowe (1709) onwards are usually identified by the editor's name, which may need modifying to indicate precisely which edition by that editor; sometimes a further distinction needs to be recognized between the editor who accepted the reading and an earlier editor or critic who first conjectured it:

130 bawds] POPE 1728 (*conj.* Theobald); bonds F, Q2

i.e. the reading 'bawds' was first instated in Pope's revised edition of 1728, following a conjecture by Theobald; the Folio and Q2 agree in reading 'bonds'.

Collation lines record the various changes made to stage directions, including (as well as normal emendation of textual error): regularization of names, alteration in the position printed, other alterations to clarify staging, and variants between the early texts in wording or staging:

4.1.0.1 *Enter Claudius*] F (*Enter King*); *Eenter King, and Queene, with Rosencraus and Guyldensterne* Q2; *Enter the King and Lordes* Q1

This note records three forms of wording in the substantive editions, potentially three different stagings, an editorial normalization of '*King*' to '*Claudius*', and, incidentally, a typographical error in Q2 '*Eenter*'.

Collation lines often also record changes to lineation, though where these are extensive they are sometimes located in a separate appendix instead.

Collations might limit themselves to identifying the first edition to adopt a particular reading. Sometimes it is necessary to record also the reading of a collateral text; for instance, in the example of 'bonds' above, F is cited as the reading of the *control text* and Q2 as a text that is both earlier and *substantive*. The extent to which a collation line records the readings in a derivative edition will vary.

composition   In printing, the compositor's assembling of type pieces to make up lines and eventually pages of text.

composition by formes   The composition of type so as to complete the setting of one *forme* before beginning the next. In the case of a *quarto* book, this would involve setting pages 1, 4, 5, and 8 of a sheet (the outer forme), then pages 2, 3, 6, and 7 (the inner forme), or *vice versa*. In the Shakespeare

Folio, with its 'folio in sixes' *format*, setting by formes was standard. The compositors would begin with the inner forme of the inner sheet of the *quire*, and work outwards towards the first and last page.

composition seriatim   The composition of type according to the sequence of the text, as opposed to *composition by formes*.

concurrent printing   The practice, more widespread than was once realized, of dividing the printing of a book between more than one stationer. The reason might be to speed up completion, or to slot in the production of a small book around larger jobs already in hand. Q1 *Romeo and Juliet* was divided between Danter (sheets A to D) and Allde (sheets E to K). In this case the division between printers is obvious. Allde's compositor(s) used a smaller typeface, and had to fill up the alloted space by introducing ornamental devices and making other adjustments. Work between the two printers of *Richard III*, Wise (sheets A to G) and Short (sheets H to M), was better coordinated. Here the typefaces are superficially similar, and there is no obvious difference in the general appearance of the page except that the type has been imposed a little higher.

conflation   The editorial practice of combining as much as possible of the text as printed in different *substantive* texts, on the assumption that the texts are imperfect witnesses to a single underlying version, as when Quarto and Folio *Lear* are combined to produce a single conflated text. A comparable practice is found in the preparation of some Folio texts, where the quarto copy is annotated with readings from an independent manuscript source.

conjectural emendation   (*a*) an emendation introduced by an editor that is not exampled in the early printed texts and so is of the editor's devising, or (*b*) a reading conjectured (i.e. hypothesized) but not actually adopted by an editor. The second sense applies to the abbreviation 'conj.' often found in the *collation lines* of editions, and might usefully be distinguished as a 'conjectured emendation'.

continuous copy   A phrase coined by John Dover Wilson to encapsulate his view, based on the example of *Sir Thomas More*, that a play manuscript would evolve over the years with an accumulation of additions, alterations, and cancellations, to become a highly complex and multilayered document.

control text   The early text on which a modern edition is primarily based. Distinct from the term *copy-text* in that it implies that the text is the predominant basis for the edition but not the only one. For instance, the text in question may not be followed for the *incidentals*. The Oxford Shakespeare describes Folio *Hamlet* as the 'control text for *substantive* variants' and Q2 as 'copy-text for *incidentals*'.

copy-text The early text that an editor follows as the basis for the edited text, with defined categories of exception. Greg explained that in an old-spelling edition the copy-text will be the one closest in spelling, punctuation, and other *incidentals* to the habits of the author. This enables a more eclectic approach to *substantives*. See also *base text* and *control text*. 'Copy-text' also refers to the text followed by a compositor. It is often shortened to 'copy', as in 'the printer's copy'. In this form it can be confused with the book itself as a 'copy' (reproduction) of the 'copy' (copy-text).

derivative text A text printed from an earlier printing and so without independent *authority*; in contrast with a *substantive* text.

F See *folio*.

fair copy A transcript copied out by a scribe or an author, and so a document that is beyond the main stage of authorial composition and ready for use by others. Often used as a semi-technical term to refer to the manuscript that was to act as the basis for the playbook, as distinct from *foul papers*.

folio Book format obtained by folding the sheet of paper once. In the Shakespeare Folio (F) three sheets were folded together, so that the first leaf was on the same sheet as the sixth, the second paired with the fifth, and the third with the fourth. A folio was a large, expensive, and prestigious volume.

format The design of a book with respect to the number, size, and layout of pages to be printed on a single sheet of paper. See *folio*, *octavo*, and *quarto*.

forme The body of type after *composition, imposition* and locking in the chase, at which point it is ready for printing. There would be two pages of type in one forme in a *folio* book, four in a *quarto*, and more in other formats. By extension, 'forme' also refers to one side of a sheet of paper, as printed from the forme of type.

forme-mate The *forme* printed on the opposite side of the sheet to the forme first in question.

foul papers In terminology of the New Bibliography, the dramatist's complete draft of a play prior to transcription for use in the theatre, 'foul' in that it would retain inconsistencies and alterations many of which would be eliminated through transcription. As it had high authorial authority it could give rise to a *'good' quarto*. But manuscripts that have been described as 'foul papers' have also been thought to underlie a few Folio texts, such as *Henry V* and *Timon of Athens*.

'good' quarto   A *quarto* text thought to have been printed from a pre-theatrical *autograph* manuscript or a manuscript close to that document.

Hand D   The writer of one of the revisions to *Sir Thomas More*. Most textual scholars regard Hand D as probably Shakespeare's.

historical collation   A *collation of variants* that records the readings of all editions, irrespective of their presumed textual authority.

hypertext   Electronic text embedded in an associative network of nodes and links that the reader can traverse non-sequentially on the computer screen (W. Chernaik, C. Davis, and M. Deegan, *The Politics of the Electronic Text* (1993), p. 6). Hypertext can also encompass digitized images and soundtrack. The 'nodes' are the files of text or other material; the 'links' allow navigation between them.

imposition   In printing, the placement of completed pages of type in the correct position to make up a *forme*. The pages would then be locked into position in the chase with wooden wedges.

impression   In the first instance, 'impression' is the act of pressing the paper against the inked type during printing. The term also refers to the product of this process, in various senses. In the identification and bibliographical description of books, it indicates all the copies of an edition printed at any one time. In the hand-press period, this usually amounts to the same as the edition itself.

imprint   The details printed towards the foot of the title page of a printed book, naming the copy holder, and the place and date of publication. The imprint also usually names the printer, and identifies the bookseller if he or she is distinct from the copy holder. See Appendix 2 for examples.

incidentals   A term adopted in the Oxford Shakespeare and elsewhere as an alternative to *accidentals*. The objection to 'accidentals' is that it is a misleading Latinism: the features in question are not products of chance, as 'accidentals' might now suggest, but features of incidence.

interlineation   The insertion into a passage in a manuscript of a word or phrase squeezed in between the lines already written.

justification   Occurs after a *compositor* had set a line of type in the *measure*, when he would make the line tight by adjusting the width of the spacing pieces between words, altering the spelling of a word to make it longer or shorter, splitting a word between two type-lines, and making use of abbreviations. Justification was necessary so that the type would lock into a solid block without side-play or danger of types falling out.

licence (*a*) A playbook would need to be inscribed with an official licence for performance from the Master of the Revels. (*b*) See *allowance* and *Stationers' Register* for the separate regulation of the book trade.

ligature A single *type* that combines two letters. The commonest ligatures in roman type were ae, ct, ff, ffi, fi, ffl, oe, oo, ss, si, sh, st, ssi, and sl. Italic type often added as, fr, ij, is, ll, sp, and us.

literary transcript A copy of a play made for use outside the theatre—for example, for presentation to a patron or for use as printer's copy. Most known examples derive from after 1616.

massed entry The usual term to describe a stage direction that follows the classical convention of listing all the characters in the scene at the beginning of a scene.

In translated classical texts such as the Seneca plays collected as *Ten Tragedies* (1581) a new scene would begin whenever a character was thought to enter or depart. Each scene would be headed with a list of characters who appeared in it. The practice was copied in the academic or 'closet' drama, and, in preparing his plays from the public stage for publication, Jonson followed it too.

It is probably the example of Jonson that led to the appearance of 'massed' stage directions in Shakespeare plays, most persistently in *The Two Gentlemen of Verona, The Merry Wives of Windsor*, and *The Winter's Tale*, which are some of the Folio plays thought to have been transcribed by Crane.

Master of the Revels Court official under the authority of the Lord Chamberlain, responsible for court entertainments in the first instance, and consequently the regulation and censorship of plays in the public and other theatres. For a few years in the early seventeenth century (1606–13) the Master of the Revels George Buc also licensed plays for the press.

memorial reconstruction A text hypothetically put together on the basis of what some of the players, or perhaps other people, could remember from the play in performance.

metrical emendation The practice of emending the text to correct perceived errors of metre. Associated particularly with eighteenth-century editors, above all Pope. Now usually considered a doubtful or poor basis for emendation, though certain metrical irregularities can safely be said to lie outside a

given writer's usual practice, and the case for identifying error is strengthened when a difficulty in meaning coincides with a non-authorial metrical
irregularity.

modernization   The common editorial practice of altering spellings and
punctuation so as to accord with modern usage (e.g. modern *due* or *dew* for
old-spelling *dewe*). Obsolete inflexions, words, and idioms are left intact.

octavo   Book *format* obtained by folding the sheet three times, so as to
divide it, after the outer edges are trimmed, into eight leaves. *The Passionate
Pilgrim*, a collection of poems by Shakespeare and others, was published in
octavo format in 1599 and reprinted in 1599 and 1612. *Richard Duke of York* was
originally published in octavo in 1595, but the later reprints were in *quarto*.

Pavier Quartos   An irregular collection of reprinted quartos of plays attributed to Shakespeare issued by Thomas Pavier in 1619. It includes five plays that
were substantially variant on the texts later published in F (*The Whole Contention* [the second and third parts of *Henry VI*], *Henry V*, *The Merry Wives of
Windsor*, *King Lear*), two plays similar to the texts in F (*A Midsummer Night's
Dream*, *The Merchant of Venice*), and three plays excluded from F (*Pericles*, *A
Yorkshire Tragedy*, *Sir John Oldcastle*).

perfecting   The printing of the second side of a pile of sheets already printed
on one side with the second *forme*.

playbook   A term sometimes used to replace 'prompt book'. Would typically
be a *fair copy* that had been annotated for use in the theatre and that might
hold the licence of the Master of the Revels. But among extant playbooks the
characteristics vary considerably.

press correction   Alterations made by stopping the press during the main
print run of a *forme*. Though a standard practice, it was not routine. The
changes might be 'mechanical' (correcting imperfections of printing resulting
from loose or uneven type, etc.) or 'textual' (altering actual or perceived errors
of spelling, punctuation, or wording). Textual changes might be based on
the printer's copy (as evidently in Q1 *2 Henry IV*) or merely informed by
guesswork (as evidently in Q1 *King Lear*).

prompt book   The more traditional term for the document otherwise referred
to as the *playbook*.

quarto   Book *format* obtained by folding the sheet first downwards and then
laterally, so as to divide it, after the outer edges are trimmed, into four leaves.
The outer *forme* contains the first, fourth, fifth, and eighth pages of the sheet
(1 paired with 8, opposite 4 paired with 5); the inner forme contains the

second, third, sixth, and seventh pages (2 paired with 7, opposite 6 paired with 3). The main fold in the sheet runs along the tops of all the pages. Quarto format was relatively small and therefore affordable. It was suitable for single plays. 'Quarto' is commonly abbreviated 'Q', 'Q1' denoting the First Quarto of a text, 'Q2' the second, etc.

quire   A collection of sheets in a book that are folded together to make a single gathering of leaves with a single *signature*.

rough draft   A less precise and accordingly less contentious term than *foul papers* that might refer to any authorial working script.

scrivener   scribe

speech prefix   The abbreviation, word, or words identifying the speaker of the lines that follow it. Alternatively, 'speech heading' (a less accurate term, as in most early modern play manuscripts and printed books the identifier appears to the left of the first line of the speech, not above it).

standing type   Type left locked in the chase after printing (see *imposition*) in anticipation of further printing, instead of being distributed to the compositors' type cases. This would apply in situations such as: (*a*) a *cancel* that involved a page of type that could be re*imposed*, as was the case with the last page of Folio *Romeo and Juliet;* (*b*) a title page or preliminaries that were retained in anticipation of a reprint; (*c*) a second edition that was partially reprinted from the same type as the first, as was the case with Thomas Dekker and Thomas Middleton's *1 Honest Whore.*

Stationers' Register   Account books of the Stationers' Company recording various transactions including the issue of *allowances* to print. A stationer planning to print from a manuscript would need to obtain a licence from the Stationers' Company. This would establish his or her right to the text. For an extra fee, licences could be recorded as entries in the Register. Entrance was not obligatory, and the absence of an entry therefore does not mean that the book in question was printed without licence. But entrance was nevertheless usual, and enabled the wardens and other stationers to check licences that had previously been granted.

stemma   A diagram showing the known or inferred derivation of extant texts from extant and lost predecessors.

substantive text   A printed text that does not simply rely on an earlier printed text, but instead is based wholly or partly on a manuscript of independent authority. The words 'wholly or partly' in this definition show that the term can be relative, especially as 'partly' can refer to a variety of situations, such as: (*a*) a text that is substantive for one passage only (Q4 *Richard II*, which contains the earliest printed text of the deposition scene but is otherwise a reprint of Q3); (*b*) a reprint that is very lightly modified through reference to a manuscript (such as Folio *A Midsummer Night's Dream*); (*c*) a text that transfers as many readings as possible from a manuscript onto printed copy, through heavy annotation of printed copy and/or fresh transcription (such as Folio *Richard III*); (*d*) a text based on a transcript belonging to a manuscript line of descent that nevertheless incorporates some minor features of a printed quarto (such as Folio *2 Henry IV*). An example of two entirely substantive texts would be *The Merry Wives of Windsor*. In this case the Quarto is usually considered to be memorially transmitted, but this challenge to its *authority* does not compromise is integrity as a substantive text.

substantives (textual) Typically refers to the words of the text as conveyors of meaning. A key term in Greg's 'Rationale of Copy-Text', but based on a problematic distinction: see *accidentals*.

tagging The marking-up of electronic text with conventionalized symbols to represent textual layout (indented part-line of verse, prose, etc.), font (italic, small capitals, etc.), etc., or the function of text (stage direction, speech prefix, etc.), in such a way that the tagged characteristics can be realized in terms of font and layout on the screen or on the printed page, or be subjected to selective electronic searches.

type A small rectangular piece of cast metal with the raised shape of an inverted letter etc. at the end. Type-metal was an alloy of lead, antimony, and tin. Printing involves assembling pages of type in such a way that the raised letters will present a flat surface that can be pressed on the paper (see *composition*); the type is inked so that the paper will take an inked impression. Types had a 'nick' running across the underside of the body, so that a compositor could tell by touch which way up it should go. Compositors' type-trays were divided into boxes each of which contained types of a single letter.

type analysis A technique for determining the page-by-page sequence of work in printing a book by identifying the recurrence of damaged or otherwise distinctive types. It works effectively for a large-format book where there is a large quantity of type per page, such as the Shakespeare Folio, which was studied in detail by Charlton Hinman. Distinctive types reappear in clusters, which mark the point at which an earlier page has been distributed. The pattern of setting and distribution can be charted through the book as a whole.

unediting   A rejection of critical editing in favour of studying directly from photofacsimiles (McLeod); a deconstruction of editorial tradition (Marcus).

variants   Readings that differ between different texts of the same work.

watermarks   Patterns that can be seen in hand-made paper when held up to the light. They take shapes such as letters of the alphabet, vases, pots, shields, fleurs de lys, coats of arms, and bunches of grapes. These shapes are made in wire sewn onto the mould in which the sheet of paper is formed. Watermarks can be used to identify the manufacturer of a stock of paper, or to distinguish one stock from another.

INTRODUCTION

1. David Scott Kastan, *Shakespeare and the Book* (Cambridge: Cambridge University Press, 2001); Andrew Murphy, *Shakespeare in Print: A History and Chronology of Shakespeare Publishing* (Cambridge: Cambridge University Press, 2003).
2. The term appears in Jerome McGann, 'What Is Critical Editing?', *Text*, 5 (1991), 15–30, and elsewhere in his work. See also D. F. McKenzie, 'Typography and Meaning: The Case of William Congreve', in Peter D. McDonald and Michael F. Suarez, SJ (eds.), *Making Meaning: 'Printers of the Mind' and Other Essays* (Amherst and Boston: University of Massachusetts Press, 2002), 198–236.

CHAPTER I

1. See M. C. Bradbrook, 'Beasts and Gods: Greene's *Groats-worth of Witte* and the Social Purpose of *Venus and Adonis*', *Shakespeare Survey 15* (1962), 62–72.
2. Quotations are modernized throughout this book, unless there is significance in the spellings or form of the text quoted.
3. Quotations from Shakespeare are based on *The Complete Works*, gen. eds. Stanley Wells and Gary Taylor, 2nd edn. (Oxford: Oxford University Press, 2005). I follow the form of titles as given in this edition, except when citing alternative early versions or modern editions published under different titles.
4. If *Arden of Faversham* is partly by Shakespeare, the 1592 Quarto is the first part-Shakespearian play to appear in print, even preceding *Venus and Adonis* (see Appendix 2). As mentioned later in this chapter, *Titus* is itself now generally regarded as a collaboration.

5. The attribution of non-canonical plays to 'W.S.' or 'W.Sh.' continued in *Thomas Lord Cromwell* (1602), *The Puritan Widow* (1607), and *The Troublesome Reign of King John* (1611).

6. Lukas Erne, *Shakespeare as Literary Dramatist* (Cambridge: Cambridge University Press, 2003).

7. Thomas Heywood, 'To the Reader', in *The English Traveller* (1633), sig. A3.

8. Erne, *Shakespeare as a Literary Dramatist*, 115–28.

9. For more detail on the Stationers' Company and Register, see Chapter 3.

10. For a conclusive recent reappraisal, see MacD. P. Jackson, 'The Date and Authorship of Hand D's Contribution to *Sir Thomas More*: Evidence from "Literature Online"', *Shakespeare Survey 59* (2006), 69–78.

11. Quoted with modifications from *The Book of Sir Thomas More*, ed. W. W. Greg, 2nd edn., with supplement by Harold Jenkins (Oxford: Malone Society, 1961).

12. Grace Ioppolo, *Dramatists and their Manuscripts in the Age of Shakespeare, Jonson, Middleton and Heywood: Authorship, Authority and the Playhouse* (London: Routledge, 2004), 102–9, argues from the fluency of the handwriting that the passage is a copy that shows Shakespeare continuing to adjust the script as he transcribed his first draft, but the more usual view is that it shows Shakespeare in the process of initial composition.

13. Gary Taylor, 'Shakespeare and Others: The Authorship of *Henry the Sixth Part One*', *Medieval and Renaissance Drama in England*, 7 (1995), 145–205.

14. MacD. P. Jackson, 'Stage Directions and Speech Headings in Act 1 of *Titus Andronicus* Q (1594): Shakespeare or Peele?', *Studies in Bibliography*, 49 (1996), 134–48.

15. Jonathan Hope, *The Authorship of Shakespeare's Plays: A Socio-Linguistic Study* (Cambridge: Cambridge University Press, 1994), 133–7.

16. Gary Taylor and John Jowett, *Shakespeare Reshaped 1606–1623* (Oxford: Clarendon Press, 1993).

17. E. K. Chambers, 'The Disintegration of Shakespeare', in J. W. Mackail (ed.), *Aspects of Shakespeare: Being British Academy Lectures* (Oxford: Clarendon Press, 1933), 23–48 (reprinting Chambers's British Academy Shakespeare Lecture of 1924).

18. Samuel Schoenbaum, *Internal Evidence and Elizabethan Dramatic Authorship: An Essay in Literary History and Method* (London: Edward Arnold, 1966).

19. Karl Klein (ed.), *Timon of Athens* (Cambridge: Cambridge University Press, 2001), 63–5.

20. The case for John Ford's authorship is advanced by G. D. Monsarrat, '*A Funeral Elegy*: Ford, W.S. and Shakespeare', *Review of English Studies*, 53 (2002), 186–203, and Brian Vickers, *Counterfeiting Shakespeare: Evidence, Authorship, and John Ford's 'Funerall Elegye'* (Cambridge: Cambridge University Press, 2002); Foster's acceptance, based on Monsarrat, was posted in the Internet discussion forum *Shaksper*, 12 June 2002.

21. MacD. P. Jackson, 'Compound Adjectives in *Arden of Faversham*', *Notes and Queries*, 53 (2006), 51–5; Jackson, 'Shakespeare and the Quarrel Scene in *Arden of Faversham*', *Shakespeare Quarterly*, 57 (2006), 249–93.

22. Cyrus Hoy, 'The Shares of Fletcher and his Collaborators in the Beaumont and Fletcher Canon', 7 parts: *Studies in Bibliography*, 8 (1956), 129–46; *SB* 9 (1957), 143–62; *SB* 11 (1958), 85–106; *SB* 12 (1959), 91–116; *SB* 13 (1960), 77–108; *SB* 14 (1961), 45–68; *SB* 15 (1962), 71–90.

23. MacD. P. Jackson, *Studies in Attribution: Middleton and Shakespeare* (Salzburg: Universität Salzburg, 1979; see also *Jackson, 'Hand D', 'Stage Directions', and 'Compound Adjectives'*; Hope, *Authorship*.

24. H. J. Oliver (ed.), *Timon of Athens* (London: Methuen, 1959), pp. xix–xxi; David Lake, *The Canon of Thomas Middleton's Plays* (Cambridge: Cambridge University Press, 1975), 284–5; Jackson, *Studies in Attribution*, 55–6.

25. Jeffrey Masten, *Textual Intercourse: Collaboration, Authorship, and Sexualities in Renaissance Drama* (Cambridge: Cambridge University Press, 1997).

26. Gerald Eades Bentley, *The Profession of Dramatist in Shakespeare's Time, 1590–1642* (Princeton: Princeton University Press, 1971).

27. Gary Taylor, 'The Canon and Chronology of Shakespeare's Plays', in Stanley Wells and Taylor, with John Jowett and William Montgomery, *William Shakespeare: A Textual Companion* (Oxford: Clarendon Press, 1987), 69–144. This book is subsequently identified throughout as *Textual Companion*.

28. For an elaboration of these ideas, see John Jowett (ed.), *Timon of Athens* (Oxford: Oxford University Press, 2004).

CHAPTER 2

1. Tiffany Stern, *Rehearsal from Shakespeare to Sheridan* (Oxford: Clarendon Press, 2000), 53.

2. Arthur Brown (ed.), *The Captives*, by Thomas Heywood (Oxford: Malone Society, 1953), p. xii.

3. James Purkis, 'Foul Papers, Prompt-Books, and Thomas Heywood's *The Captives*', forthcoming in *Medieval and Renaissance Drama in England* 2008.

4. Janet Clare, *'Art made tongue-tied by authority': Elizabethan and Jacobean Dramatic Censorship* (Manchester: Manchester University Press, 1990).

5. Richard Dutton, *Mastering the Revels: The Regulation and Censorship of English Renaissance Drama* (London: Macmillan, 1991).

6. Quotations and line numbers in these and the following examples from the Malone Society editions: *Believe As You List*, ed. Charles J. Sisson (1928, for 1927); *The Captives*, ed. Arthur Brown (1953); *Sir Thomas More*, ed. W. W. Greg (1911).

7. David Kathman, 'Actors' Names as Textual Evidence' (forthcoming).

8. William B. Long, '"A Bed/for woodstock"', *Medieval and Renaissance Drama in England*, 2 (1985), 91–118. Long's chronology of productions reflected in the manuscript may need revising in the light of MacD. P. Jackson's argument for the original composition and performance being in the early Jacobean period: see his 'Shakespeare's *Richard II* and the Anonymous *Thomas of Woodstock*', in *Medieval and Renaissance Drama in England*, 14 (2001), 17–65.

9. Stern, *Rehearsal*, 88.

10. Andrew Gurr, 'Maximal and Minimal Texts: Shakespeare v. The Globe', *Shakespeare Survey 52* (1999), 68–87.

11. Ibid. 81–2, 86.

12. The figure is as in Lukas Erne, *Shakespeare as a Literary Dramatist* (Cambridge: Cambridge University Press, 2003), 141.

13. Cited in Eric Rasmussen, 'The Revision of Scripts', in John D. Cox and David Scott Kastan (eds.), *A New History of Early English Drama* (New York: Columbia University Press, 1997), 441–60 (p. 442).

14. *Textual Companion*, 9.

15. Stern, *Rehearsal*, 98. Grace Ioppolo suggests that there may be no difference between the documents, in *Dramatists and Their Manuscripts in the Age of Shakespeare, Jonson, Middleton and Heywood* (Abingdon: Routledge, 2006), p. 55. But it seems unlikely that details of casting would be undertaken before a script was available.

16. See Greg, *Dramatic Documents* from the Elizabethan Playhouses, 2 vols. (Oxford: Clarendon, 1933), vol. i, for photographic reproductions and type facsimiles.

17. Greg's dating of *2 Seven Deadly Sins* as *c.* 1590 and attribution to Lord Strange's Men (*Dramatic Documents*, ii. 11) are persuasively reassigned to the Lord Chamberlain's Men in the later 1590s, in David Kathman,

'Reconsidering *The Seven Deadly Sins*', *Early Theatre*, 7/1 (2004), 13–44. Kathman's work has implications for the dating of the other plot Greg placed at '*c.* 1590', *The Dead Man's Fortune*. The surviving examples therefore probably belong to a much narrower range of dates than Greg indicated.

18. David Bradley, *From Text to Performance in the Elizabethan Theatre: Preparing the Play for the Stage* (Cambridge: Cambridge University Press, 1992), 120.

19. Stern, *Rehearsal*, 98.

20. Photographed and transcribed in Greg, *Dramatic Documents*, vol. i.

21. Orlando's part, ll. 130–1 and ll. 138–9, in *Two Elizabethan Stage Abridgements: 'The Battle of Alcazar' and 'Orlando Furioso'*, ed. W. W. Greg (Oxford: Malone Society, 1922). The directions are more concerned with bodily action than is typical of a playbook.

22. Michael Warren, 'Quarto and Folio *King Lear* and the Interpretation of Albany and Edgar', in David Bevington and Jay L. Halio (eds.), *Shakespeare, Pattern of Excelling Nature* (Newark: University of Delaware Press, and London: Associated University Presses, 1978), 95–107 at 105.

23. Gary Taylor, 'The Canon and Chronology of Shakespeare's Plays', in *Textual Companion*, 69–144, at 131.

24. Robert Clare, '"Who is it that can tell me who I am?": The Theory of Authorial Revision between the Quarto and Folio Texts of *King Lear*', *Library*, 6/17 (1995), 34–59.

25. Gary Taylor and Michael Warren (eds.), *The Division of the Kingdoms: Shakespeare's Two Versions of 'King Lear'* (Oxford: Clarendon Press, 1983); René Weis (ed.), *'King Lear': A Parallel Text Edition* (London: Longman, 1993).

26. The adaptation of both *Macbeth* and *Measure for Measure* is best studied in Thomas Middleton, *Collected Works*, gen. ed. Gary Taylor and John Lavagnino (Oxford: Oxford University Press, 2007), which responds to the doubtful proposition that Shakespeare was himself involved in the adaptation of *Macbeth*.

27. Gary Taylor, 'Shakespeare's Mediterranean *Measure for Measure*', in Tom Clayton, Susan Brock, and Vicente Forés, *Shakespeare and the Mediterranean: The Selected Proceedings of the International Shakespeare Association World Congress, Valencia, 2001* (Newark: Delaware University Press, and London: Associated University Presses, 2004), 243–69.

28. John Kerrigan, 'Revision, Adaptation, and the Fool in *King Lear*', in Taylor and Warren (eds.), *Division*, 195–245.

CHAPTER 3

1. A superscript 'r' is sometimes added to the signature of recto pages. This is hard on the eye but technically more correct, as 'B1' strictly speaking identifies a leaf rather than a page.

2. The facts relating to entries or transfers of ownership in the Stationers' Register of Shakespeare's plays are recorded in Appendix 2, which also provides a transcript of first and other substantive editions and a brief record of reprints.

3. Susan Cyndia Clegg, *Press Censorship in Elizabethan England* (Cambridge: Cambridge University Press, 1997), 17; P. W. M. Blayney, 'The Publication of Playbooks', in J. D. Cox and D. S. Kastan (eds.), *A New History of Early English Drama* (New York: Columbia University Press, 1997), 383–422.

4. Blayney, 'Publication', 408–9.

5. Alan B. Farmer and Zachary Lesser, 'The Popularity of Playbooks Revisited', *Shakespeare Quarterly*, 56 (2005), 1–32.

6. Blayney, 'Publication', 405.

7. This description refers to quarto format and other formats with one-sheet gatherings. Folio in sixes format is discussed later in this chapter.

8. See Philip Williams, 'The "Second Issue" of Shakespeare's *Troilus and Cressida*, 1609', *Studies in Bibliography*, 2 (1949), 25–33; Alice Walker's edition (Cambridge: Cambridge University Press, 1957); and Kenneth Palmer's Arden 2 edition (London: Methuen, 1982).

9. Trevor H. Howard-Hill, 'The Compositors of Shakespeare's Folio Comedies', *Studies in Bibliography*, 26 (1973), 61–106.

10. *The Norton Facsimile: The First Folio of Shakespeare*, ed. Charlton Hinman (London and New York: Paul Hamlyn, 1968), app. A, plates VI and VII; J. K. Moore, *Primary Materials Relating to Copy and Print in English Books of the Sixteenth and Seventeenth Centuries* (Oxford: Oxford Bibliographical Society, 1992), plates 50–57.

11. In recognition that editing, unlike printing, does not involve mere copying, I refer to the editor's 'base text' rather than 'copy-text'.

12. The term 'paratext' is advanced in Gérard Genette, *Seuils* (Paris: Éditions de Seuil, 1987), trans. Jane E. Lewin as *Paratexts: Thresholds of Interpretation* (Cambridge: Cambridge University Press, 1997).

13. Most influentially, Oscar James Campbell, *Comicall Satyre and Shakespeare's 'Troilus and Cressida'* (San Marino: Huntington Library, 1938).

14. *Textual Companion*, 424.

15. Charlton Hinman, *The Printing and Proof-Reading of the First Folio of Shakespeare*, 2 vols. (Oxford: Clarendon Press, 1963).

16. For a detailed examination of the play's theatrical orientation and genre as articulated in Q1 and F, see Gary Taylor, '*Troilus and Cressida*: Bibliography, Performance, and Interpretation', *Shakespeare Studies*, 15 (1982), 99–136.

17. Zachary Lesser, *Renaissance Drama and the Politics of Publication: Readings in the English Book Trade* (Cambridge: Cambridge University Press, 2004), 21.

CHAPTER 4

1. This was the first collection of more than one Shakespeare play under a single title page, and the first edition of the two plays to attribute them to Shakespeare.

2. As argued by Sonia Massai, in *Shakespeare and the Rise of the Editor* (Cambridge: Cambridge University Press, forthcoming).

3. Peter W. M. Blayney, 'Introduction to the Second Edition', in *The Norton Facsimile: The First Folio of Shakespeare*, ed. Charlton Hinman, 2nd. edn., with a new introduction by Blayney (New York and London: W. W. Norton, 1996), p. xxviii.

4. David Scott Kastan, *Shakespeare and the Book* (Cambridge: Cambridge University Press, 2001), 61–2.

5. Titles are modernized in spelling but given in the form in which they appear in the Catalogue.

6. Charlton Hinman, *The Printing and Proof-Reading of the First Folio of Shakespeare*, 2 vols. (Oxford: Clarendon Press, 1963), i. 363.

7. For further discussion of the nature of playbooks, see Chapter 2.

8. This statement needs qualifying in that there is minor influence from Q1 to F in *2 Henry IV*, most plausibly explained by Q1 influence on the manuscript that served as Folio copy, and probably similarly in *Othello*.

9. Trevor H. Howard-Hill, 'Shakespeare's Earliest Editor, Ralph Crane', *Shakespeare Survey 44* (1992), 113–29.

10. 'TLN' refers to the through line-numbers in *The Norton Facsimile*.

11. Margreta de Grazia, *Shakespeare Verbatim* (Oxford: Clarendon Press, 1991), 14–48.

12. Lukas Erne, *Shakespeare as Literary Dramatist* (Cambridge: Cambridge University Press, 2003), 255–8.

13. W. W. Greg, *The Editorial Problem in Shakespeare: A Survey of the Foundations of the Text*, 3rd edn (Oxford: Clarendon Press, 1954), p. 6 n. 1.

14. De Grazia, *Shakespeare Verbatim*, 90–2; Julie Stone Peters, *Theatre of the Book, 1480–1880* (Oxford: Oxford University Press, 2000), 141.

15. In fact, like the texts, the engraving is not an immediate copy, despite Jonson's claim that Droeshout struggled with Nature to 'out-do the life'.

16. *Sir Thomas More*, ed. Harold Jenkins, in C. J. Sisson (ed.), *Complete Works* (London: Odhams, 1953).

17. *Timon of Athens*, ed. John Jowett (Oxford: Oxford University Press, 2004).

18. Charles Knight, 'A Biography of William Shakspere', in Knight (ed.), *The Works of Shakspere: Imperial Edition*, 2 vols. in 2 parts (London: Virtue, n.d.), separately paginated supplement to vol. ii, pt. 2, p. 105.

CHAPTER 5

1. Jerome J. McGann, *The Textual Condition* (Princeton: Princeton University Press, 1991), 13, 56, 78, etc.

2. On this distinction see Paul Eggert, 'Textual Product or Textual Process: Procedures and Assumptions of Critical Editing', in Philip Cohen (ed.), *Devils and Angels: Textual Editing and Literary Theory* (Charlottesville and London: University Press of Virginia, 1991), 57–77.

3. Alfred W. Pollard, *Shakespeare Folios and Quartos: A Study in the Bibliography of Shakespeare's Plays 1594–1685* (London: Methuen, 1909); Pollard, *Shakespeare's Fight with the Pirates and the Problems of the Transmission of his Text* (Cambridge: Cambridge University Press, 1920).

4. Pollard, *Shakespeare Folios and Quartos*, 64–80.

5. W. W. Greg, *The Editorial Problem in Shakespeare: A Survey of the Foundations of the Text*, 3rd edn. (Oxford: Clarendon Press, 1954), 10.

6. Pollard, 'Preface', in *Shakespeare Folios and Quartos*, p. vi.

7. W. W. Greg (ed.), *Shakespeare's 'Merry Wives of Windsor' 1602* (London: Tudor and Stuart Library, 1906).

8. Greg, *Editorial Problem*, 11–12.

9. Ibid. 9.

10. George Ian Duthie, *The 'Bad' Quarto of 'Hamlet': A Critical Study* (Cambridge: Cambridge University Press, 1941), 12–18.

11. Hardin Craig, *A New Look at Shakespeare's Quartos* (Stanford: Stanford University Press, 1961). The view was espoused in the 1980s and 1990s in various articles by Steven Urkowitz, though Urkowitz is more concerned to describe the effects of textual differences than to determine their causes.

12. Gary Taylor, in *Textual Companion*, 84–6.

13. Kathleen O. Irace, *Reforming the 'Bad' Quartos: Performance and Provenance of Six Shakespearean First Editions* (Cranbury, London, and Mississauga: Associated University Presses, 1994).

14. See especially Paul Werstine, 'Narratives about Printed Shakespeare Texts: "Foul Papers" and "Bad" Quartos', *Shakespeare Quarterly*, 41 (1990), 65–86. The critique of the term 'bad quartos' as an enabling category goes back to Random Cloud [Randall McLeod], 'The Marriage of Good and Bad Quartos', *Shakespeare Survey 33* (1982), 421–31; and Steven Urkowitz, 'Good News about Bad Quartos', in Maurice Charney (ed.), *'Bad' Shakespeare: Revaluations of the Shakespeare Canon* (Rutherford: Fairleigh Dickinson University Press, 1988), 189–206.

15. Laurie E. Maguire, *Shakespearean Suspect Texts: The 'Bad' Quartos and their Contexts* (Cambridge: Cambridge University Press, 1996).

16. Ibid. 286, 310, 256, 295.

17. As witnessed by the New Cambridge Early Quartos series, and readings of 'bad' quartos such as in Leah Marcus, *Unediting the Renaissance: Shakespeare, Marlowe, Milton* (London: Routledge, 1996).

18. Andrew Gurr, 'Maximal and Minimal Texts: Shakespeare v. The Globe', *Shakespeare Survey 52* (1999), 68–87.

19. *The Tragedy of King Richard III*, ed. John Jowett (Oxford: Clarendon Press, 2000); *The History of King Lear*, ed. Stanley Wells (Oxford: Clarendon Press, 2000).

20. Pollard, *Shakespeare's Fight*, 60, 63–4, 66.

21. Alfred W. Pollard (ed.), *Shakespeare's Hand in the Play of Sir Thomas More* (Cambridge: Cambridge University Press, 1923).

22. Greg, *Editorial Problem*, 29.

23. Ibid. 33, 107.

24. R. B. McKerrow, 'The Elizabethan Printer and Dramatic Manuscripts', *Library*, 4/12 (1931–2), 253–75; McKerrow, 'A Suggestion regarding Shakespeare's Manuscripts', *Review of English Studies*, 11 (1935), 459–65.

25. Greg, *Editorial Problem*, 95–7.

26. W. W. Greg, *The Shakespeare First Folio: Its Bibliographical and Textual History* (Oxford: Clarendon Press, 1955), 103.

27. Fredson Bowers, *On Editing Shakespeare and the Elizabethan Dramatists* (Philadelphia: University of Pennsylvania Library, 1955), 11–12.

28. Bowers, 'The Copy for Shakespeare's *Julius Caesar*', *South Atlantic Bulletin*, 43 (1978), 23–36. For a critique, see *Textual Companion*, 387.

29. Bowers, *On Editing Shakespeare*, 19–20.

30. *Textual Companion*, 145–6.

31. Ibid. 147.

32. The fullest study is J. K. Walton, *The Quarto Copy for the First Folio of Shakespeare* (Dublin: Dublin University Press, 1971).

33. T. H. Howard-Hill, *Ralph Crane and Some Shakespeare First Folio Comedies* (Charlottesville: University Press of Virginia, 1972).

34. See *Textual Companion*, 329–40, 549, 593.

35. In Gary Taylor and John Jowett, *Shakespeare Reshaped 1606–1623* (Oxford: Clarendon Press, 1993), 3–50.

36. Ibid. 51–106.

37. Ibid., esp. 237–43.

38. Werstine, 'McKerrow's "Suggestion" and Twentieth-Century Shakespeare Textual Criticism', *Renaissance Drama*, NS 19 (1988), 149–73.

39. Edward Pechter, 'Crisis in Editing?', *Shakespeare Survey 59* (2006), 20–38, at 35.

40. W. W. Greg, 'The Rationale of Copy-Text', *Studies in Bibliography*, 3 (1950–1), 19–36. For the purpose of this discussion based on Greg I retain his term 'copy-text', where elsewhere in this book 'base text' is the usual preferred (and less precise) term.

41. Ibid. 26.

42. Ibid.

43. Ibid. Greg had previously addressed the identification and correction of error in *Principles of Emendation in Shakespeare* (London: British Academy, 1928).

44. *Textual Companion*, 399, 402.

45. See R. B. McKerrow, *Prolegomena for the Oxford Shakespeare* (Oxford: Oxford University Press), 13.

46. Michael J. Warren, 'Quarto and Folio *King Lear* and the Interpretation of Albany and Edgar', in David Bevington and Jay L. Halio (eds.), *Shakespeare, Pattern of Excelling Nature* (Newark: Delaware University Press, and London: Associated University Presses, 1978), 95–107; Gary Taylor and Michael Warren (eds.), *The Division of the Kingdoms: Shakespeare's Two Versions of 'King Lear'* (Oxford: Clarendon Press, 1983).

47. Peter W. M. Blayney, *The Texts of 'King Lear' and Their Origins*, vol. 1, *Nicholas Okes and the First Quarto* (Cambridge: Cambridge University Press, 1983).

48. Thomas Clayton, ' "Is this the promis'd end?": Revision in the Role of the King', in Taylor and Warren (eds.), *Division*, 121–41.

49. *Textual Companion*, 34, 63 n. 34; citing Jerome J. McGann's influential *A Critique of Modern Textual Criticism* (Chicago: Chicago University Press, 1983).

50. McKerrow, *Prolegomena*, 6.

51. *Textual Companion*, 64 n. 53, citing James Thorpe, 'The Aesthetics of Textual Criticism', *PMLA* 80 (1965), 465–82: the 'integrity of the work

of art' derives from 'those intentions which are the author's, *together with those others of which he approves or in which he acquiesces'*. See also T. H. Howard-Hill, 'Modern Textual Theories and the Editing of Plays', *Library*, 6/11 (1989), 89–115.

52. For a summary, see R. A. Foakes (ed.), *King Lear* (Walton-on-Thames: Nelson, 1997), esp. 128–37.

53. Ann R. Meyer, 'Shakespeare's Art and the Texts of *King Lear*', *Studies in Bibliography*, 47 (1994), 128–46.

54. Jay L. Halio (ed.), *The First Quarto of 'King Lear'* (The New Cambridge Shakespeare, The Early Quartos; Cambridge: Cambridge University Press, 1994), text at 3.4.86, discussed pp. 16–17.

55. E. A. J. Honigmann, *The Texts of 'Othello' and Authorial Revision* (London: Routledge, 1996).

56. See especially Margreta de Grazia, 'The Essential Shakespeare and the Material Book', *Textual Practice*, 2 (1988), 69–85; De Grazia and Peter Stallybrass, 'The Materiality of the Shakespearean Text', *Shakespeare Quarterly*, 44 (1993), 255–83.

57. Donald Reiman, '"Versioning": The Presentation of Multiple Texts', in *Romantic Texts and Contexts* (Columbia: University of Columbia Press, 1987), 167–80; Jack Stillinger, *Coleridge and Textual Instability: The Multiple Versions of the Major Poems* (New York and Oxford: Oxford University Press, 1994), 118–40 ('A *version* of a work is a physically embodied text of the work', p. 132). But when Hans Zeller writes 'In the most extreme case a version is constituted by a single variant', in 'A New Approach to the Critical Constitution of Literary Texts', *Studies in Bibliography*, 28 (1975), 231–64, at 236, he is referring specifically to *authorial* variants.

58. Peter Shillingsburg, *Scholarly Editing in the Computer Age: Theory and Practice* (Athens, Ga.: University of Georgia Press, 1986; rev. edn. Ann Arbor: University of Michigan Press, 1996), 44.

59. Graham Holderness, Bryan Loughrey, and Andrew Murphy, '"What's the Matter?": Shakespeare and Textual Theory', *Textual Practice*, 9 (1995), 93–119.

60. Jonathan Goldberg, 'Textual Properties', *Shakespeare Quarterly*, 37 (1986), 213–17, at 214, 217.

61. McKerrow, *Prolegomena*, 6, 7; Greg, *Editorial Problem*, p. ix; *Textual Companion*, 2, 18.

62. David Scott Kastan, *Shakespeare and the Book* (Cambridge: Cambridge University Press, 2001); Andrew Murphy, *Shakespeare in Print: A History and Chronology of Shakespeare Publishing* (Cambridge: Cambridge University Press, 2003).

63. Valerie Wayne, 'The Sexual Politics of Textual Transmission', in Laurie E. Maguire and Thomas L. Berger (eds.), *Textual Formations and Reformations* (Newark: Delaware University Press, 1998), 179–210; Maguire, *Suspect Texts*, 26–32; Marcus, *Unediting*.

64. See, for instance, Randall McLeod, 'UN Editing Shak-speare', *Sub-stance*, 33–4 (1982), 26–55.

65. Shillingsburg, *Scholarly Editing*, 17, 22.

66. Barbara Mowat, 'The Problem of Shakespeare's Text(s)', in Maguire and Berger (eds.), *Textual Formations*, 131–48.

67. Lukas Erne, *Shakespeare as Literary Dramatist* (Cambridge: Cambridge University Press, 2003).

CHAPTER 6

1. W. W. Greg, 'Principles of Emendation in Shakespeare', in J. W. Mackail (ed.), *Aspects of Shakespeare: Being British Academy Lectures* (Oxford: Clarendon Press, 1933), 128–210 (reprinting and expanding on Greg's British Academy lecture of 1928), 133.

2. The issue here is the relation between the text the author penned and its meaning. Hand C's intervention (see Chapter 2) is a separate issue.

3. There are complications. Folio texts replacing shortened and theatrically experienced texts such as Q1 *Henry V* might revert to an earlier version of the play. Critics still debate whether Q1 or F *Troilus and Cressida* is the earlier state.

4. See John Jowett and Gary Taylor, 'Sprinklings of Authority: The Folio Text of *Richard II*', *Studies in Bibliography*, 38 (1985), 151–200.

5. Charles R. Forker (ed.), *King Richard II* (London: Thomson Learning, 2002), 514.

6. Confusingly, this term is often limited so as to refer only to emendations that editors propose but do not actually adopt.

7. A. E. Housman, *M. Manilii Astronomicon liber primus recensuit* (1903), pp. xxx–xxxi.

8. 'Conservatism or liberalism, skill or folly': the phrase is not exactly either a parallelism or a chiasmus. It should be confessed that I alter Housman's point, which is that in classical editing even a fool can be unleashed on a text surviving in a solitary manuscript because he or she does not have to choose between variants: 'he cannot exhibit his impotence to judge and choose.' This ignores the need for conjectural emendation, which is more limited in scope, but more susceptible to both wisdom and folly.

9. Gary Taylor (ed.), *Henry V* (Oxford: Clarendon Press, 1984), 295.

10. A. E. Housman, 'The Application of Thought to Textual Criticism', *Proceedings of the Classical Association*, vol. 18 (1921), repr. in *Selected Prose*, ed. John Carter (Cambridge: Cambridge University Press, 1961), 131–50. See also James Ernest Thorpe, *Principles of Textual Criticism* (San Marino: Huntington Library, 1972).

11. Edmond Malone (ed.), *The Plays and Poems of William Shakespeare*, 10 vols. (1790), vi. 620–1 (note on *Othello*, 5.2.7).

12. M. H. Abrams, *The Mirror and the Lamp: Romantic Theory and the Critical Tradition* (New York: Oxford University Press, 1953).

13. For further discussion and a review of previous scholarship, see Ronald A. Tumelson II, 'Ferdinand's Wife and Prospero's Wise', *Shakespeare Survey 59* (2006), 79–90.

14. Jeanne Addison Roberts, ' "Wife" or "Wise"—*The Tempest* l. 1786', *Studies in Bibliography*, 31 (1978), 203–8.

15. Valerie Wayne, 'The Sexual Politics of Textual Transmission', in Thomas L. Berger and Laurie Maguire (eds.), *Textual Formations and Reformations* (Newark: University of Delaware Press, 1998), 179–210.

16. Stephen Orgel, 'Prospero's Wife', in *The Authentic Shakespeare and Other Problems of the Early Modern Stage* (New York: Routledge, 2002), 173–86.

17. *The Tempest*, ed. Virginia Mason Vaughan and Alden T. Vaughan (Walton-on-Thames: Nelson, 1999), 136–8.

18. Stanley Wells and Gary Taylor, *Modernizing Shakespeare's Spelling, with Three Studies in the Text of 'Henry V'* (Oxford: Clarendon Press, 1979); Wells, *Re-Editing Shakespeare for the Modern Reader* (Oxford: Clarendon Press, 1984).

19. Joseph Moxon, *Mechanick Exercises on the Whole Art of Printing (1683–4)*, ed. Herbert Davis and Harry Carter (London: Oxford University Press, 1958), 192.

20. See Percy Simpson, *Proof-Reading in the Sixteenth, Seventeenth and Eighteenth Centuries* (London: Oxford University Press, 1935), and J. K. Moore, *Primary Materials Relating to Copy and Print in English Books of the Sixteenth and Seventeenth Centuries* (Oxford: Oxford Bibliographical Society, 1992).

21. Moore, *Primary Materials*, plates 14 (Bodleian Library, MS Ashmole 765, fo. 76ᵛ) and 15 (Daniel King, *The vale-royall of England* (printed by John Streater, 1656), sig. M4ᵛ).

22. Quoted from *Richard III*, ed. John Jowett (Oxford: Clarendon Press, 2000).

23. The passage is variant in F, which here reads 'Euen so'.

CHAPTER 7

1. Past-participle '-ed' is in some texts regularly preserved when it is non-syllabic if it is preceded by a vowel. Hence 'buried' could either be a feminine ending or (less likely) make up a hexameter.

2. In these hypothetical examples capitalization for verse-lines and a final full stop are introduced, but spellings and other punctuation are left unchanged.

3. It is possible, indeed, that Clarence's first line similarly fell at the end of the page.

4. Paul Werstine, 'Line Division in Shakespeare's Dramatic Verse: An Editorial Problem', *Analytic and Enumerative Bibliography*, 8 (1984), 73–125.

5. For instance, N. W. Bawcutt in his edition (Oxford: Oxford University Press, 1991).

6. Marco de Marinis, *The Semiotics of Performance*, trans. Áine O'Healy (Bloomington and Indianapolis: Indiana University Press, 1993), 28–9.

7. This statement illustrates de Marinis's point that stage directions lack a key characteristic of a notational system in that the movement from text to 'performance text' (all aspects of the play as realized in a particular performance) is not reversible.

8. This statement needs qualifying. Some plays, notably *The Tempest*, printed from a Crane manuscript, may contain directions supplied by Crane that come after and describe stage performance. These are not the 'original' directions, but they are embedded in the earliest text we have.

9. The present analysis may be compared with M. J. Kidnie, 'Text, Performance, and the Editors', *Shakespeare Quarterly*, 51 (2000), 456–73. Kidnie also refers to de Marinis, concluding that the 'gaps in the dramatic text' should be treated 'as an invitation to play' (p. 473). For an illustration of what this might mean, see her 'The Staging of Shakespeare's Drama in Print Editions', in Lukas Erne and Kidnie (eds.), *Textual Performances: The Modern Reproduction of Shakespeare's Drama* (Cambridge: Cambridge University Press, 2004), 158–77.

10. W. W. Greg, *The Shakespeare First Folio: Its Bibliographical and Textual History* (Oxford: Clarendon Press, 1955), 135.

11. Stanley Wells, *Re-Editing Shakespeare for the Modern Reader: Based on Lectures Given at the Folger Shakespeare Library, Washington, DC* (Oxford: Clarendon Press, 1984).

12. *Textual Companion*, p. xxxvii.

13. Alan C. Dessen, *Rescripting Shakespeare: The Text, The Director, and Modern Productions* (Cambridge: Cambridge University Press, 2002), 234.

14. This practice came gradually into use in the Arden series. Early examples are the 1955 editions of *Merchant of Venice*, ed. John Russell Brown, and *Julius Caesar*, ed. T. S. Dorsch.

CHAPTER 8

1. John Jowett (ed.), *The Tragedy of King Richard III* (Oxford: Oxford University Press, 2000).
2. The phrase is attributed to Thomas L. Berger.
3. W. W. Greg (ed.), *'Doctor Faustus' 1604–1616: Parallel Texts* (Oxford: Clarendon Press, 1950).
4. Kristian Smidt (ed.), *The Tragedy of King Richard the Third: Parallel Texts of the First Folio with Variants of the Early Quartos* (Oslo: Universitetsforlaget, 1969).
5. Stephen Booth (ed.), *Shakespeare's Sonnets* (New Haven and London: Yale University Press, 1977).
6. Steven Urkowitz, '"Brother, Can You Spare a Paradigm?": Textual Generosity and the Printing of Shakespeare's Multiple-Text Plays by Contemporary Editors', *Critical Survey*, 7 (1995), 292–8.
7. In my own edition of *Richard III*, for example, lineation notes are subordinated to an appendix. So too are rejected readings from quartos printed after Q1 that influence the transmission to F. But the edition entirely omits rejected 'derivative quarto readings that are altered back to the Q1 reading in subsequent pre-1623 reprints' and 'readings from quartos that appeared after the quarto that is assumed to be the Folio copy at the point in question' (p. 366). The latter leads to a partial record of Qq4–6, as the Folio copy alternated between Q3 and Q6.
8. An early example of a multimedia electronic project combining text and performance is the 1994 Voyager *Macbeth* on CD-ROM, which includes a full audio recording and extracts from different film adaptations.
9. Guidelines online at http://www.tei-c.org.uk/P5/Guidelines/index.html.
10. Accessible online from the homepage at http://ise.uvic.ca/index.html.
11. Jerome J. McGann, *The Textual Condition* (Princeton: Princeton University Press, 1991), 120.
12. In her challenging account of digital textuality, N. Katherine Hayles notes of the editors of the electronic William Blake Archive: 'surely they know better than anyone the extensive differences between the print and electronic Blake. Nevertheless, they make the rhetorical choice to downplay these differences ... there is little or no theoretical explanation of what it means to read an electronic text produced in this fashion rather than the print original' (*My Mother was a Computer: Digital Subjects*

and Literary Texts (Chicago and London: Chicago University Press, 2005), 91).

13. As a point of comparison, Elizabeth L. Eisenstein's *The Printing Press as an Agent of Change: Communications and Cultural Transformations in Early-Modern Europe*, 2 vols. (Cambridge: Cambridge University Press, 1979) argues that the Reformation, Renaissance, and rise of science were, in a strong sense, cultural changes driven by the adoption of print technology, but the technological determinism of her account may well be overstated.

Further Reading

REFERENCE WORKS

Bibliographical details of all early printed plays including Shakespeare can be found in W. W. Greg, *A Bibliography of the English Printed Drama to the Restoration*, 4 vols. (London: Bibliographical Society, 1939–59). The standard listing of modern studies in the field is the revised edition of T. H. Howard-Hill, *Shakespearian Bibliography and Textual Criticism* (Signal Mountain, TN: Summertown, 2000). For more recent material, this can be supplemented by annual reviews in yearbooks such as *Shakespeare Survey* and the online subscription-based *World Shakespeare Bibliography*, ed. James L. Harner.

PLAY MANUSCRIPTS

The physical details of surviving play manuscripts can be studied, as far as print transcription allows, in the editions of the Malone Society. A concise list of them appears in W. W. Greg, *The Editorial Problem in Shakespeare*, 3rd edn. (Oxford: Clarendon Press, 1954), 23–4 n. 1. See also Greg, *Dramatic Documents from the Elizabethan Playhouses*, 2 vols. (Oxford: Clarendon Press, 1933); William B. Long, 'Precious Few: English Manuscript Playbooks', in *A Companion to Shakespeare*, ed. David Scott Kastan (Oxford: Blackwell, 1999), 414–49; and Grace Ioppolo, *Dramatists and their Manuscripts in the Age of Shakespeare, Jonson, Middleton and Heywood* (Abingdon: Routledge, 2006).

The manuscript of *Sir Thomas More* is best studied in *The Book of Sir Thomas More*, ed. W. W. Greg, 2nd edn, with supplement by Harold Jenkins (Oxford: Malone Society, 1961), along with the photofacsimile *The Book of Sir Thomas Moore*, ed. John S. Farmer (London: Tudor Facsimile Texts, 1910). The play has appeared in full in C. J. Sisson's *Complete Works* (London: Odhams, 1953) and in the second edition of the Oxford Shakespeare *Complete Works* (Oxford: Oxford University Press, 2005). There is a Revels Series edition edited by Vittorio Gabrieli and Giorgio Melchiori (Manchester: Manchester University Press, 1990). The Hand D passages have been printed in the complete works as edited by Peter Alexander (London: Collins, 1951) and many of the most important subsequent editions. Shakespeare's authorship of the Hand D sections was urged in A. W. Pollard (ed.), *Shakespeare's Hand in the Play of Sir Thomas More* (Cambridge: Cambridge University Press, 1923), and accepted in Stanley Wells and Gary Taylor, with John Jowett and William Montgomery, *William Shakespeare: A Textual Companion* (Oxford: Clarendon Press, 1987), 124–5, and by the contributors to T. H. Howard-Hill (ed.), *Shakespeare and Sir Thomas More: Essays on the Play and its Shakespearian Interest* (Cambridge: Cambridge University Press, 1989).

SHAKESPEARE IN PRINT

The early printings of Shakespeare's plays can be examined in high-resolution digital images. For quartos, see the British Library website at http://www.bl.uk/treasures/shakespeare/homepage.html. This includes reprints as well as first editions, though omits rarities that are not in the British Library collection such as Q1 *Titus Andronicus*. The Furness Shakespeare Library copy of the 1623 Folio is available online at http://dewey.library.upenn.edu/sceti/furness/index.cfm, and the Brandeis University First Folio along with the State Library of New South Wales copies of all four Folios and selected quartos are available on Shakespeare Internet Editions at http://ise.uvic.ca/index.html.

A standard guide to the process of early modern printing is in the hand-press sections of Philip Gaskell, *New Introduction to Bibliography* (Oxford: Clarendon Press, 1972). See also its predecessor, Ronald Brunlees McKerrow, *Introduction to Bibliography for Literary Students* (London: Oxford University Press, 1928); and George Walton Williams, *The Craft of Printing and the Publication of Shakespeare's Works* (Washington: Folger Shakespeare Library, 1985).

The general field of book history is well represented in David Finkelstein and Alistair McCleery (eds.), *The Book History Reader* (London and New York: Routledge, 2002). Adrian Johns, *The Nature of the Book* (Chicago: Chicago University Press, 1998), though it focuses on the middle decades of the seventeenth century and on scientific rather than literary books, is instructive on issues of standardization and control in the book industry, and in particular the workings of the Stationers' Company. The Stationers' Register can be consulted in *A Transcript of the Registers of the Company of Stationers of London, 1554–1640 A.D.*, ed. Edward Arber, 5 vols. (London: privately printed, 1875–94). Entries pertaining to all plays of the period are transcribed more accurately in Greg, *Bibliography*, i. 1–78. Those relating to Shakespeare's works are photographically reproduced in S. Schoenbaum, *William Shakespeare: Records and Images* (London: Scolar, 1981), 208–35.

The issue of press censorship in the period as a whole, without specific reference to Shakespeare, is analysed in Cyndia Susan Clegg, *Press Censorship in Elizabethan England* (Cambridge: Cambridge University Press, 1997), and Clegg, *Press Censorship in Jacobean England* (Cambridge: Cambridge University Press, 2001). W. W. Greg, *Licensers for the Press &c. to 1640: A Biographical Index Based Mainly on Arber's Transcript of the Registers of the Company of Stationers* (Oxford: Oxford Bibliographical Society, 1962), identifies personnel.

On Shakespeare's early readers, see Heidi Brayman Hackel, ' "Rowme" of its Own: Printed Drama in Early Libraries', in J. D. Cox and D. S. Kastan (eds.), *A New History of Early English Drama* (New York: Columbia, 1997), 113–30; Sasha Roberts, 'Reading the Shakespearean Text in Early Modern England, *Critical Survey*, 7 (1995), 299–306; and Lena Cowen Orlin, 'The Private Life of Public Plays' (forthcoming).

THE FIRST FOLIO

A major study of the book's production and use of copy, still valuable, is W. W. Greg, *The Shakespeare First Folio* (Oxford: Clarendon Press, 1955). Charlton Hinman, *The Printing and Proof-Reading of the First Folio of Shakespeare*, 2 vols. (Oxford: Clarendon Press, 1963), provides an almost definitive account of the sequence of work and its distribution between compositors. More recent developments are summarized in Blayney's introduction to the revised edition of Hinman's Norton Facsimile (New York and London: Norton, 1996). Anthony West's multivolume and ongoing *The Shakespeare First Folio* (Oxford: Oxford University Press) includes in vol. i (2001) a review of the history of its sales and in vol. ii (2002) a census of all known copies.

HISTORY OF EDITING

Andrew Murphy, *Shakespeare in Print: A History and Chronology of Shakespeare Publishing* (Cambridge: Cambridge University Press, 2003), provides a historical overview and a listing of all significant editions. Modern editing is generally understood to originate in the eighteenth century. Key studies are Margreta de Grazia, *Shakespeare Verbatim* (Oxford: Clarendon Press, 1991); Simon Jarvis, *Scholars and Gentlemen* (Oxford: Clarendon Press, 1995), and Marcus Walsh, *Shakespeare, Milton, and Eighteenth-Century Literary Editing* (Cambridge: Cambridge University Press, 1997). Beyond Murphy, the nineteenth century is less well charted. For the twentieth century, F. P. Wilson's laudatory *Shakespeare and the New Bibliography*, as revised by Helen Gardner (Oxford: Clarendon Press, 1970), may be supplemented, especially with reference to memorial reconstruction, with more recent and more sceptical approaches, in Laurie E. Maguire, *Shakespearean Suspect Texts* (Cambridge: Cambridge University Press, 1996), 21–94, and in a series of articles by Paul Werstine, notably 'A Century of Bad Quartos', *Shakespeare Quarterly*, 50 (1999), 310–33. Recent theorizing work that has developed textual studies away from the New Bibliography is subject to hostile review in G. Thomas Tanselle, *Textual Criticism since Greg: A Chronicle, 1950–1985* (Charlottesville: University Press of Virginia, 1987).

Issues of editing and gender are addressed in Ann Thompson, 'Feminist Theory and the Editing of Shakespeare: *The Taming of the Shrew* Revisited', in D. C. Greetham (ed.), *The Margins of the Text* (Ann Arbor: University of Michigan Press, 1997), 83–103; Lois Potter, 'Editing Desdemona', in Ann Thompson and Gordon McMullan (eds.), *In Arden: Editing Shakespeare* (London: Thomson, 2003), 81–94; Jeanne Addison Roberts, 'Women Edit Shakespeare', *Shakespeare Survey 59* (2006), 136–46; and Suzanne Gossett, ' "To foster is not always to preserve": Feminist Inflections in Editing *Pericles*', in Thompson and McMullan (eds.), *In Arden*, 65–80.

EDITORIAL THEORY AND PRACTICE

Readers seeking to familiarize themselves with the theoretical dimension of textual studies should read D. C. Greetham's compendious *Theories of the Text* (Oxford: Clarendon Press, 1999). On the principles of emendation, see in addition to Greg (without reference to Shakespeare) Eugène Vinaver, 'Principles of Textual Emendation', *Studies in French Language and Medieval Literature* (1930), 351–69, and (with reference to Shakespeare) Gary Taylor, ' "Praestat difficilior lectio": *All's Well That Ends Well* and *Richard III*', *Renaissance Studies*, 2 (1988), 27–46.

Shakespeare's metre has been explored in detail most influentially by George Thaddeus Wright, in *Shakespeare's Metrical Art* (Berkeley and Los Angeles, and London: University of California Press, 1988). Taylor provides a summary statement of the 'predictable deviations' from iambic pentameter in *Textual Companion*, 638. A formal description is found in Marina Tarlinskaya, *Shakespeare's Verse* (New York: Peter Lang, 1987). In addition to Werstine's article cited in Chapter 7, lineation issues are discussed by Gary Taylor in *Textual Companion*, 637–40, and David Bevington, 'Textual Analysis', in his edition of *Antony and Cleopatra* (Cambridge: Cambridge University Press, 1990), 266–70.

The overall scope of early modern stage directions can be explored through Alan C. Dessen and Leslie Thomson, *A Dictionary of Stage Directions in English Drama, 1580–1642* (Cambridge: Cambridge University Press, 1999). Francis Teague, *Shakespeare's Speaking Properties* (Lewisburg, PA: Bucknell

University Press, and London and Toronto: Associated University Presses, 1991), provides a discursive treatment. In addition to Dessen, as cited in Chapter 7, other discussions of the scope of editorial stage directions include Leslie Thomson, 'Broken Brackets and 'Mended Texts: Stage Directions in the Oxford Shakespeare', *Renaissance Drama*, NS 19 (1988), 175–93, and George Walton Williams, 'To Edit? To Direct?—Ay, There's the Rub', in Thompson and McMullan (eds.), *In Arden*, 111–24.

In addition to the Oxford *Textual Companion*, recent editions of individual plays in the Arden, Oxford, and Cambridge series usually have thorough and up-to-date discussion of their textual matters.

TEXTS FOR READERS

On types of editions, see D.C. Greetham, *Textual Scholarship* (New York and London: Garland, 1992). A useful if soon dated collection of essays on electronic editing is *Electronic Text*, ed. Kathryn Sutherland (Oxford: Clarendon Press, 1997). In addition to the online facsimiles mentioned above and the projects discussed in Chapter 8, see Bernice Kliman's 'Enfolded *Hamlet*', at http://www.leoyan.com/global-language.com/enfolded/enfolded.html.

Index